15. Hadzas — Tanzania
16. Bushmen — Kalahari Region, Africa
17. Marsh Arabs — Iraq
18. Kafirs — Pakistan
19. Tibetans, Sherpas, Bhutanese — Himalayas
20. Bondos — India
21. Nilgiri Tribes — India
22. Veddas — Ceylon
23. Nagas — India
24. Lua — Thailand
25. Ainus — Japan
26. Bununs — Taiwan
27. Dusuns — Sabah, Island of Borneo
28. Ibans — Sarawak, Island of Borneo
29. Asmats — Island of New Guinea
30. Highlanders — Island of New Guinea
31. Australian Aborigines

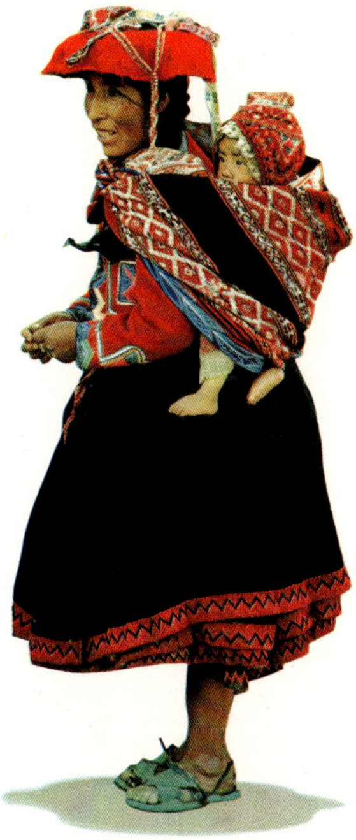

Vanishing Peoples of the Earth

Foreword by Leonard Carmichael, Vice President for Research and Exploration, National Geographic Society

Produced by the National Geographic Special Publications Division, Robert L. Breeden, Chief

National Geographic Society, Washington, D. C.
Melvin M. Payne, President
Melville Bell Grosvenor, Editor-in-Chief
Frederick G. Vosburgh, Editor

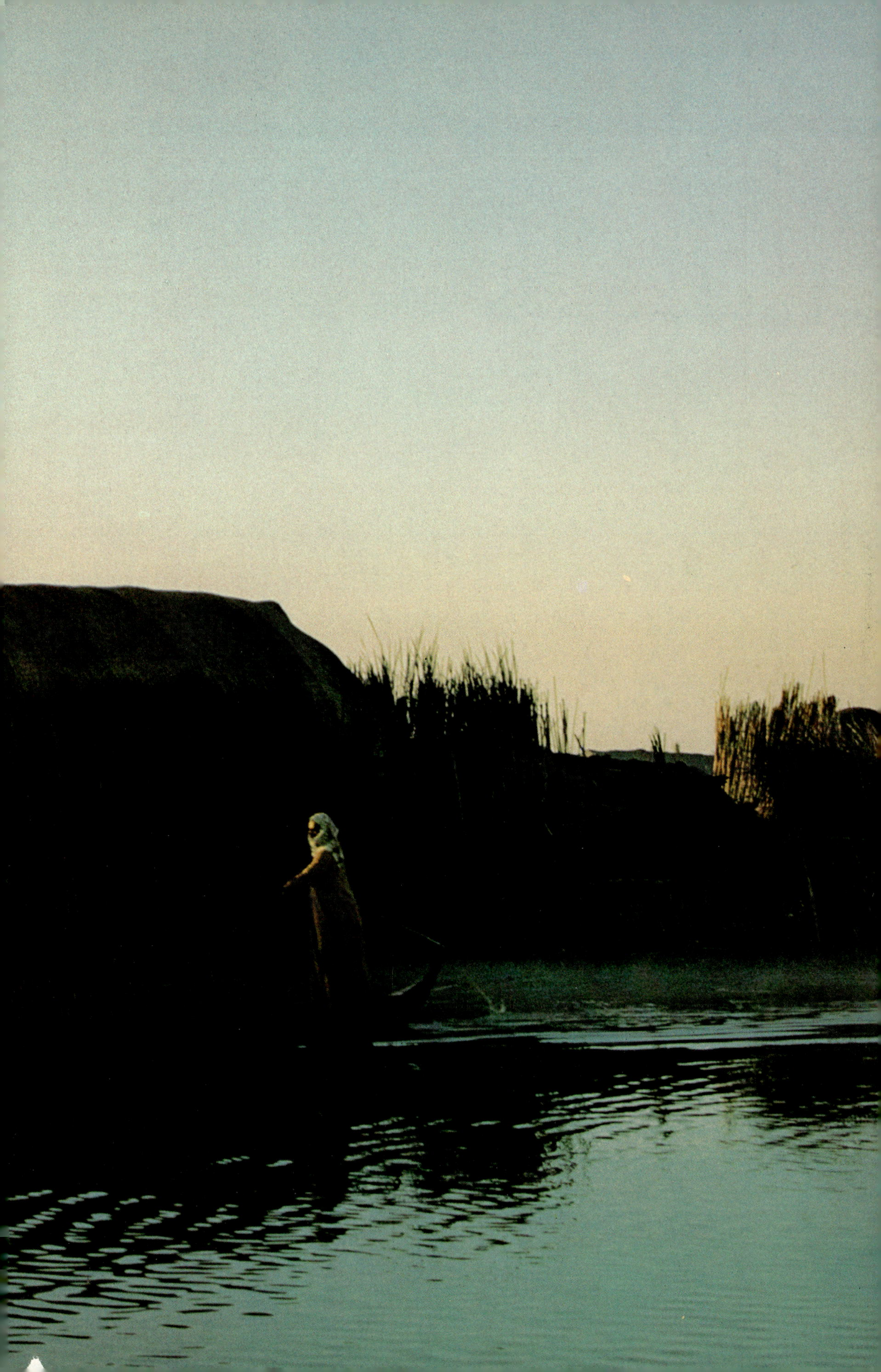

VANISHING PEOPLES OF THE EARTH

Published by
THE NATIONAL GEOGRAPHIC SOCIETY
MELVIN M. PAYNE, *President*
MELVILLE BELL GROSVENOR,
  Editor-in-Chief
FREDERICK G. VOSBURGH, *Editor*
GILBERT M. GROSVENOR, *Executive
  Editor for this Series*
ALLAN C. FISHER, JR., *Consulting Editor
  for this Book*

Prepared by
THE SPECIAL PUBLICATIONS DIVISION
ROBERT L. BREEDEN, *Editor*
DONALD J. CRUMP, *Associate Editor*
PHILIP B. SILCOTT, *Senior Assistant
  to the Editor*
LEON M. LARSON, *Assistant to the Editor*
CYNTHIA R. RAMSAY, *Project Editor*
TEE LOFTIN SNELL, PENELOPE W. SPRINGER,
  BETTY I. STRAUSS, PEGGY D. WINSTON,
  Research
RICHARD M. CRUM, RONALD M. FISHER,
  WILLIAM R. GRAY, JR., *Picture Legends*
BRUCE G. BRANDER, ABIGAIL T. BRETT,
  RICHARD M. CRUM, TEE LOFTIN SNELL,
  Editorial Staff
MARGARET S. DEAN, CAROL R. OAKES,
  SABINE PARKS, SANDRA A. TURNER,
  BARBARA J. WALKER, *Editorial Assistants*

Illustrations and Design
BRYAN D. HODGSON, *Picture Editor*
JOSEPH A. TANEY, *Art Director*
JOSEPHINE B. BOLT, *Assistant Art Director*
BOBBY G. CROCKETT, *Maps*
MUNRO KINSEY, *Map Research*

Production and Printing
ROBERT W. MESSER, *Production*
JUDY L. STRONG, *Production Assistant*
JAMES R. WHITNEY, *Engraving and
  Printing*
JOHN R. METCALFE, *Assistant, Engraving
  and Printing*
BRIT PETERSON, TONI WARNER, *Index*

Copyright © National Geographic Society. All rights reserved. Reproduction or use of the whole or any part of the contents without written permission is prohibited. Library of Congress Catalog Card No. 68-59196.

Devout Sherpas of Nepal (right) chisel Buddhist prayers into a cliff overhanging the trail to a monastery at the foot of Mount Everest. Overleaf: Sunlight gilds a house of reeds as a Marsh Arab of southern Iraq poles his mashuf *along a village waterway. Page 1: A Quechua Indian of Peru carries a baby in a brightly patterned shawl.* Copyright © 1968 National Geographic Society

Foreword

ALL OVER THE GLOBE, around flickering campfires, in thatched huts and skin tents, men find joy in friendship, summon courage in moments of despair, and see a kind of immortality in the faces of their children. Emotions and aspirations, common to us all, bind us together in the community of man. However, men meet life in distinctly different ways. People vary in their languages, in their religious beliefs, and in their goals. Each culture reflects all that a people develop and create to meet their special needs.

Today, many human societies, such as Africa's Bushmen, the Australian Aborigines, and the Eskimos, once isolated from the mainstream of civilization by scorching deserts, steaming jungles, or snowy tundras, find themselves caught between the old and the new. They seek to adapt their way of life to opportunities and alternatives offered by the 20th century. As they meet these challenges, peoples alter or discard in varying degrees many skills, values, and attitudes that once served them well.

For a century cultural anthropologists and ethnologists have been concerned with the securing of food, with courtship, with the rituals related to birth and death, and with all the behavior patterns and ideals of the world's isolated tribes and clans. Scientists who study man and his societies know that much of the infinite variety of such groups is fast fading. It has become increasingly apparent that the way of life of these peoples must be recorded and studied, or we will lose all knowledge of how each group has solved the problems of survival.

Your Society has recognized the importance of such research and has supported varied expeditions to the remote corners of the globe to document the many facets of human life. Accounts of this research have appeared year after year in the Society's journal. For example, almost 70 years ago the NATIONAL GEOGRAPHIC described the Yahgan Indians of Tierra del Fuego. Today, their culture has vanished, but fortunately it was studied in time to give us a glimpse into the Yahgans' beliefs and traditions.

The Society's Special Publications Division has prepared *Vanishing Peoples of the Earth* to help preserve for our members a record of many disappearing traditions before they are lost to the history of mankind. Here we present a sampling of tribes and peoples in the process of rapid and dramatic change. We have journeyed to six continents to share the special ways people have secured their food, raised their children, arranged marriages for their daughters, and prayed to their gods.

When boys and girls of today become adults, many of the customs, institutions, and beliefs described in the pages of this book will have altered so much that, in effect, they will have vanished. It is our hope, therefore, that this record of the diversity of man's social life and of the variety of his tools, his weapons, his works of art, and his religions will enrich the understanding of each modern reader.

LEONARD CARMICHAEL
Vice President for Research and Exploration,
National Geographic Society

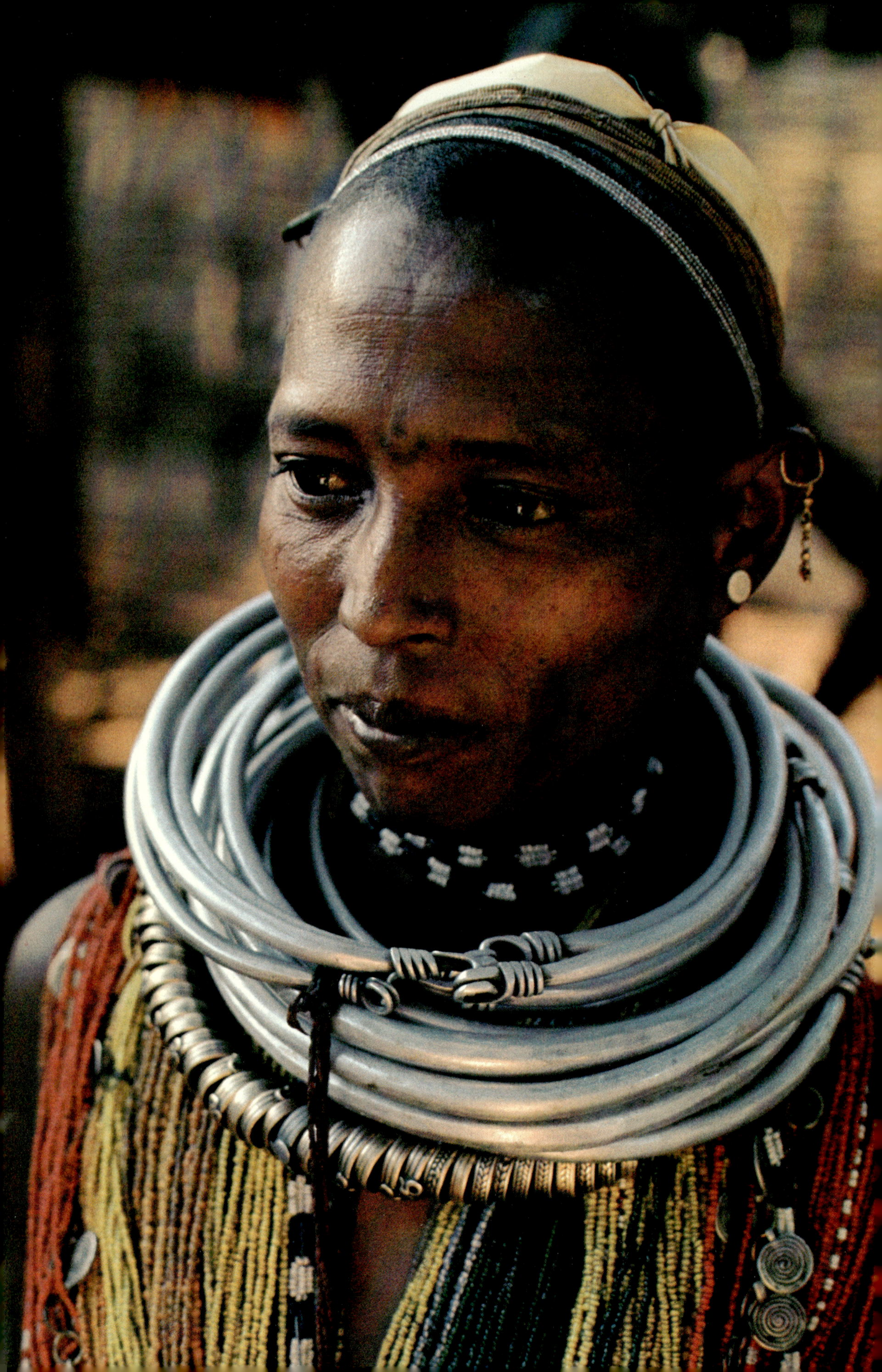

Contents

Foreword 5

1 *Vanishing Cultures Mirror the Yesterdays of Man* 8

2 *Lapps in a Modern World Face Timeless Realities* 36

3 *The Bushmen: Gentle Nomads of Africa's Harsh Kalahari* 58

4 *Nilgiri Peoples of India: An End to Old Ties* 76

5 *Mysterious "Sky People": Japan's Dwindling Ainu* 92

6 *Australian Aborigines: Blending Past and Present* 114

7 *The Indomitable Eskimo: Master of a Frozen World* 132

8 *Indians of Central Brazil: A Struggle to Survive* 152

9 *Hopis: "The Peaceful Ones" Confront the 20th Century* 170

10 *New Guinea's Fierce Asmat: A Heritage of Headhunting* 186

Index 204

Tribal finery adorns a Bondo woman of India; the complexities of the 20th century may change drastically the culture of the Bondos and that of other once-remote peoples of the earth.

NATIONAL GEOGRAPHIC PHOTOGRAPHER JAMES P. BLAIR

1

Vanishing Cultures Mirror The Yesterdays of Man

By MATTHEW W. STIRLING, Ph.D.

*Research Associate, Smithsonian Institution;
Member, Committee for Research and Exploration of the
National Geographic Society*

CHILL ANTARCTIC GUSTS whipped the flames on the tiny sand hearth in the center of the frail bark canoe. Cowilij, his yellow-brown body sleek with seal oil, speared a large salmon. His wife, as naked as he, with only a tiny otter-skin apron, then turned the canoe toward their campground, paddling steadily in the rough waters around Cape Horn. With her infant daughter straddling her back, she maneuvered close enough to the rocky coast for her husband and son to clamber ashore with the day's catch and embers from the hearth for the campfire.

Mooring the canoe was woman's work. Men hunted otter, seal, and guanaco, and snared birds. Women fished with a sinew line and gathered mussels. Cowilij's wife steered to a thick kelp patch nearby, and tied ropelike branches of the seaweed to the canoe's mooring lines. A film of frost covered the leathery leaves. She slid into the waters of Tierra del Fuego and swam ashore, her baby still clinging to her.

Once there was a family like this, fearless sailors at home among bleak islands and storm-tossed seas. Once there was a hardy people, the Yahgans. They lived on the islands off the southern tip of South America. Fortunately, a few of my fellow anthropologists studied and worked among the tribe, so we know something of their life. Today possibly two full-blooded Yahgans survive, but nothing of their old culture remains except vague memories, a love for the islands and the sea, and their language, spoken by a few Indians of mixed blood.

Col. Charles W. Furlong, who studied the Yahgans, captured in somber paintings the rigorous life of these people. Simply seeing his portrait of a medicine man, now part of a collection in the Smithsonian Institution in Washington, D. C., made me want to study the tribe myself. But it was too late; by the time I saw the picture, only a few of the people remained, living near the settlement of Puerto Williams, Chile, their old life gone.

Iban children of Sarawak, on the island of Borneo, frolic on a mossy log in the shallows of the Baleh River. Like many isolated peoples, these children—descendants of headhunters—face life in a modern world that debases old values and introduces alien ones to remote villages.

N.G.S. PHOTOGRAPHER WINFIELD PARKS

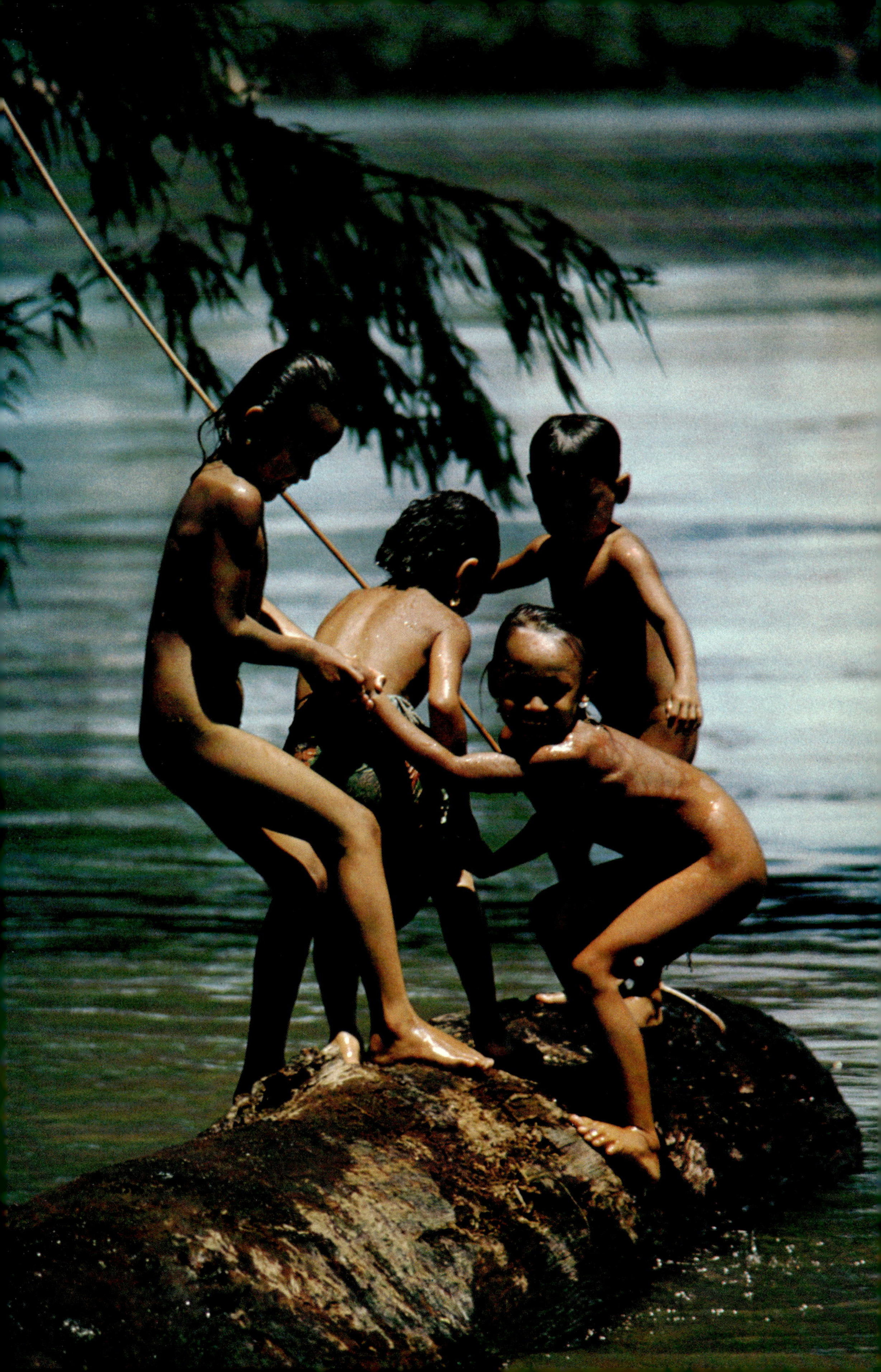

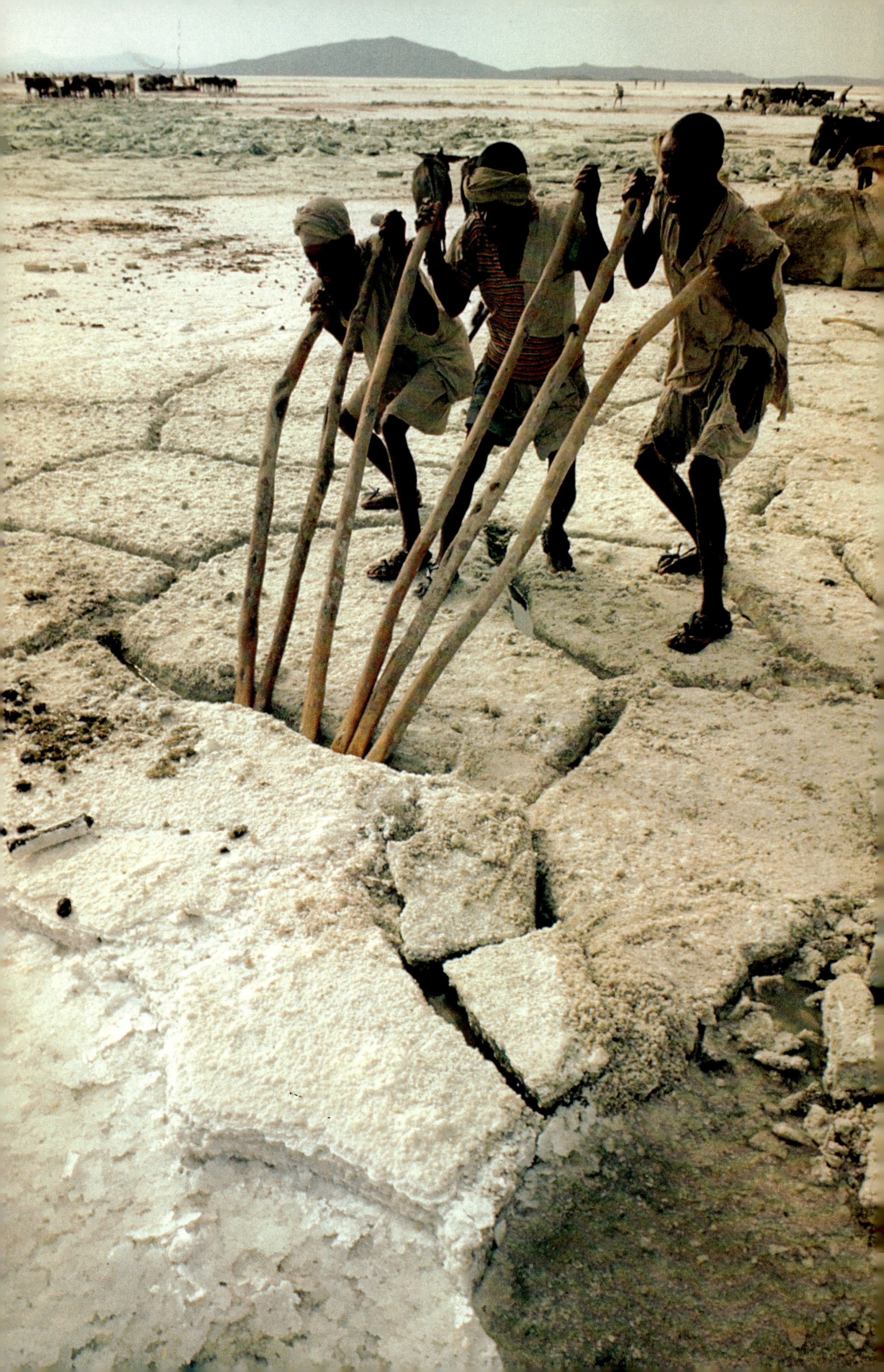

When Charles Darwin sailed around Cape Horn in H.M.S. *Beagle* in 1832, he could have counted some 3,000 Yahgans. By 1884 they numbered fewer than 1,000; in 1933 there were about 40.

What happened to wipe out an entire tribe? Why did a people who could endure the raw Fuegian climate more than half naked, who lived in rude shelters of branches, grass, and skins, and who bathed their newborn in icy seas vanish from the face of the earth?

About a hundred years ago the Yahgans felt the impact of new diseases and new ways of life. Since the 16th century, Western civilization has swept across the globe, challenging customs and beliefs steeped in tradition. I have seen the effect of civilization on mud-walled villages, jungle-girt settlements, and desert oases. Sometimes disease, violence, and confusion cast their shadows on a people. Sometimes change disrupts the lives of the people so drastically that their old culture disappears. Sometimes the combination of circumstances makes the crisis so acute that, as in the case of the Yahgans, it destroys the population.

Respiratory diseases, measles, and typhoid brought to the Yahgans by white intruders caused a rapid decline of the population in the 1880's. Then clothing from well-meaning Europeans compounded the disaster. Reading Darwin's accounts of how the Yahgans lived, I can imagine the pity many of his contemporaries must have felt for the Indians. He described a woman "suckling a recently born child... whilst the sleet fell and thawed on her naked bosom, and on the skin of her naked baby!" Before long, boxes of cast-off clothes arrived at missionary posts in the area.

Dressed, the Yahgan returned to his damp canoe. Water continued to seep in through its seams; waves continued to break over it. The canoe fire gave too little heat to dry his wet clothes, and he soon became an easy victim of pneumonia, influenza, and tuberculosis.

Darwin related a whaling captain's description of cannibalism among the Yahgans, and the stigma persisted for decades; but careful study proved the story false. Confronted with unfamiliar patterns of conduct, European travelers often misjudged and misinterpreted the simplest actions and motives of the peoples they encountered in new lands.

For example, when Capt. James Cook visited the island of Tasmania off the southeast coast of Australia in 1777, one of his crewmen described the aborigines there as "mild and chearfull" but rather slow-witted because they showed less interest and surprise than he expected when he put beads around their necks. He failed to consider that the etiquette of the people may have required a show of indifference.

We will never know with certainty why the Tasmanians failed to show interest. The entire population died out less than a century after the first sealers set up camp on the island in 1798. We have only the accounts of travelers, settlers, and government officials to give us clues to the Tasmanians' life. Records of Cook's voyage tell us: "They daub their Faces, Hair, Beards & their Bodies with red Earth, and their Bodies are ornamented in several Places, all on the forepart with large

Danakils of Ethiopia pry a block of salt—a major source of income—from a sun-baked pan. Only in the last 20 years have they started to sell their goats, sheep, camels, and salt, once bartered for clothing and grain.

VICTOR ENGLEBERT

Dark-eyed Danakil maiden braids her hair in tight plaits to attract suitors; tiny ringlets cover the head of the man in tribal fashion. The government has converted pastures into orchards and cropland, and many Danakils have given up their nomadic life to work on farms.

Bira woman from the Lake Albert region of Africa (above) wears a wooden disk in her pierced upper lip, stretched during childhood by inserting progressively larger plaques. The dying practice originated in tribal initiation rites. An Elmolo girl in Kenya (opposite) rests against a stack of marsh grass and reeds used for building huts. More warlike peoples forced the small Elmolo tribe to take refuge on islands in Lake Rudolf.

Scars...." We also know that the men wore their hair in corkscrew ringlets two to three inches long, and the women shaved their heads, leaving only a patch of hair at the crown. The men hunted kangaroo and wallaby with simple spears—a lance with its point hardened in fire, and a large stick called a waddy.

According to some reports, Tasmanian women abducted by sealers killed their half-caste children. In the Black Wars from 1804 to 1830, shepherds, outlaws, soldiers, and convicts hunted down and killed most of the estimated 1,200 aborigines. In 1835, missionary George Robinson persuaded the nearly 200 survivors to settle on Flinders Island, off the north coast of Tasmania.

Massacred, degraded, bewildered, wrenched from their homeland, the refugees lost the will to live. Mourning the tribal life shattered by the Europeans, afflicted by disease and malnutrition, the Tasmanians literally pined and died, finding the white man's civilization as fatal as his musket. Within seven years after their voluntary exile, their numbers had declined to 50; the last full-blooded native Tasmanian died in 1888. A few mixed-bloods still live in Australia—none of them more than one-quarter aboriginal.

Although anthropologists never had a chance to study the Tasmanians, they had a unique opportunity to observe the very last of the Yahi Indians of California, for in August 1911, the lone survivor of the tribe stumbled into the modern world from the Stone Age.

The Yahis, a branch of the Yana Indians of California, had lived in the foothills around Lassen Peak in northern California until the gold rush brought prospectors and settlers to their hunting grounds and salmon runs. The Indians treated the ranchers' sheep and cattle as game to replace deer, elk, bear, and rabbit that had grown scarce. Soldiers and vigilante bands hunted and massacred the Yahis, who numbered about 3,000, until all but 12 had died. In 1872 the tiny group found sanctuary in the caves, gorges, and chaparral around Deer Creek. Old age and illness reduced them even more. Finally one man remained.

Starved, his hair singed close to his head in mourning, he wandered into the small town of Oroville not far from Sacramento to await his fate. He expected death, but instead he acquired friends, a home, a job, a bank account, and a new name.

An anthropologist who had quickly identified the man as a Yahi arranged for him to stay at the Museum of Anthropology in San Francisco. I first met him there when I was a high-school student and watched as he demonstrated how to flake arrowheads, shape bows, and make fire with a fire drill. He patiently taught anthropologists how to pronounce Yahi words, but he could never bring himself to violate custom and speak his own name. Dr. Alfred Kroeber, under whom I later studied at the University of California, decided to call him Ishi, the Yahi word for "man."

At about age 50, Ishi had entered the 20th century abruptly and alone. I saw him face with courage the complexity of life in San Francisco—window shades and trolley cars, traffic signs and safety pins. One afternoon I joined Ishi for a ride on a streetcar. After he settled into a seat, he calmly began to pluck his whiskers with wooden tweezers, to the astonishment of the other passengers and me.   *Continued on page 21*

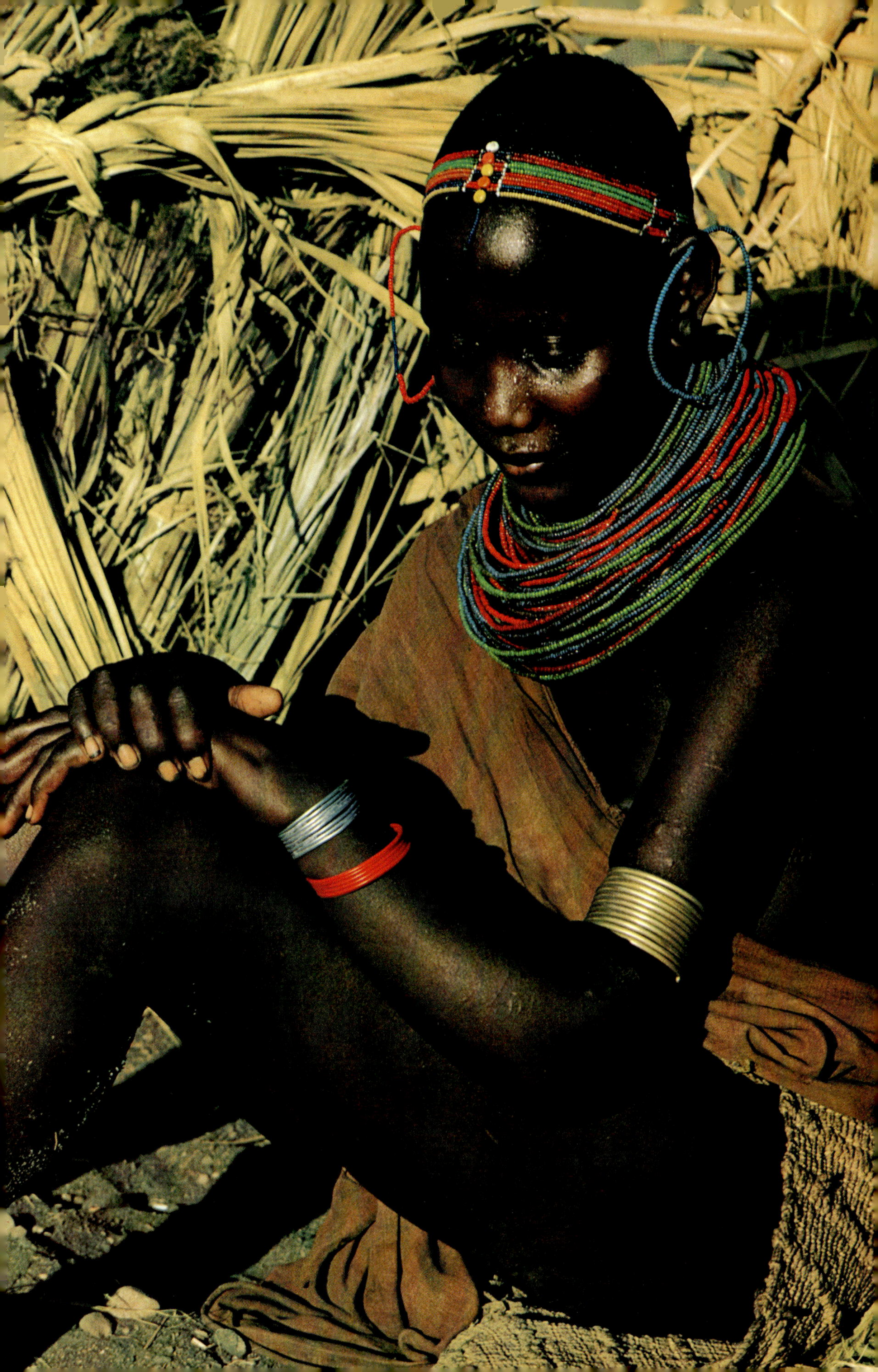

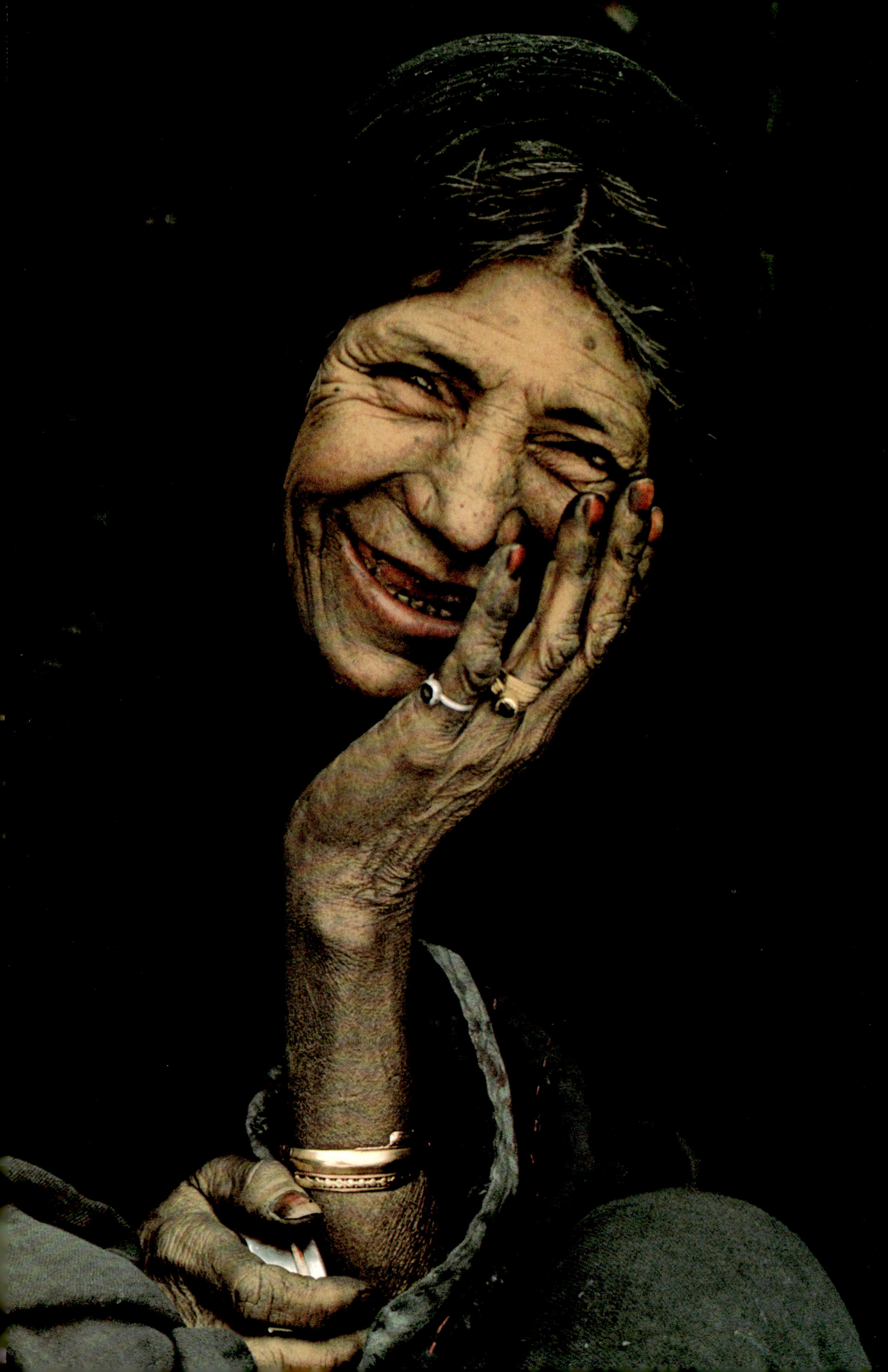

Shyly smiling Kafir matron relaxes after many hours of gathering wood. She and about 3,000 of her people live in the remote valleys of the towering Hindu Kush mountains in West Pakistan. Some of the Kafirs still dance, bury the dead, and worship in pagan ways. Nearly life-size funerary figures, carved to represent and to honor the dead, mark graves. This art has declined with the conversion of many tribesmen to Islam. At right, cowrie shells and medallions adorn the tufted headdress of a young woman.

HELEN AND FRANK SCHREIDER, NATIONAL GEOGRAPHIC STAFF

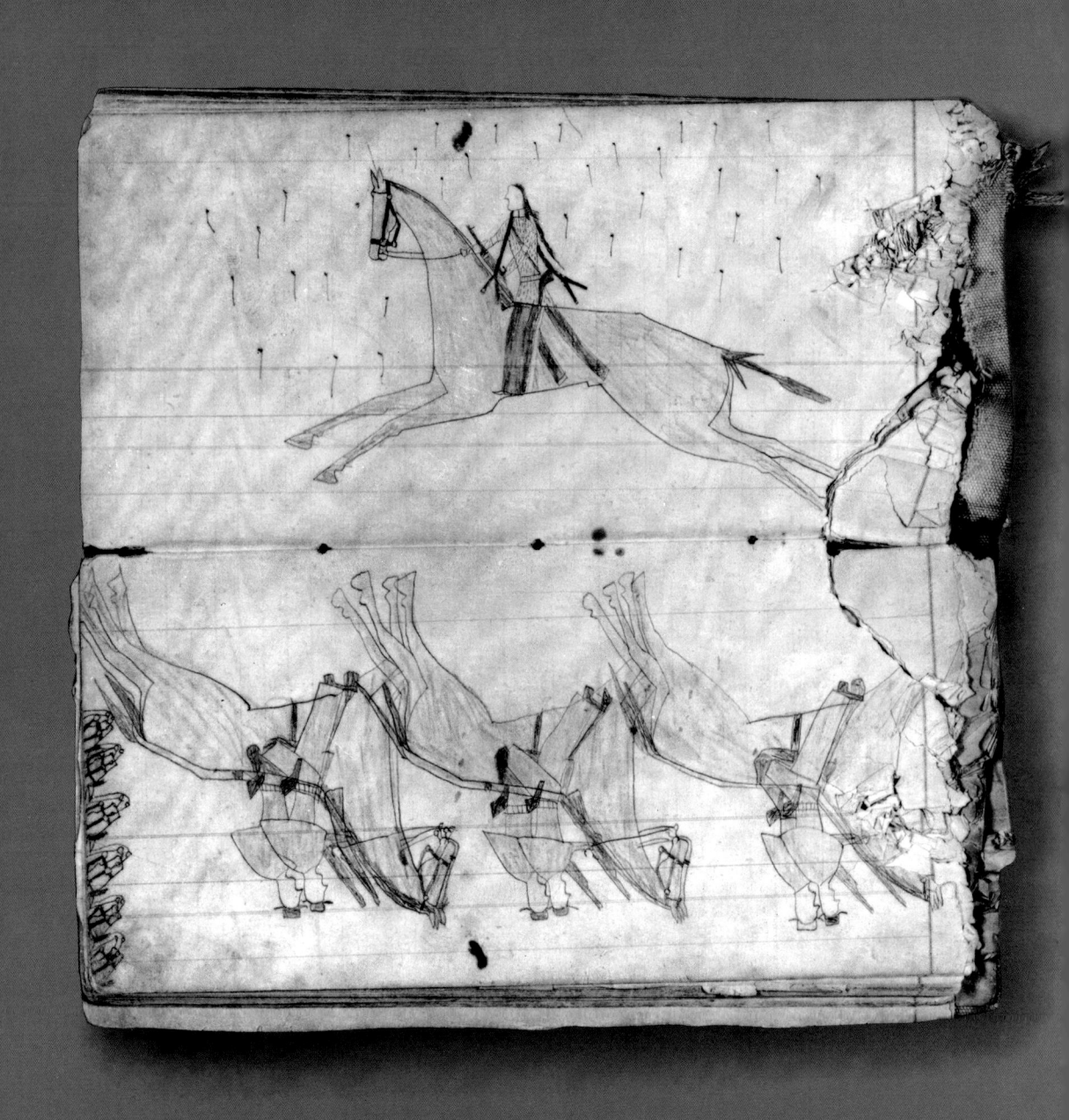

A YAHI SURRENDERS

Near starvation, and certain he would soon die at the hands of his white enemies, the last of northern California's Yahi Indians emerged from hiding in 1911. Butchers at a slaughterhouse near Oroville, California, found him one morning crouching against a fence, held at bay by barking dogs. A scientist from the University of California recognized him as a survivor of the Yahi and took him to live at the Museum of Anthropology in San Francisco. A tribal taboo prevented him from speaking his own name, so the professors called him Ishi—the Indian word for "man." His people, once numbering perhaps 3,000, had lived in the foothills around Lassen Peak, hunting, fishing, and gathering wild food, until the mid-19th century when the gold rush brought swarms of prospectors and settlers to their land. The Yahi, forced to raid for food, provoked attacks by soldiers and vigilantes, and by 1872 only 12 Indians survived. The small band hid in rough, inaccessible country, where old age and illness gradually killed them off. Ishi lived alone for nearly three years before despair and loneliness drove him to the white men he feared. He spent the remainder of his life at the museum, where he acquired friends and a job and a measure of happiness before tuberculosis killed him in March 1916.

A CHEYENNE DIES FIGHTING

While imprisoned in a U.S. Army guardhouse, a Cheyenne brave recorded on the pages of a ledger the conflict between his tribe and uniformed soldiers. After his release he refused an adjutant's offer to buy the book at any price and carried it, strapped to his side, into battle. In 1879, fighting in the Wyoming Territory, he died from a bullet that grazed the margin of the volume. The bottom leaf portrays mounted troops advancing with carbines; a row of horses' heads indicates reserves. At top, a Cheyenne gallops through a barrage of enemy gunfire.

R. H. LOWIE MUSEUM OF ANTHROPOLOGY,
UNIVERSITY OF CALIFORNIA, BERKELEY

A. M. BAILEY AND FRED BRANDENBURG

Trailed by Navajo herdsmen, a flock of sheep cascades over a sand dune in Arizona's bleak Monument Valley. Young Navajos, like the girl above, learn to weave rugs and tend sheep and goats. New vistas and opportunities open as industry, roads, and commercial ventures come to the desert reservation. Mohawks have successfully adapted to the modern world. Like many of his people, Michael Chuck Sky (below) pursues a perilous vocation, rigging steel girders of skyscrapers.

VICTOR R. BOSWELL, JR., N.G.S. STAFF (ABOVE) AND MARGARET DURRANCE

18

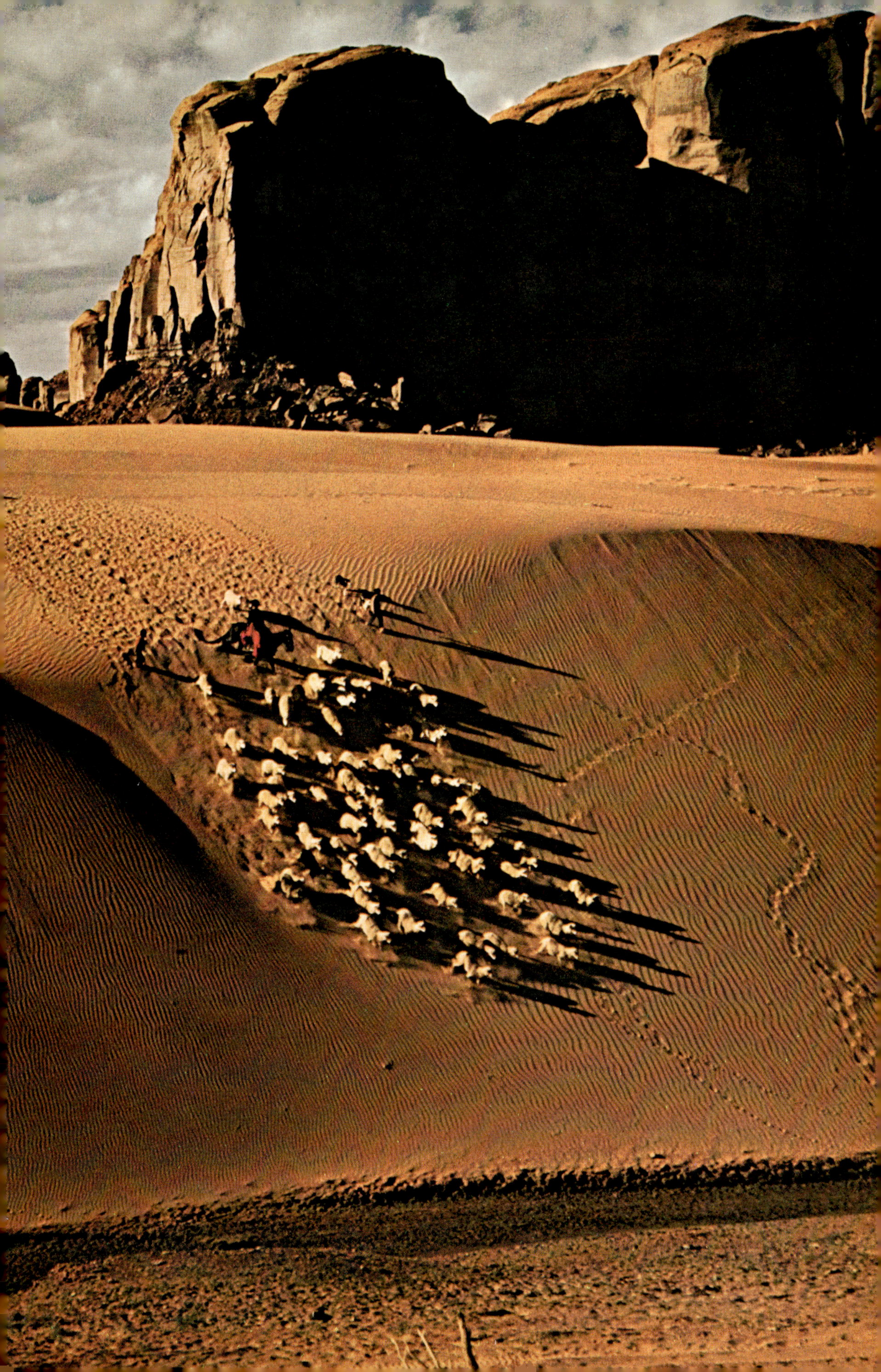

ARTHUR TRESS (ABOVE) AND NATIONAL GEOGRAPHIC PHOTOGRAPHER B. ANTHONY STEWART

Musicians of the Chamula Indians of southern Mexico, playing large wooden harps that date from the 16th century, celebrate during a spring festival in San Cristóbal de las Casas. These farmers descend from the powerful Maya who built great temple-cities in Mexico more than a thousand years ago. A Maya sculpture found in a tomb at the Palenque Ruins bears a strong resemblance to the Chamula.

Ishi saw the *saltu* — the white man — as fortunate, inventive, and clever, but lacking in restraint and in an understanding of nature. Glue he rated next to matches as the most useful invention. He believed that the long hours spent indoors — in offices, autos, and houses — accounted for the white man's ills. An anthropologist observed, . . . "he took very kindly to civilization." But Ishi viewed the world through Yahi eyes, just as all of us see through the lens shaped by our own culture.

A web of culture binds us to a style of life, to a moral order, and a definition of human nature. We see, understand, and make judgments based on the codes and values we grow up with. Knowledge of the diverse ways of mankind can give us a new perspective on man — who he is, what he can hope to become. Folklore, art, religion, technology, and social order reflect the way a people come to terms with life. Each culture embodies an experiment in the human potential. Each culture stands as a monument to man's achievement, and each testifies to the human capacity to find a formula for survival. Yet each web may have so intricate and fragile a pattern that cutting the strands of religion, political life, or economic base can sometimes cause the whole delicate structure to collapse. The people stay on, but their special way of adapting to life may vanish.

When myths fade from a people's memory, when their traditions lose importance, when old values no longer serve a need — the world loses something unique and precious. Throughout this book you will meet tribes, clans, and families who have survived exposure to new diseases and an encounter with the modern world. As a people they may be increasing in number, but some part of their old way of life is disappearing. Contact with civilization steadily erodes their old culture, posing problems and offering opportunities. The people must adapt, for better or for worse.

WHITLAW'S STUDIOS, COURTESY QUEEN VICTORIA MUSEUM, LAUNCESTON, TASMANIA

COURTESY MITCHELL LIBRARY, SYDNEY, AUSTRALIA

I have found many examples in history of people who surrendered traditions slowly or suddenly in the wake of expanding civilization. As Islam swept from Arabia, it transformed much of the Middle East. Only a few groups—such as the mountain Berbers of North Africa, the remnants of the Zoroastrians of Iran, and the Copts of Egypt—retained a distinct identity and way of life as a powerful civilization flowed around them.

THE KAFIRS of the Hindu Kush mountains on the border of Afghanistan and present-day Pakistan remained such an enclave until the turn of the century. Sir George Robertson, a British official, traveled to the high valleys of Kafiristan in 1890, just five years before the Afghan Emir Abdur Rahman converted the Kafirs in Afghanistan from their pagan ways to Islam. Known as Nuristanis thereafter, the people abandoned their stone temples, outdoor altars, and wooden statues honoring the dead.

In his book, *The Káfirs of the Hindu Kush*, Robertson reported a complex ceremonial life of a people whose customs may have echoed those of the ancient Persians. Robertson wrote: "Káfirs dance when they are happy, and when they are plunged in grief. . . . When any one is sorely hurt from an accident, or when he is sick or dying . . . people congregate in his room to amuse him, as they say; but my own idea is that . . . it is a form of supplication to the gods. . . . The Káfir gods are propitiated by songs, dancing, and feasting. . . ."

Their funeral ceremonies Robertson called "curious and fantastic." One year after the death of an adult, the Kafirs erected a wooden effigy to his memory. The family of the dead person earned the right to mark the grave with a figure by feasting the community. An ordinary carving required a day of feasting, but an effigy placed on a throne or astride a horse merited a banquet lasting three days. Today only the Kafirs, in Pakistan, make statues to honor the dead, and dance to the trill of flutes and the beat of drums. The Nuristanis have abandoned these old skills and customs. The two groups less than 75 years ago shared the same culture; in their contrasting ways, they present a case study in social change.

Like the Nuristanis, the once tall, proud Marquesans survive, but their unique culture has vanished. Although a core of traditions persists, contact with the Western world in the 19th century—with soldiers, seamen, and missionaries—snuffed out the soul of the vigorous, sensual Polynesian civilization that blossomed in the deep valleys of the Marquesas Islands of the South Pacific.

The war clubs of intricately carved and polished wood now on display in museums all over the world once ran with human blood. Brave warriors, their naked bodies a mosaic of ornate and artistic tattoos, smeared their clubs with the blood of enemies to give their weapons added strength. In warfare Marquesans devoured human flesh in fierce cannibalistic rites; a host of gods and goddesses demanded human sacrifice.

Raids and counter-raids for victims alternated with life's routine. Men in fleets of long slender canoes fished in the bays and the ocean beyond for bonito, tuna, and giant manta rays. Marquesans cultivated

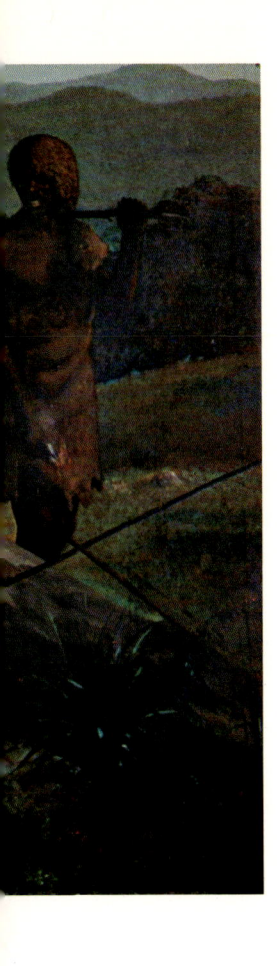

Cloaked in kangaroo skins, Tasmanian aborigines gather around a fire at dusk in an artist's conception painted in 1859. The intrusion of the white man led to the extinction of an estimated 1,200 natives of Tasmania in less than a century. Hundreds died in the Black Wars of 1804-30; contagious diseases killed many more. The remaining 200 resettled on Flinders Island off Tasmania in 1835. Four survivors (left) posed stiffly in Victorian dress several years later. The last aborigine died in 1888.

DANIEL LEAHY

plots of sweet potatoes, yams, taro, and bananas, gathered the bounty of the coconut palm and breadfruit tree, and eagerly awaited ceremonies in their village plaza.

Then missionaries frowned upon the old moral code and banned the ancient songs and dances in honor of tribal gods. The newcomers contradicted all that the Marquesans knew and believed.

Rough sailors from whaling ships descended on the population, bringing disease from the waterfronts of the world. Epidemics afflicted the people; bewilderment and despair ravaged their spirit. Marquesans still walk the shores of their islands, but the people have been effectively cut off from their past. The impact of civilization convulsed the very foundations of Marquesan life.

The world has intruded more slowly and more gently on the Veddas, short, wiry, primitive hunters of the remote forests of eastern Ceylon. As the Sinhalese and Tamil people of Ceylon have moved in and pushed back the frontiers of the Veddas' forest home, they gradually have absorbed nearly all of the population. Some Veddas lost their heritage and identity by marrying Ceylonese. Others simply ceased to be Veddas when they chose to adopt the language, dress, manners, and customs of the village society nearby.

Roads are breaking down isolation everywhere, spanning distances and obliterating barriers that once helped to create and preserve isolated cultures. I made my first trip deep into Mexico 32 years ago over almost impassable roads. In the 1940's the Pan American Highway cut through the mountains of the state of Chiapas in southern Mexico and blazed a trail for trade, industry, and government in an area where virtually no road existed, where Indians lived in small, close-knit villages.

More than 270,000 Indians of Chiapas speak languages descended from early Maya and cling to a folk religion that echoes pagan beliefs. For the Chamula Catholics, God becomes "our father the sun" and the Virgin Mary "our mother the moon." A Chamula believes in two souls —one that dies and one that goes to the underworld—"the sky below." Although many Chamulas leave the village for work on coffee plantations in the lowlands or jobs in the city of San Cristóbal de las Casas, they return to the family altar on *Todos Santos,* All Saints' Day, to await the souls of ancestors with feasts of tamales, cabbage, meat, and *posol,* or corn gruel.

NO GROUP HAS HELD to its Maya traditions more tenaciously than the Lacandon Indians. On a trip to Chiapas in 1937, I saw the Lacandons worshiping before the ruins of the Maya city of Yaxchilán. I watched as they burned copal, sacred resin of the celebrated Maya. Wisps of smoke from the incense rose in the dense mahogany and chicozapote forests. In those days the Lacandons numbered a scant 200. As a result of the Mexican Government's campaign against malaria, the population has risen to 300. Even today, the Lacandons set incense ablaze in clay god-pots to carry prayers and offerings to Maya gods. The men, women, and children smoke large cigars of cured tobacco leaves as their ancestors did centuries ago.

In a special hut where women may not enter, the men shape new pots, working without a potter's wheel. The craftsmen shape the face of a god on each pot in a style that faintly recalls the art gracing the temple-cities of Palenque and Yaxchilán. The Lacandons, with their heavy-lidded eyes, strong aquiline noses, and drooping lower lips, might have stepped out of the glowing frescoes of the ruined temple of Bonampak, except for the crudeness of their billowing sacklike tunics. Gone are the enormous feathered headdresses, the jaguar-skin skirts, the long cloaks fastened with jade. Although the Lacandons descend from the Maya builders, they have forgotten the writing, medicine, calendar, and architecture of their ancestors. Only diluted elements of the old religion survive.

Until recently the shy Indians camouflaged the way to their *caribals,* or family settlements, by meticulously covering the trail with fallen

Stone Age New Guinea Highlanders greet the first white man they have ever seen—Daniel Leahy, member of a 1933 expedition into the rugged country. Today the sons of these men, accustomed to the sight of airplanes landing on fields throughout the interior, herd cattle, grow coffee and tea, and shop in small, prosperous towns.

Bamboo rafts (opposite) rigged with gossamer fishing nets glide across placid Sun Moon Lake, as Taiwan aborigines paddle shoreward in evening mist. Wearing beads and a headdress, a girl of the Bunun tribe of Taiwan pauses after a dance for tourists. Following World War II, tribesmen began to leave the island's mountainous interior to seek jobs in coastal towns.

HELEN AND FRANK SCHREIDER, N.G.S. STAFF

trees and branches. Since the 1940's, foreign influences have found their way into the jungle as more and more airstrips mark the green landscape. The people no longer hide their trails. Women wove cotton cloth on crude looms until factory-made cloth became increasingly available. Now most of them buy it, using money earned principally from the sale of tobacco. Many Indians have acquired transistor radios, flashlights, and cigarette lighters. They still treat their ills with prayer and offerings of incense, but they try to get aspirin as well. A few years ago their numbers started to decrease; before the trend changed, an old belief grew stronger among the people: When the last Lacandon dies, the world will come to an end.

Nowhere has the airplane leaped barriers with such dramatic and profound impact as in the Highlands of New Guinea. Sealed off by dense jungle and soaring mountains, the area remained untouched by Western civilization until 1930. Its people lived in the Stone Age, had never seen a wheel or a white man, and felt the perpetual fear of sorcery.

Anthropologist James B. Watson relates one New Guinea Highlander's recollection of the first moments in the meeting of two worlds. "The strangers were ghosts and women would burst out wailing at the sight of them, thinking to recognize dead ancestors. They came from the direction ... where dwelt the ghosts of the departed. Pigs were hastily killed so that the men might smear themselves and their women and children with the blood, the strongest protection they knew against sickness or death from the nameless danger."

Today many of these people send their children to school, sell coffee and other crops for Australian dollars, and elect representatives to the House of Assembly of the Territory of Papua and New Guinea. They have recovered from the head-on collision between a world governed by magic and a world ruled by reason. But the disruption and dislocation spawned a series of prophetic cults in parts of the Highlands and throughout the South Pacific. These promised a new world that would bring the people the "cargo" of the European, and on occasion threatened the white man with violence.

We can only imagine the effect of shipment after shipment of bicycles, radios, matches, lamps, cloth, and food in cans on people who knew nothing of factories, mass production, and banking. The white man made signs on paper, and he received goods he neither paid for nor worked for. Many islanders believed that he held the secret of cargo and kept it from them—intercepting this wealth of goods sent by their ancestors.

Day after day they waited for the secret. They performed all the rites; they gathered in front of mock radios with antennas of bamboo and rope and made signs on paper. Sometimes, in a climax of mass hysteria, men and women danced and sang in eager expectation of the cargo. When it failed to come, disillusionment set in, but belief in the cargo persisted, and the strong emotions it engendered continued to smolder, perhaps to erupt again.

While in the Highlands not long ago, I sat on the floor of a hut in a village near the town of Kainantu, and dined as a guest of Wanamera, a gracious host and leader of a cargo cult. With the help of a friend who speaks Pidgin—the lingua franca of the Australian half of the island—

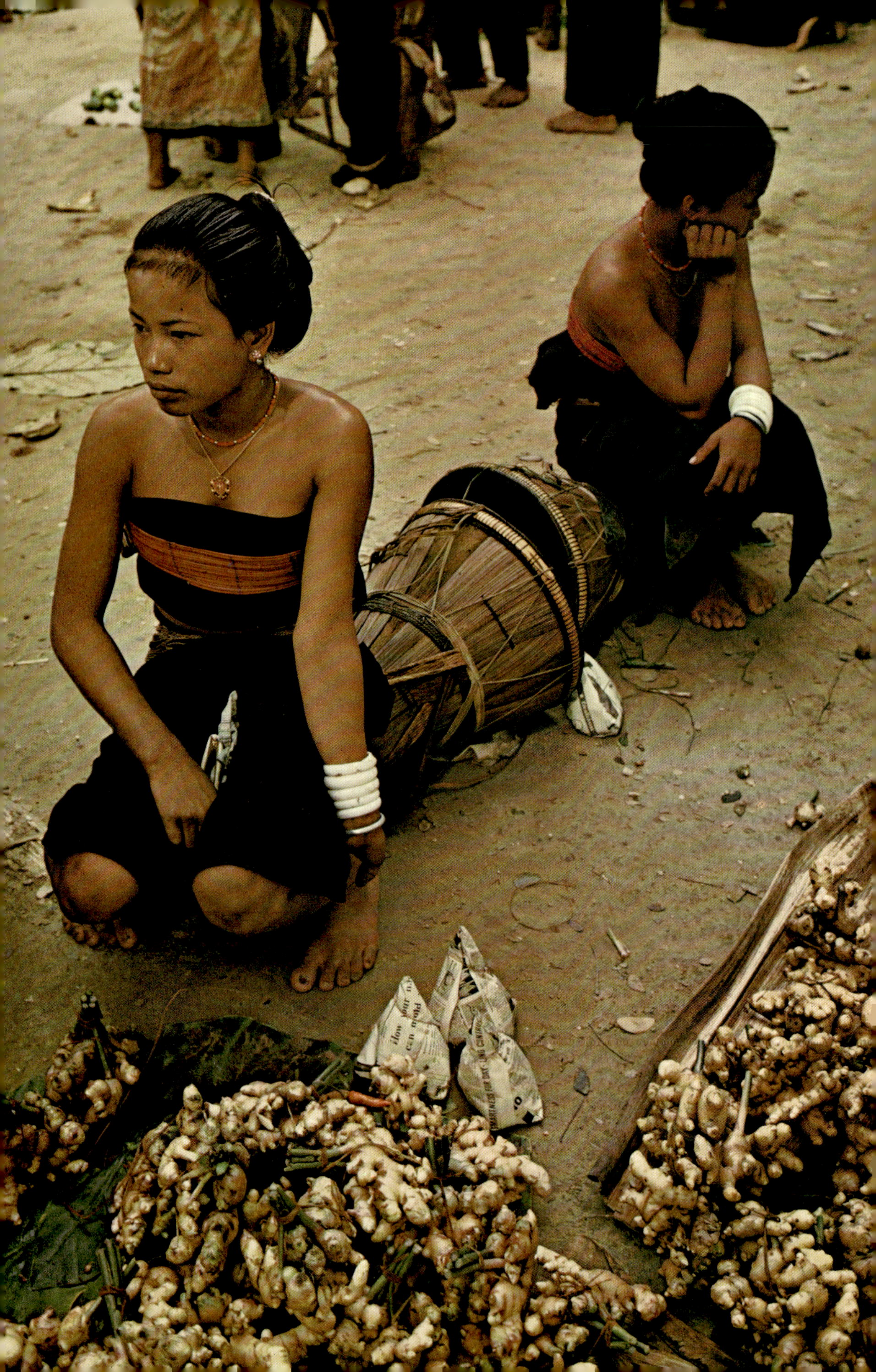

Sitting on baskets of tree bark, Dusun, or Kadazan, girls of Sabah, on the island of Borneo, vend ginger in the market square of Kota Belud. The Kadazans—once head-hunters—now lead a peaceful life. They grow rubber trees and rice and take an increasingly active part in the government of Malaysia. The majestic peak of Kinabalu (right), revered as the resting place of Kadazan souls, towers over the island's hill country.

NATIONAL GEOGRAPHIC PHOTOGRAPHER WINFIELD PARKS

we talked about the carved wooden figures that "lived" in his hut. Wanamera believed they would help him in the spirit world.

Not far from the village, people had built a crude wooden airplane. Many cults believe that the possession of an airplane offers the key to getting cargo; anticipating its arrival, some of the people have constructed runways.

Forty years ago I flew into the interior of New Guinea in a single-engine pontoon plane. The pilot and I picked a campsite near a river and landed. As we began to unload supplies, screaming warriors in canoes suddenly appeared, shooting arrows that bounced off the plane and fell all around us. We quickly jumped back into our seats and took off. When our plane roared over the tribesmen who had reached the bank, they fell face down in the sand.

A cosmopolitan civilization forged by an industrial urban society is rapidly spreading across the globe. The tempo of change accelerates as the modern nations with great resources converge on tribal cultures. Governments everywhere exert more power, exercise more control and influence, and make plans that reach out into all spheres of life.

For generations, five or six hundred dark-skinned Hadza hunted eland, impala, zebra, and other animals of the bush around Lake Eyasi in Tanzania. The Hadza built no houses, only rude, temporary shelters of grass and branches. The people roamed in bands of several families, easily plucking all the fruits and nuts they needed. Then the nomads moved on. They had no gardens to cultivate, no domestic animals to care for, and very little to carry. They acknowledged no chief and knew no authority; only the struggle for existence governed them. But the struggle was not harsh, and no one starved. Much of the food had little flavor, and the Hadza relished the millet porridge and other foods grown by neighboring tribes. Still they did not think the taste made all the work of cultivation worthwhile.

PETER KUNSTADTER

Bamboo-and-thatch homes in a peaceful village rimmed by the mountains of northern Thailand house Lua farmers who raise chickens and pigs and grow rice on precipitous slopes. A young girl harvests the crop (top left), and an elder weaves an umbrella frame from split bamboo. A tattoo, a symbol of manhood, covers his knee and extends to his waist. The 10,000 Lua maintain their own culture amid an increasing number of Karen tribes who have migrated from Burma during the past 150 years.

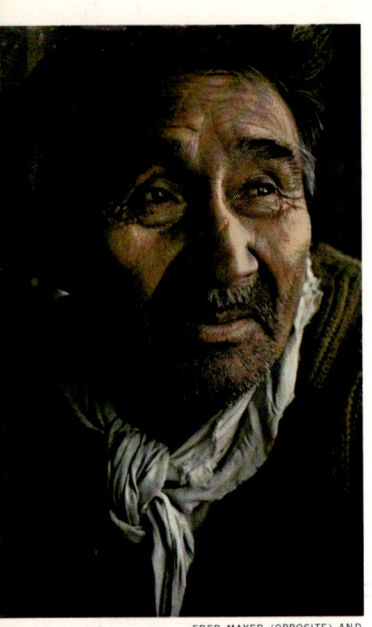

FRED MAYER (OPPOSITE) AND
N.G.S. PHOTOGRAPHER JAMES STANFIELD

Felipe Alvarez Victoria (above), a 79-year-old half-breed of the Yahgan tribe, lives in Tierra del Fuego—homeland of the Yahgans. In the late 1800's many of these Indians died of measles, typhoid, and influenza. A Tibetan boy (opposite), who moved from the Himalayas to the Swiss Alps with 600 fellow refugees to escape the Communist Chinese, stands before a painting of the Potala in Lhasa, palace of Tibet's exiled god-king, the Dalai Lama.

In two hours the women could pick enough fruits and berries to last the day. They spent the rest of their time sewing, stringing beads, and amusing themselves with songs and dances around the evening campfires. The men enjoyed gambling and smoking tobacco in stone pipes, until hunger or opportunity sent them out on a hunt.

The Tanzanian Government settled all the Hadza on a reservation in 1965, granting them land for cultivation. We can only guess how the Hadza, uprooted and thrust into a new setting, finally will adjust to an agricultural life. Cast adrift in a different setting amid strangers, the people find that their old skills and values no longer hold answers and guides to life's challenges.

In the mid-1800's British civil servants crossed rain-drenched Assam in northeastern India; they brought new laws, trade, and religion to the terraced rice fields and villages of the Naga tribes. Missionaries, bureaucrats, and traders from the hot plains of India and the crowded cities of Europe and America breached the stone walls, thorn fences, and spiked palisades guarding the Naga villages spread across the land between the Brahmaputra River and the Burmese border.

Trade introduced implements and novelties difficult to resist. Plastic ornaments, enamel, and cheap glass ousted the old decorations of shells and beads, feathers, and flowers. Brass and aluminum pots took the place of handmade bamboo vessels. Shirts and trousers replaced black and crimson togas and collars of beads and bone.

Other changes went much deeper, attacking a basic premise of Naga culture. Manhood, marriage, and the arts all depended on the taking of human heads in battle or ambush. A human head, the Nagas believed, contained great powers. It made rice and cotton grow better. It increased a man's chances of finding a wife.

For a time, demoralization and a sense of frustration beset the Nagas in the face of disruptive change. Then, in the period after World War II the Nagas clamored for more schools, more roads, more trade. At the same time, with new self-confidence, they took greater pride in their own traditional culture, reviving the dances, songs, and skills of their ancestors. Given time and the opportunity to shape their own destiny, the Nagas themselves have opened the door to change.

In North America the life of the Indian furnishes a well-documented example of what can transpire when two cultures meet. The introduction of the horse by the Europeans in the 16th century transformed the life of the Plains Indians much as the automobile has shaped life in the 20th century. They learned to hunt and fight in new ways, acquired more leisure, and enlarged their domain.

Disease brought by intruders took a heavy toll of many tribes. The Mandan, a tall, striking people who lived on the upper Missouri River near what is now Bismarck, North Dakota, suffered repeated scourges of smallpox that decimated the tribe; fewer than 125 survived a severe epidemic in 1837. The pitiful remnants joined the neighboring Hidatsa tribe. Today no full-blooded Mandan exists.

Other Indians found a new life, making a successful transition to a once-alien world. Well into the 1800's the Chiricahua Apaches kept faith with a warlike heritage, raiding the Pueblo villages, and settlements in Mexico and the American Southwest. But by the time their leader

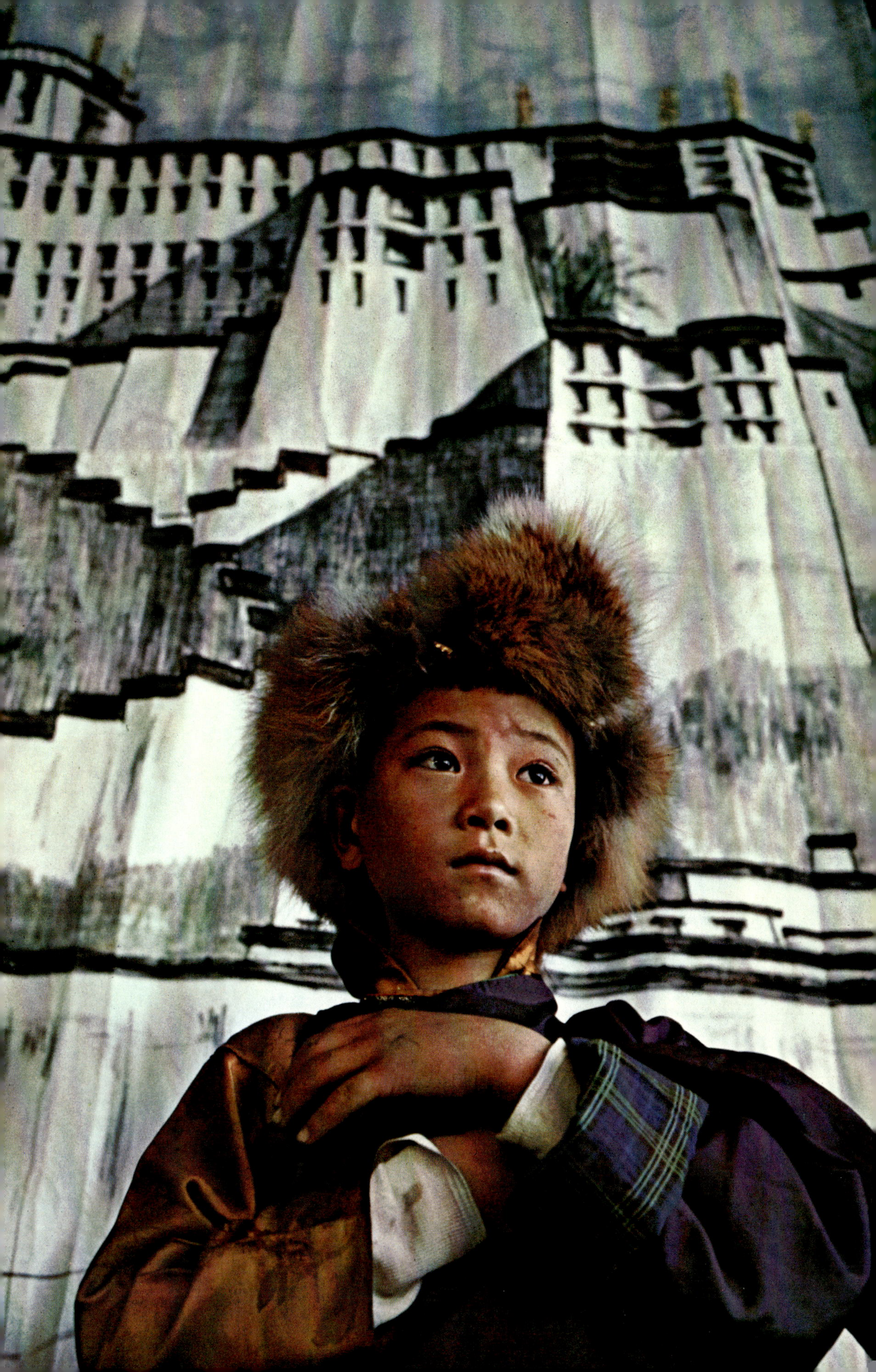

Geronimo voluntarily surrendered in 1886, other Apaches had begun to expand their interest in agriculture. Now the Apaches, who once took pride in hunting and marauding, take pride in their outstanding success as ranchers. Many of them own automobiles and electrical appliances—and get top prices for their fine cattle.

For more than a hundred years the Seminole Indians of Florida have guarded the mysteries of their religion and performed secret ceremonies, aloof from the world of the white man. Determined warriors fought the United States in three wars, the last one ending in a stalemate in 1857. Over several years the Government deported some 4,600 Seminoles to the West, most of them to Oklahoma, where descendants now live.

After the last Seminole war a small band of the Indians, less than 200, remained in the trackless swamps of the Everglades area, eyeing outsiders with suspicion and mistrust and avoiding contact with them whenever possible. They lived in thatched-roof huts called *chickees*, hunting, gardening on small hammocks, or marsh islands, and fishing from dugouts that moved silently through the swamp.

Today the airboat replaces the canoe, and roads cut a bold swath on the green landscape linking the Seminole to the 20th century. The children are learning to speak English. Cars, radios, and television sets are bringing the people a new style of life, as they embark on such economic ventures as selling timber, leasing land to vegetable growers, and selling dolls, costumes, and wood carvings to tourists.

Although the Seminoles still hold the sacred Green Corn Dance to assure good health throughout the year, the ceremony has lost some of its sanctity. The women continue to wear their distinctive style of colorful full-skirted dress, but as more and more families move from the Everglades region to new homes on Florida's east coast, the Seminoles are abandoning their isolation and joining the life of those they once shunned.

SOME PEOPLES surrender and submit to change. Others resist. Some are shattered and overwhelmed by change; others find strength to build a new future. Some suffer from epidemics of new diseases; others find new health and vigor through modern medicine. Yet whatever the reaction and response, the old order in many places is yielding to the new. Scientists and philosophers have felt the urgent need to investigate these peoples' life, language, and folklore before they vanish, before the modern world dilutes the myriad local customs and beliefs.

Claude Lévi-Strauss, the eminent French anthropologist, has eloquently expressed the need to study existing but little-known cultures before they disappear: "Let us suppose for a moment that astronomers should warn us that an unknown planet was nearing the Earth and would remain for 20 or 30 years at close range, afterwards to disappear forever.... neither effort nor money would be spared to build telescopes and satellites [to study the planet].... If the future of anthropology could be seen in this light, no study would appear more urgent or more important. For native cultures are disintegrating faster than radioactive bodies; and... we may never again be able to recognize and study this image of ourselves."

High in the Himalayas, Bhutanese schoolboys peer through a weathered classroom window. Technology slowly transforms their mountain kingdom. Roads and airstrips scar the countryside, and electric lights illuminate old cities as the Bhutanese begin to adapt their traditions to the demands of a modern society.

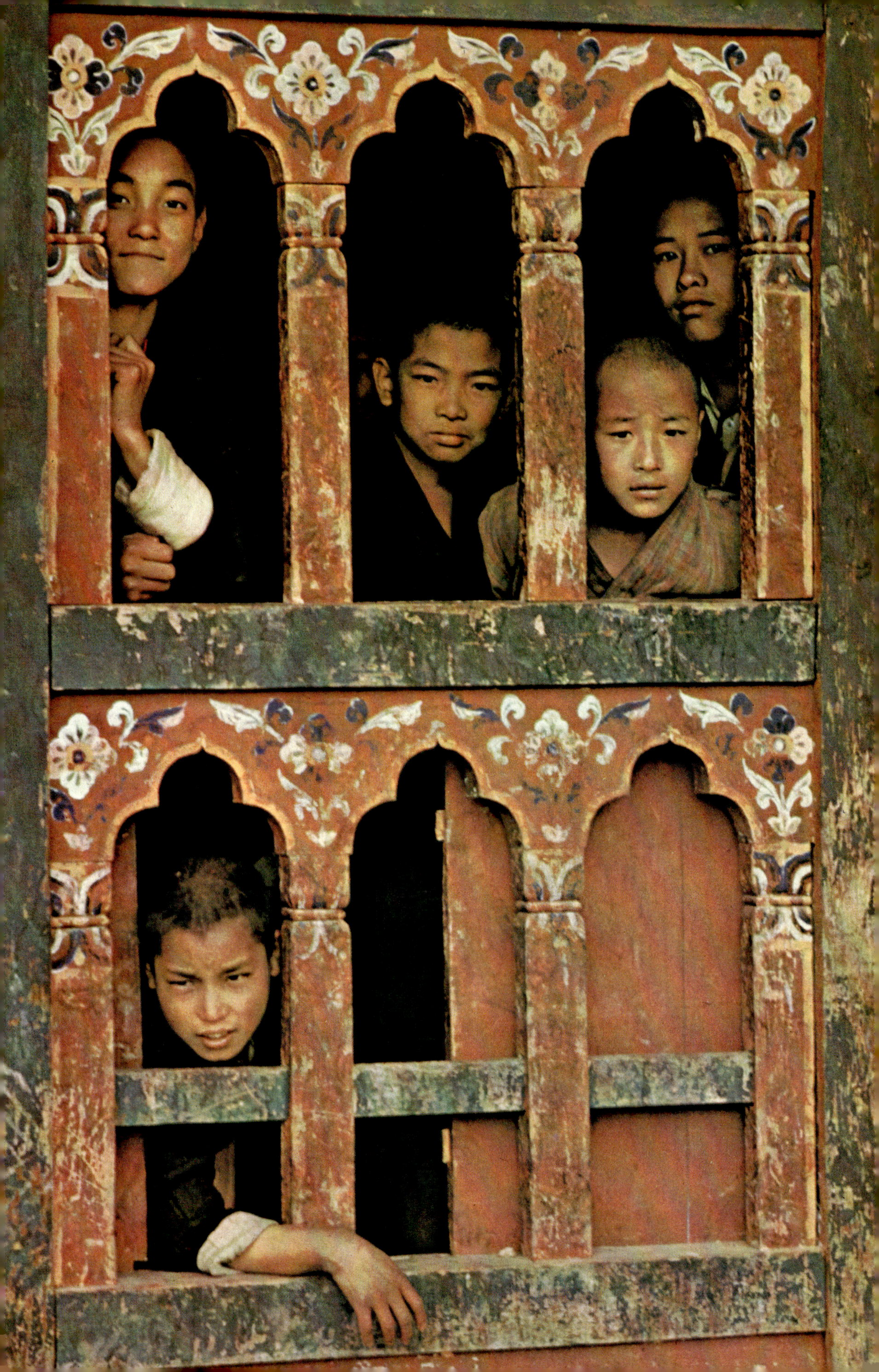

2

Lapps in a Modern World Face Timeless Realities

By GEORGE F. MOBLEY, *National Geographic Staff*
Illustrations by the Author

LAPPS OF NORWAY tell about a man, grown too old to follow the reindeer migration to summer pastures, who had three sons. One entered the army and gained an education that eventually led to a respected job in town. Another won a university scholarship and went on to bring great honor to his family. Finally, it came time for the third son to choose what he would do.

"Father," the young man began, "I have decided to become a reindeer herder like you and your father before you."

"At last," the old man cried. "Now I have a son I can be proud of."

Relatively few of some 32,000 Lapps who live scattered across the arctic fringes of Norway, Sweden, Finland, and Russia, the rugged area known as Lapland, have ever followed the lonely life of the reindeer nomad. But those few have clung tenaciously to the customs of their forefathers, following their herds along migratory routes linking winter and summer pastures.

Today, however, a new way of life has come to a once-isolated Lapland. Automobiles and trucks speed across a countryside where some of the people still gear their everyday lives to the meandering movements of foraging reindeer.

In April of 1968, I drove a rented car along an all-weather highway toward Kautokeino, 170 miles above the Arctic Circle in Finnmark, Norway's northernmost county. Around me, beautiful rolling hills lay covered in deep snow, a chilly reminder that only a few years ago I would have been forced to use skis or a sled to make my journey in this land of some 1,500 reindeer nomads.

I arrived just before Easter to find Kautokeino in a holiday mood. Lapps—young and old—poured into the village from the surrounding *vidda*, or plateau. Lengthening days had begun to temper the bitter cold. Soon the herds of reindeer that wintered in the area would grow

Waning sunlight burnishes the tousled hair of Isak Gaup, a 30-year-old Lapp nomad on a trek across northern Norway. He and his kinsmen still follow their migrating reindeer herd in the seasonal quest for pasture, traveling by sled, on skis, or on foot, and sleeping in an old-style goatte, *or tent.*

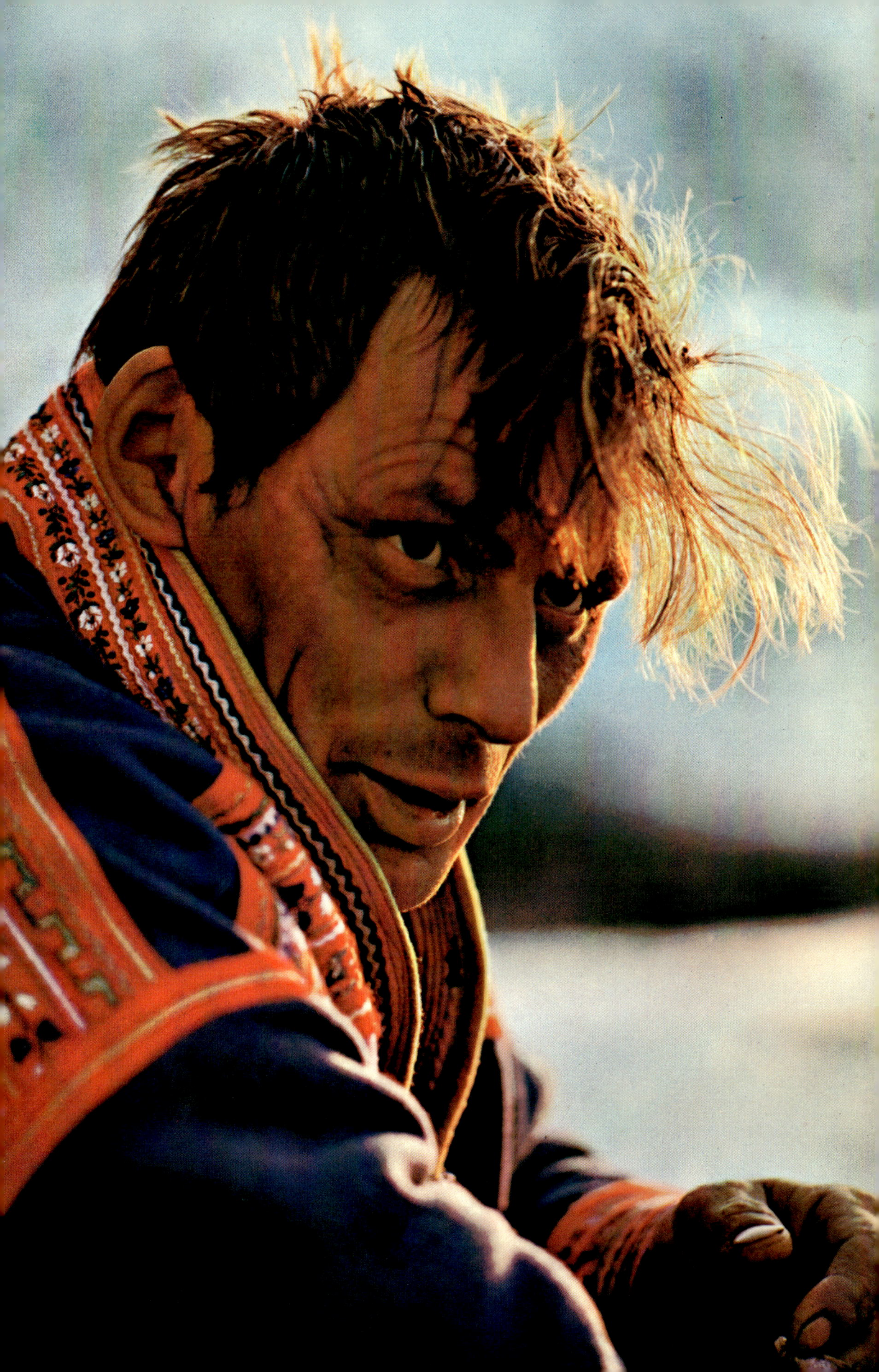

restless to begin the migration to other pasture lands. Warmly dressed tourists jammed the hotel and the smaller guest lodges, leaving latecomers like me to find beds in a boarding school, which had recessed for the holidays.

A jovial crowd filled the streets, streaming toward the annual reindeer races, and I joined in, looking for a man named Isak Gaup. I had learned he might let me accompany him and his family on their migration to the coast.

A gallery of spectators, many in gaily embroidered Lapp dress, crowded around the circular race course marked out on the frozen Kautokeino River. I watched as a spirited reindeer galloped past, snow from its flying hoofs showering the handler, who sat sidesaddle on a wooden sled. "*Giš, giš,*" the herdsman yelled, urging his animal to still-greater speed.

Skimming over the snow on his reindeer-drawn sled, a Lapp charges down the track during the Easter-eve races at Kautokeino, Norway. For many families, the holiday offers a time to gather for weddings, baptisms, and feasts before starting migrations to distant grazing lands. A proud herder of Sevettijärvi, Finland, fills a can with extra fuel for his snow scooter. Reindeer-tending Lapps now use the versatile vehicles to round up strays and to transport supplies.

Between races I was introduced to Isak, a rugged, muscular man of 30, and his attractive wife, Karen Anna. When I asked about joining the migration, Isak frowned and told me of another journalist who had accompanied him northward a few years before. The rigors of the long journey had proved too much for him.

"But you seem to be built of stronger stuff than that one," Isak said at last. I smiled, relieved.

For those reindeer-herding Lapps who remain isolated during much of the year tending their herds, holidays such as Christmas and Easter offer opportunities for entire families to gather for baptisms, confirmations, and weddings. The receptions and feasts that follow the wedding rites sometimes last for three days, with family and friends savoring time and again the *bidos,* a delicious stew of reindeer meat and vegetables simmered in a rich, thick sauce and served steaming hot from huge bowls.

The elaborate "proposal" ceremony that once preceded Lapp weddings has largely disappeared. Although the procedure varied in different parts of Lapland, in Finnmark the suitor would dress in his finest clothes on the chosen day, put his best reindeer in harness, and, accompanied by a marriage broker as his spokesman, drive up to the home of his intended.

He would circle the girl's tent on his sled three times. If she came out and unhitched the reindeer, the suitor knew he had won her favor; if not, she probably would reject his offer. Having eloquently elaborated on the suitor's many desirable qualities and countered any objections offered by the girl's family, the spokesman then prepared a festive meal. Later he would help the families settle questions of dowry and exchange of property.

"Some Lapps still adhere to this old custom," Bjørn Aarseth, secretary of the Nomadic Lapp Union in Karasjok, about 70 miles northeast of Kautokeino, had told me earlier. "But young men often modernize the ritual.

"Now some suitors carry out the ceremony with snow scooters instead of reindeer and sleds. Last year in Karasjok one Lapp even hired a snowmobile, loaded it with his spokesman, relatives, and friends, and proudly drove away to seek the hand of his love."

THE TIME for festivities, however, soon ended. Easter had come later this year than usual, and Isak and the other reindeer nomads plunged into preparations for the long, hard drive northward to summer pasture.

Isak's wife explained the reason for the migration. "In the winter pasture near Kautokeino," she said, "the herd lives on reindeer moss and other lichens which the animals reach by digging through the snow. In summer, the lichens there become dry and crumbly. If the deer stayed in the same pasture, their hoofs would soon trample it to powder. Also, warm weather brings hordes of gadflies and midges to torment the reindeer, so in spring everyone moves his herd to higher mountains or to the coast.

"Our herd moves to Arnøy, an island north of Lyngen Fjord, where there is rich pasture in summer," Karen Anna explained, "but in

Split-rail fences surround log houses in the tiny village of Lisma, Finland. With summer and winter pastures close by, the four reindeer-herding families of this hamlet do not migrate. At right, a villager unhooks a side of dried deer meat from the rafters of a storage shed. A fringed scarf covers the shoulders of a girl in traditional Lapp dress.

Lapland knows no fixed boundaries; it extends across arctic Sweden, Norway, and Finland into Russia. Ancestors of the 32,000 Lapps who live there may have roamed these lands as early as 8,000 years ago. Archeologists have established the existence of Lapps in the region in A.D. 400. Adapting to the geography over the centuries, they evolved into three distinct groups—coastal, forest, and mountain people. The more settled coastal and forest Lapps have been drawn into the mainstream of modern European life. The mountain Lapps depend on their reindeer for a livelihood, much as their forebears did more than a thousand years ago, and cling to many age-old customs in their seasonal pursuit of pasturelands. In early 1968 George F. Mobley, NATIONAL GEOGRAPHIC *writer and photographer, accompanied a family of Lapps on a numbing month-long migration across the rolling hills and coastal mountains of northern Norway. He finds the pressures of a modern world assailing these long-isolated nomads with ever-increasing force.*

winter, the snow on the coast is very deep. When rain freezes and coats the snow with ice, the reindeer can't reach the forage. That's why we move back to Kautokeino in autumn."

Although I had prepared myself for an arduous trip, I really had only an inkling of what lay ahead. Throughout the long, slow journey, herd and herder alike live at the mercy of a fickle climate; and a winter that refuses to give way to spring can spell catastrophe. Seeing man tested to his very marrow would soon add new meaning to the story of the old reindeer herder and his three sons.

On the tenth day after Easter, under a lightly overcast sky, we began the trip north. As our train of 22 supply-laden sleds fell into line behind the herd of 1,500 reindeer, Karen Anna walked beside Isak to the crest of the hill overlooking Kautokeino, where she said goodbye.

Until their second child was born two years ago, she had always accompanied her husband on the migration; but now, like an increasing number of Lapp women, she would make the trip by automobile and meet us at the coast.

Isak would not see his wife again until well into May. Making the trek with him were Karen Anna's two brothers, Aslak and Johan Logje, Johan's wife Marit and their two children, Anders and Ellen Inga, and Isak's cousin Ellen Anne Haetta.

Slowly we turned westward, following the track made by the herd as it moved onto the rolling hills and into a land of drifting snow. Only the sounds of wooden traces creaking against the sleds, the whine of the dogs, and the hiss of the wind brushing across the snow marred the stillness.

Hour after hour we trudged deeper into the white and silent world of the empty vidda, utterly barren except for an occasional clump of stunted birch trees.

Finally, at midnight, we stopped, and Isak showed me how to set up the tent. Using three birch poles, 11 feet tall and forked at the top, we formed a triangular support against which we propped ten more poles to complete the frame. Over this we tied panels of canvas, leaving an opening for the doorway. A piece of blanket with several bars of birch to hold it in place became our door.

By now, ice coated my thermal boots, and cold numbed my feet.

Deerskin gallokak, *packed with sennegrass to help hold their shape, hang inside out to dry in the sun between a pair of colorful handwoven bootstraps. Lapps use the tough, fibrous weed to insulate their feet against the bitter cold.*

Wiry Jouni Kitti, now 70, herded reindeer in the harsh climate of northern Finland for six decades. The shape, color, and pattern of a Lapp's headgear identifies his native district.

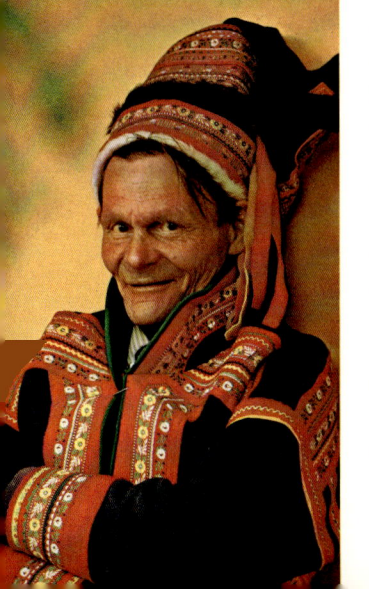

Isak handed me a pair of *gallokak*. "Here," he said, "you'd better try these." Gallokak, the shoes commonly worn by Lapps, are handmade from reindeer skin. The toes curl up and back, designed to fit into the single leather strap that Lapps use on their skis in place of bindings. Ellen Anne showed me how to pack my gallokak with sennegrass, a tough, fibrous plant that provides perfect insulation; even with only one pair of socks I found my feet stayed warm and dry.

A mountain Lapp's winter clothing also includes a heavy coat and trousers of reindeer skin. In these he can lie down in the snow to rest or to steady his telescope as he searches for strayed deer, without getting cold or wet.

A crackling fire warmed the tent, and the smell of coffee brewing renewed my appetite. I never thought I would see the day I would gladly chew a few shreds of meat from a bone, but when Isak sliced a rib off a side of dried reindeer with his heavy knife and passed it to me, I grabbed it eagerly.

Throughout the journey we lived mainly on dried reindeer meat, bread and butter, and coffee. Sometimes we ate the meat uncooked; at other times we put it in the fire to roast. Karen Anna had baked bread for days for the migration, and we ate huge chunks of it thickly coated with butter.

Hardly anyone in Lapland bothers to milk reindeer anymore; the process of catching and holding an animal becomes too laborious for the scant yield. So when our limited supply of fresh milk ran out, I turned to the Lapp practice of slicing off thin slivers of cheese and dropping them into my coffee. We jokingly called the concoction *Finnmarks middag,* Norwegian for "Finnmark dinner."

After a week on the trail Isak slaughtered a reindeer, and we had fresh, boiled meat for the first time—a real feast. Isak offered me half the tongue, a Lapp delicacy, and showed me how to cook the large leg bones in the fire and break them open for their delicious marrow.

We had no regular meals and no regular time for sleep. We ate when we camped, the same monotonous food every time. Theoretically, we were herding the reindeer, but I soon learned that in reality the deer were herding us. We moved when they moved; when they found food and stopped to graze, we stopped.

We often traveled at night when the frozen snow made the going easier for the herd. Breath condensed in my beard, forming large hunks of ice. The temperature grew too cold for us to ride the sled, so we struggled along on foot, sometimes through snow up to our knees, to generate enough body heat to stay comfortable.

Progress varied, depending on weather conditions and the movements of the herd. One day we covered only two miles. Another time, when the reindeer could find no food, we went 25 miles, traveling all day and night. Sometimes a thick, icy fog would settle over the mountains, cutting visibility to zero and forcing us to remain two or three days in the same camp.

Snow fell frequently, and often I could see nothing but the tracks behind me—no horizon, no sky, no ground. As we moved cautiously across the monochromatic sea of white, it seemed that we had somehow been suspended in a huge bottle of frozen milk. Now above the

43

timberline, we traveled for days across the high plateau, a world of endless snow broken here and there by a lonely, windblown outcropping of gray rock.

As I adapted to the life and became more a part of the group, I began to help with the herding, often traveling for miles on skis into the surrounding mountains and valleys in search of strays. One night, after a long day's drive, Ellen Anne—who had never been on a migration—said to me, "Now we too are reindeer Lapps."

I knew that I still had a way to go before I would merit such a compliment. But in facing the rigors of the migration with my newfound friends, I did sense the growth of a bond of kinship that I would remember long after the trip was over.

Isak and I often joked with each other. He laughed heartily at my attempts to speak the Lapp language; and when I tried to imitate his *juoigos,* the Lapps' own distinctive folk song, he rolled on the skin floor of the tent in near hysteria. Obviously, I had not yet mastered the strangely melodic songs—essentially a series of simple phrases which, linked together by bridges of rhythmic humming, gradually develop a lyric theme.

While many of the songs, often erotic, have been passed down through generations, Lapps are fond of creating new ones on the spur of the moment. Such melodies may give voice to the singer's feelings about the graceful movement of a reindeer fawn, the grand sweep of a mountain precipice, or perhaps something no more unusual than the warmth of a late winter sun.

As we trekked slowly across the glistening snow of the vidda one rare sunny day, Isak burst forth with a carefree demonstration of Lapp folk singing that lasted for nearly an hour. No less happy to catch a glimpse of the sun, I joined in, boisterously singing in English nearly every song I knew.

I learned that the songs, long discouraged as sinful by church leaders, now are undergoing somewhat of a revival in Lapland. But apparently the revival had not yet made much of an impression on the Lapp youngsters I met later in Finnmark's coastal towns. Much more in tune with the Beatles than the folk music of their forefathers, they gathered in small cafes to listen to deafening jukebox renditions of rock-and-roll. The fact that many of the youngsters could not understand the lyrics did nothing to dampen their enthusiasm.

The end of April came, but still winter would not let go its claim to the barren land. Sometimes we arose to find that as much as a foot of snow had fallen while we slept. Increasing numbers of reindeer, grown too weak to keep up with the herd, fell by the way. At first we tried to carry them with us, bundling them onto sleds, but we soon gave up.

Then one morning we awoke to the sound of a howling, raging wind. Snow swirled in through the smoke hole and under the edges of the tent. Aslak started a fire, and for a time the smoke mingled with our frosty breath.

"I think Biegg-olmai, the wind man, is angry," Ellen Anne said with a sudden shiver.

Isak grew perturbed and peered out of the tent. "It is not good," he said, returning to the fire. "Marit, Ellen Anne, and the children must

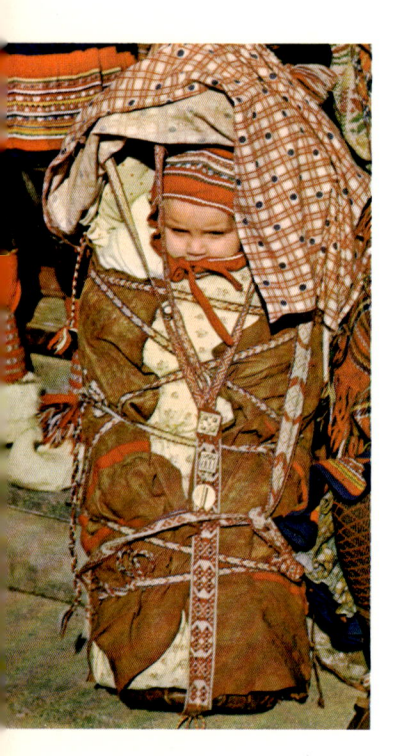

Bundled to her chin, a baby nests snugly in her gietkå; *today few Lapps still use the once-common wooden carrying cradle. Opposite, a newlywed couple stands at the altar of Kautokeino's Lutheran church. The bride wears an array of brooches, a gift from the groom.*

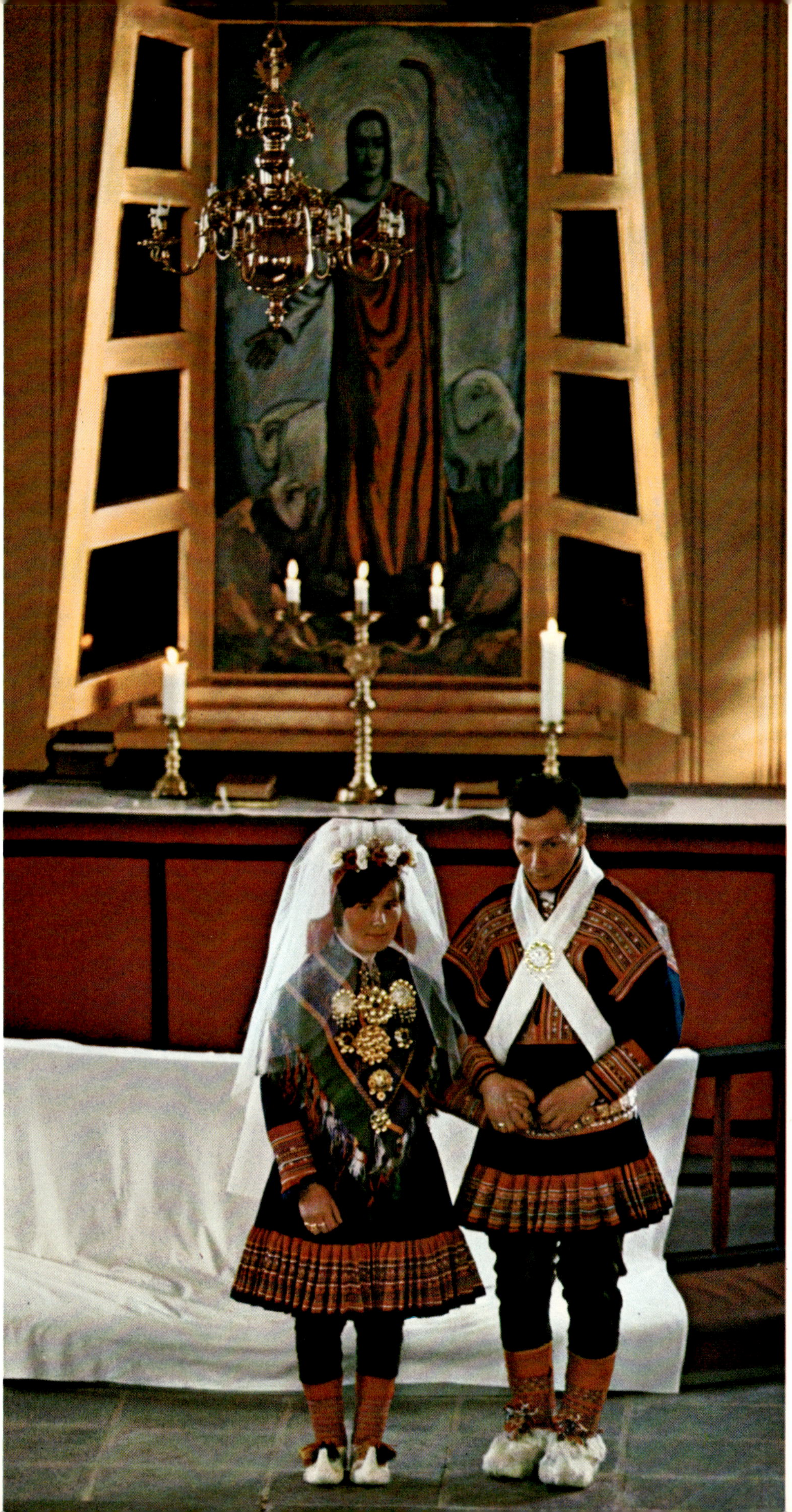

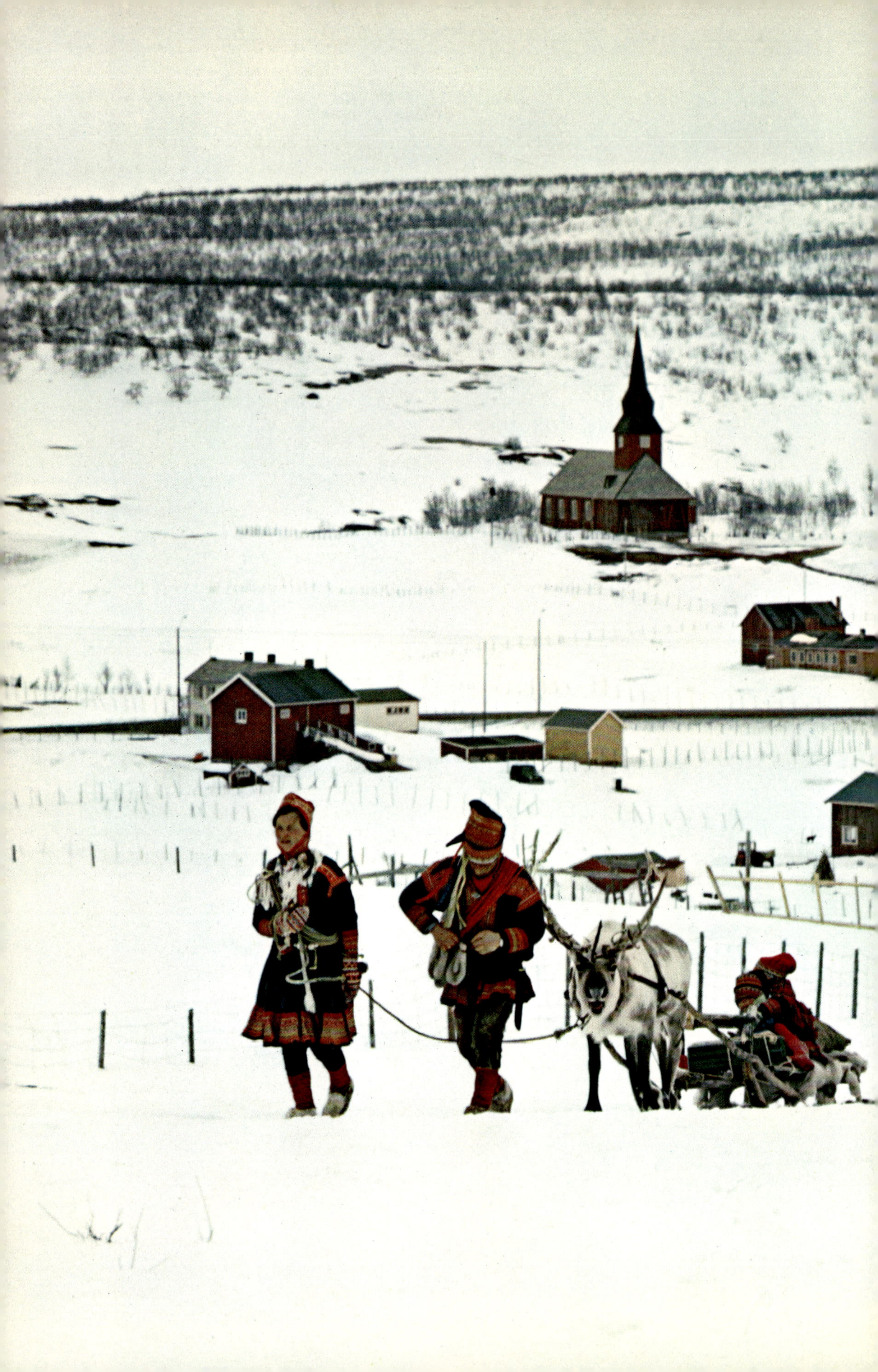

Leaving Kautokeino, Isak Gaup and his family begin their migration across a wilderness of drifting snow and freezing cold to lead their reindeer north to summer pasture on the island of Arnøy.

leave us now." Turning to me, he explained, "We are near the coastal mountains, and the weather will make the going very hard. You may stay with Aslak, Johan, and me if you wish; but I must warn you that if you fall behind you will be on your own."

"I will stay," I replied. I had gone too far to quit now.

Once the wind abated, the men took everything except four sleds and headed out of the mountains. They would go down to the road in the valley of the Reisa River; from there they could send the women, the children, and the equipment on to the coast by truck.

For the first time on the migration, I was completely alone. Relaxing in the tent beside a dying fire, I wondered how much more difficult this nomadic life must have been before the days of good roads, snow scooters, and other motor vehicles. I thought back to my conversation with Karen Anna's 68-year-old mother. "Before they built the road," she had told me, "I never knew what Kautokeino was like in the summer. Everyone followed the herd and stayed with it until we returned to winter pasture."

Early the next morning, a weird cry startled me from my sleep. I sat up and listened. Could wolves be after the herd? For a time it remained quiet; then the cry came again. This time I recognized Isak's voice and flipped open the tent door to find the wind had gone, leaving in its wake a sea of dense fog. Isak, Aslak, and Johan had been fighting their way back to the camp, barely able to see two yards in front of them. I called loudly to guide them and started a fire to make coffee.

Later, as I struggled to get back into my sleeping bag, half a dozen coins fell from my pocket onto the tent floor. I picked them up and started to put them back. "No, no," my three tired friends protested.

"You must throw them out the top of the tent," Isak explained. "It will bring good weather."

"Good weather?" I asked dubiously.

"Oh, yes," Aslak agreed.

Marit Logje hangs a kettle over a fire to melt snow as she prepares a supper of dried reindeer meat, bread, butter, and coffee. Above, lonely sentinel on a knoll, a canvas tent offers shelter from biting winds that howl across the barren tundra. Nearby, deer dig through a blanket of snow for lichens.

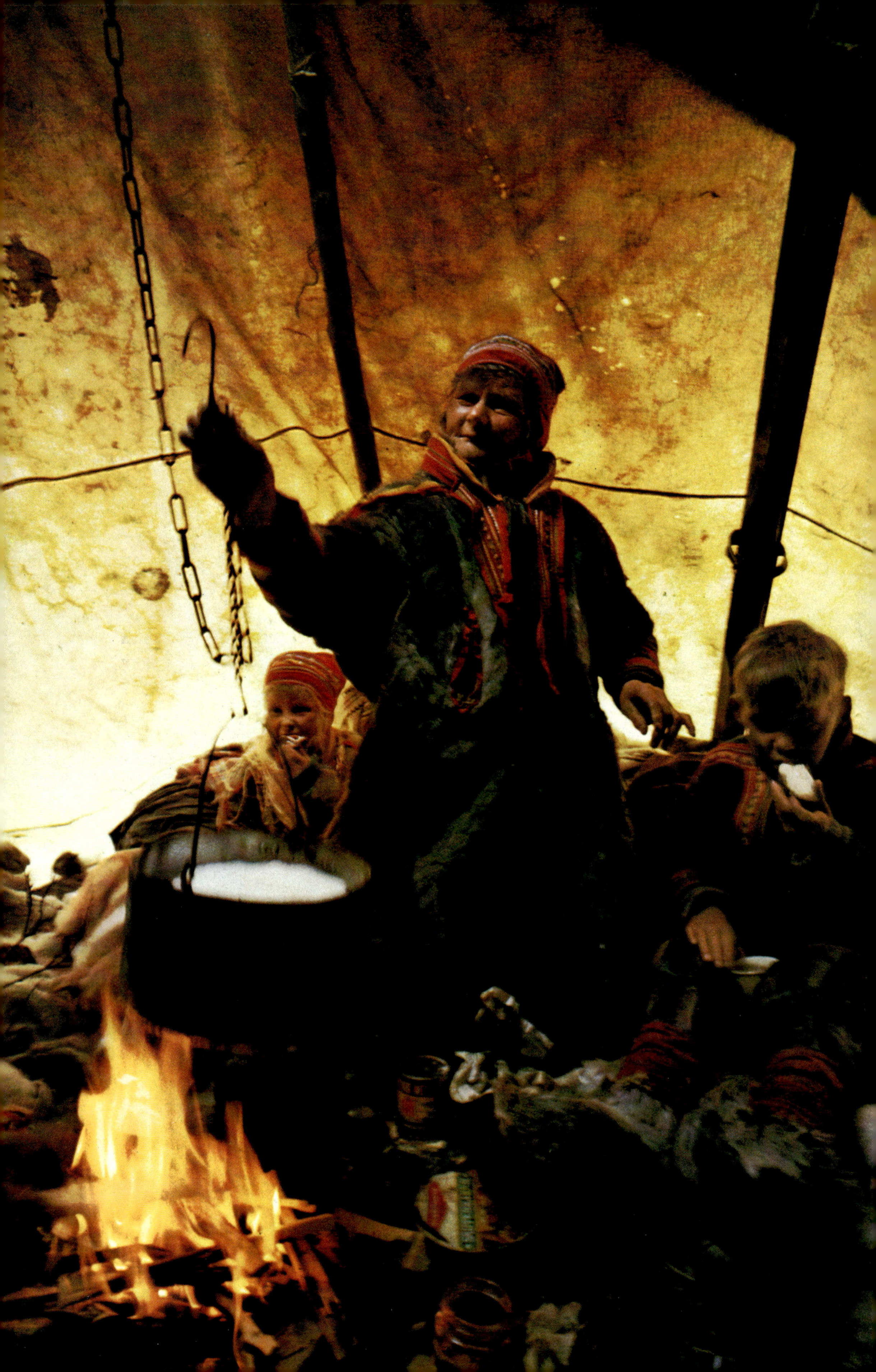

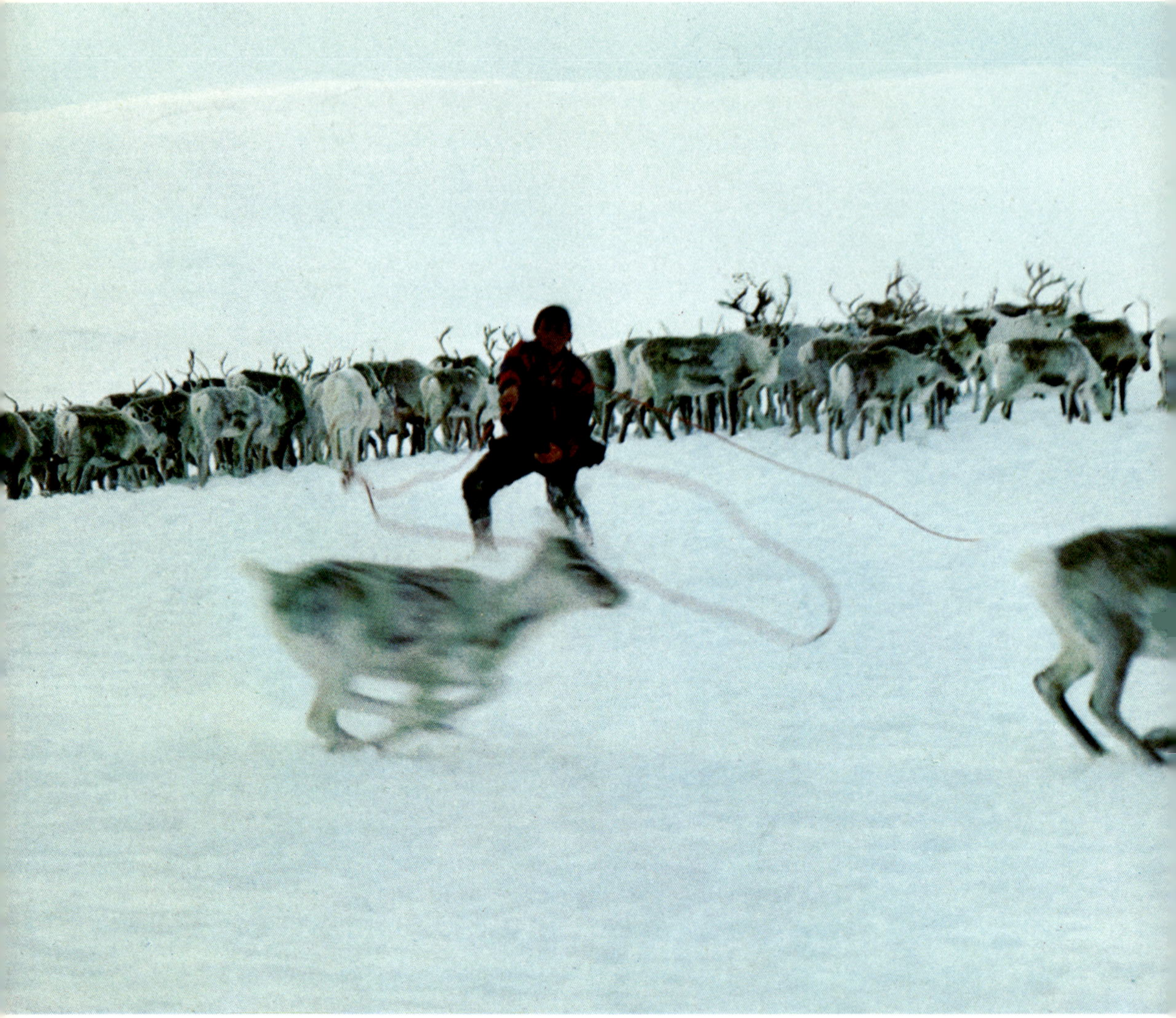

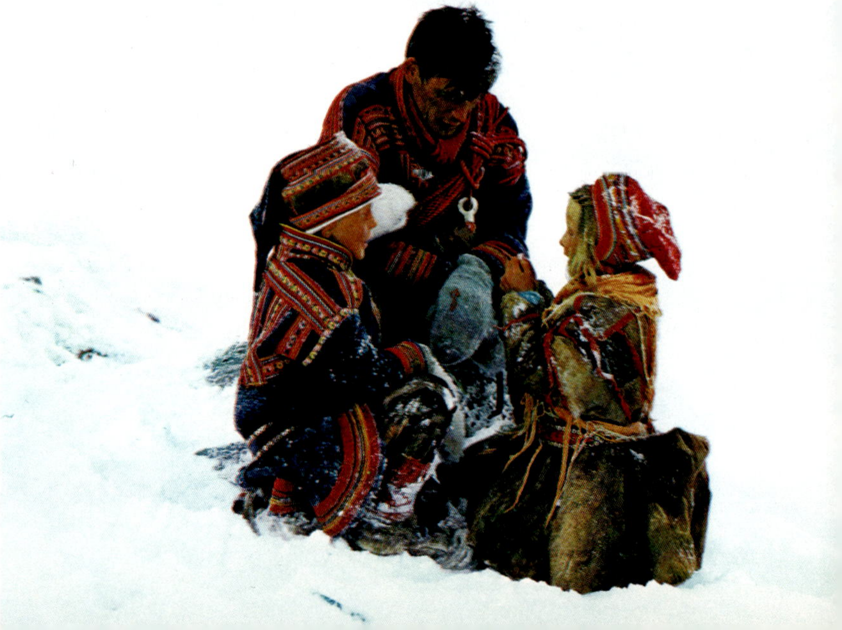

"Or you can say the names of seven bald men, throw salt into the fire, and lie down so the sparks won't reach you," said Johan. "Then surely good weather will come."

"But the men must be completely bald," Isak cautioned. "Not a hair on their heads."

"In the old days, people left offerings on a *sieide*," Aslak added. "That also brought good luck."

I had learned about such practices on an earlier visit among Lapp families of Finland. Early Lapps thought sieide—rocks, mountains, cliffs resembling animals or man-made objects—possessed magical powers. In Lisma, Finland, Jouni Kitti, now 70 years old, had told me how his grandfather used to sacrifice two white reindeer to a sieide every year. Once wolves killed all of the white deer, making a sacrifice impossible. Within the year, Jouni had said, virtually nothing remained of a herd of 10,000 reindeer.

Since I didn't know the name of even one completely bald man, much less seven, I tossed the coins out the smoke hole, and we all went to sleep. Next morning I awakened to find sunshine streaming into the tent. During the day, it grew so warm I was able to work comfortably without my parka or sweater.

B<small>Y THE TIME</small> we moved into the mountains, April had turned into May. The landscape changed abruptly as the rolling slopes of the vidda gave way to a series of cliffs and valleys which plunged into the broad basin of the Reisa River. Before us, as we stopped on the crest of a hill, sheer walls of bare rock tumbled down toward the frozen river 1,800 feet below. "You stay here and make some coffee," Isak said and quickly disappeared.

An hour later he returned, driving some 300 reindeer. I would not have known where to start searching for them, but Lapps have an uncanny instinct about such things, and their eyesight exceeds belief. With the naked eye, my comrades frequently counted off the number of deer milling on a slope so distant that I scarcely could see them with a pair of binoculars. The Lapps invariably can single out their own animals without having to check the notches that they cut into the ears for identification.

Gradually, the mountains closed in—awesome, brooding forms towering over us in frozen silence. We kept moving, trying to keep the herd together, pausing only to quench our thirst along a frozen stream where a freak pocket in the snow and ice had exposed a tiny patch of rushing water. The sun set and rose again, and still we continued the tiresome march.

As he moved to the head of the herd to lead the way, Isak gave me one of the dogs tied to a long rope. "Go back and follow the herd," he told me. "If the deer start to wander off, make Rune bark to keep them moving."

What a mistake! Rune insisted on walking between my feet and

Breaking camp for the day's journey, Isak lassoes a scurrying reindeer to pull one of the 22 sleds. During a rest stop, he shares a moment with his niece and nephew, spinning tales of past migrations.

Overleaf: Reindeer plod toward forbidding mountains at the head of Josdalen, a valley near the coast of Norway. Fog settling over the slopes sometimes forced the author and the herders to remain in camp for days.

51

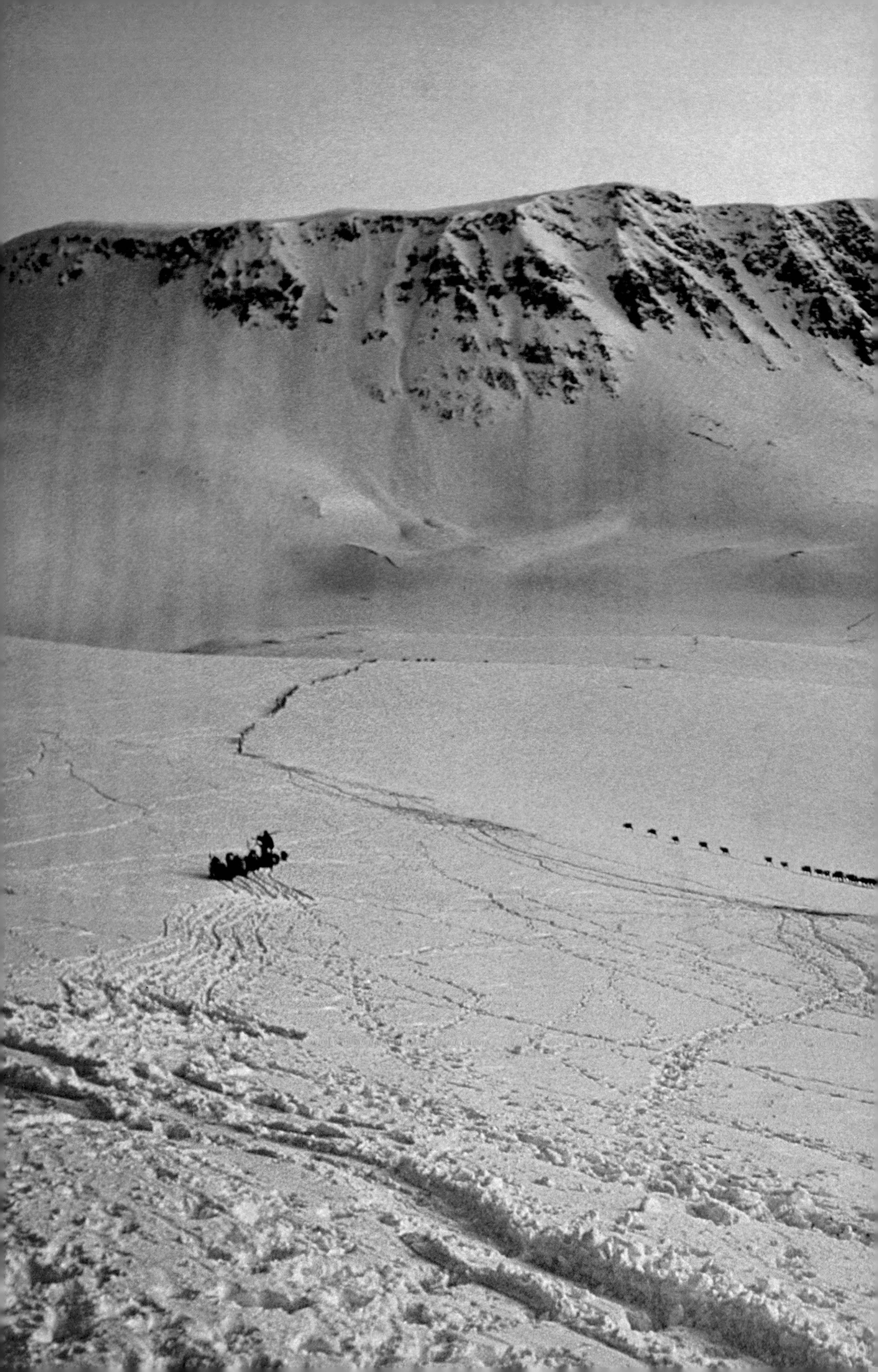

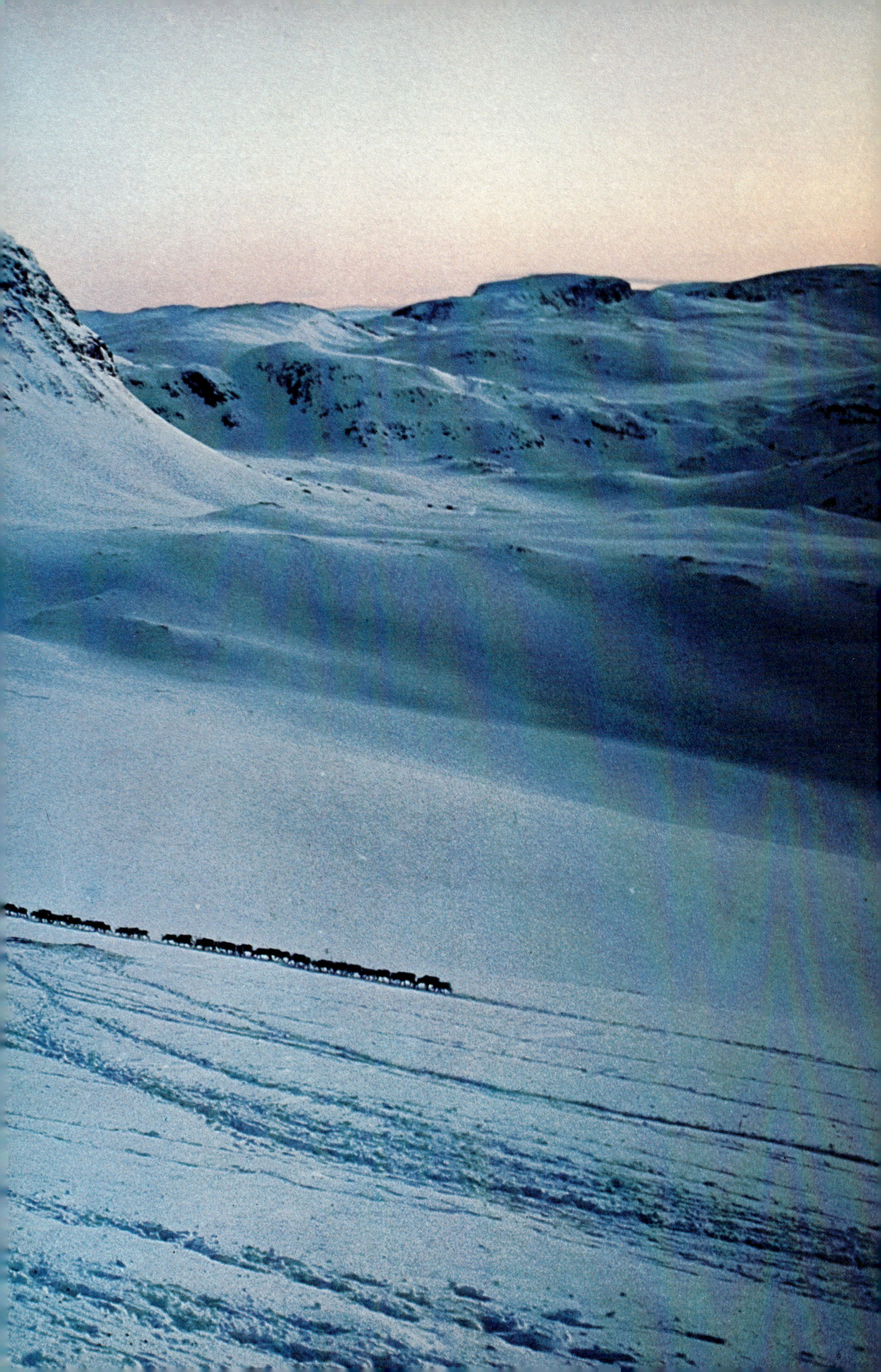

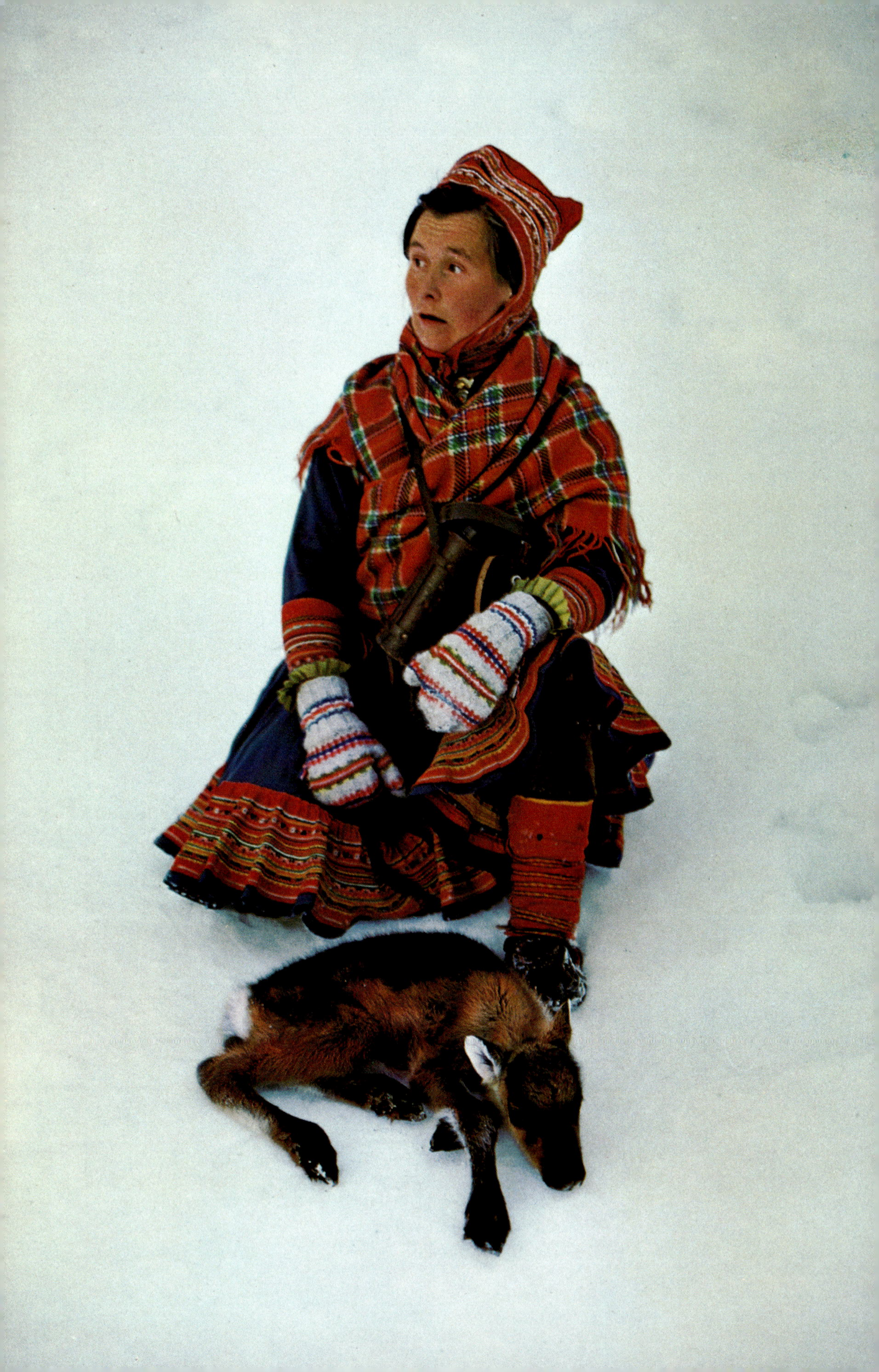

tripping me up, pulling his rope over one ski and under the other and wrapping it around my ankles. If he found a birch tree handy, he circled it for good measure. To top everything, when I wanted him to bark, he wouldn't. Finally, in disgust, I untied Rune's rope, and he immediately bounded into the herd, yapping madly and scattering the reindeer into the mountains in every direction.

Catching up with Isak as he stopped to set up camp, I lost little time in telling him what I thought of his dog. "Rune is a good dog," Isak countered. "He's just young—only six months old. It takes three years to train a good reindeer dog." Earlier, I had watched some of the older dogs, mostly mixed-breed Pomeranians, in action. The better ones could be sent to a far corner of the herd to turn strays and would follow hand signals once out of earshot.

"Until we started using snow scooters three years ago," Aslak told me, "we had to rely on the dogs a great deal more. And we had good dogs; if necessary, we could send them five and six miles after a herd. But now the snow scooter is replacing both dog and sled."

N<small>O MATTER</small> how we tried, we could not keep the reindeer from straying. For three days we stayed at the same camp while we attempted to pull the herd together, and with each day the situation grew more desperate. "This time last year we already had reached Arnøy," Isak said. "The deer have to swim two fjords to get to their summer pasture, and they must swim before the fawns are born."

Three hundred reindeer still wandered the Reisa Valley, but we could wait no longer. Any day the does would begin to drop their fawns. Aslak and Johan went after the herd while Isak and I packed the sleds and headed northward once more. As we climbed higher and higher into the mountains through deepening snow, we often had to help the deer pull the heavy sleds.

Three eagles swooped ominously low over our heads, two of them settling on a rocky pinnacle. "Bad for baby rein," Isak said, frowning.

Toward evening we topped the icy summit of a mountain the Lapps call Arasbårraš'ša, and stopped to rest, spellbound by the view. To the northwest, beyond the island of Uløy, the setting sun spread a sheet of gold over the still waters of Lyngen Fjord. But Isak's trained eyes saw little to bring him cheer as he studied distant peaks of the islands of Kågen and Arnøy. "Too much snow," he said. "It is full winter at our summer place."

Newborn reindeer struggles for life in heavy, late-season snow, still 20 miles from Arnøy. Karen Anna, Isak's wife, scans the wintry horizon for the fawn's mother. Many does—weak, hungry, and unable to find food—could not produce enough milk for their young.

The wind returned and brought with it fresh snow, forcing still another delay. Finally, three days later, we reached the water and sought shelter from the persistent gales in Johan's summer home beside Rotsund, the channel separating Uløy from the mainland. There we found Marit, Karen Anna, Ellen Anne, and the children waiting.

Northward from Rotsund, a crooked finger of mainland juts 15 miles into the sea. Across Maursund from the rocky peninsula lies Kågen, and beyond it, Arnøy. The weather had to be near perfect before we could attempt to swim the herd; some herdsmen have lost many of their animals in the tricky currents of these northern fjords. As we moved toward the water the deer scattered in a vain search for food, adding new woes to Isak's already heavy burden.

Then one day Aslak came in from the mountains. "I found two baby rein," he said, holding up a tiny skin with soft, beautiful fur. "One mother was too starved to give milk."

Isak shook his head. "The herd must swim soon, or it will be too late," he said. But the wind which had turned Maursund into a choppy sea refused to let up. More days passed. More fawns were born, and many of them starved.

In a last, desperate effort to gather the herd for the swim, we combed the icy slopes of the peninsula, only to find young fawns standing numb and silent among every group of reindeer. Karen Anna came upon a small bundle of fur lying limp and motionless in the snow. "Four hours old," she said. Maybe its mother would be back; more likely she would not.

At 1 a.m. we stood on a sharp ridge. An early morning sun burnished the peaks of Kågen with tints of gold, but farther out to sea a new snow squall darkened the horizon.

"What will we do?" Karen Anna asked.

"The deer will swim," Isak replied, "but not until late summer when the baby rein are strong enough."

For a time the migration was over. As we moved slowly back down the slope toward Maursund, where we would sleep, Isak turned to me.

"Perhaps you can come with us again next year," he said. "I think it will be better then."

I had heard such thoughts expressed before—and with the same deep faith—by farmers of the midwestern United States when the rains did not come, by crab fishermen along Chesapeake Bay, near my home, when their traps came up empty. And year after year I had watched as farmers' sons and fishermen's sons joined a growing march toward the city in search of an easier life and a wage measured in something more convertible than hope.

Today, a similar march has begun across the windswept moorland of Finnmarks Vidda. Isak, content with his life—arduous as it may be— and envious of no one, hopes his sons also will choose to become reindeer herders.

But clearly, time is not on Isak's side.

Reflection of a golden sunrise silhouettes Isak and his brother-in-law Aslak Logje, as they walk along a sharp ridge overlooking Maursund. Delayed by a renewed winter onslaught, they must wait until the fawns grow stronger before the herd can swim to summer pastures. A rock carving near Tromsø, Norway, chiseled 3,500 years ago, suggests the early association of these northern people with reindeer.

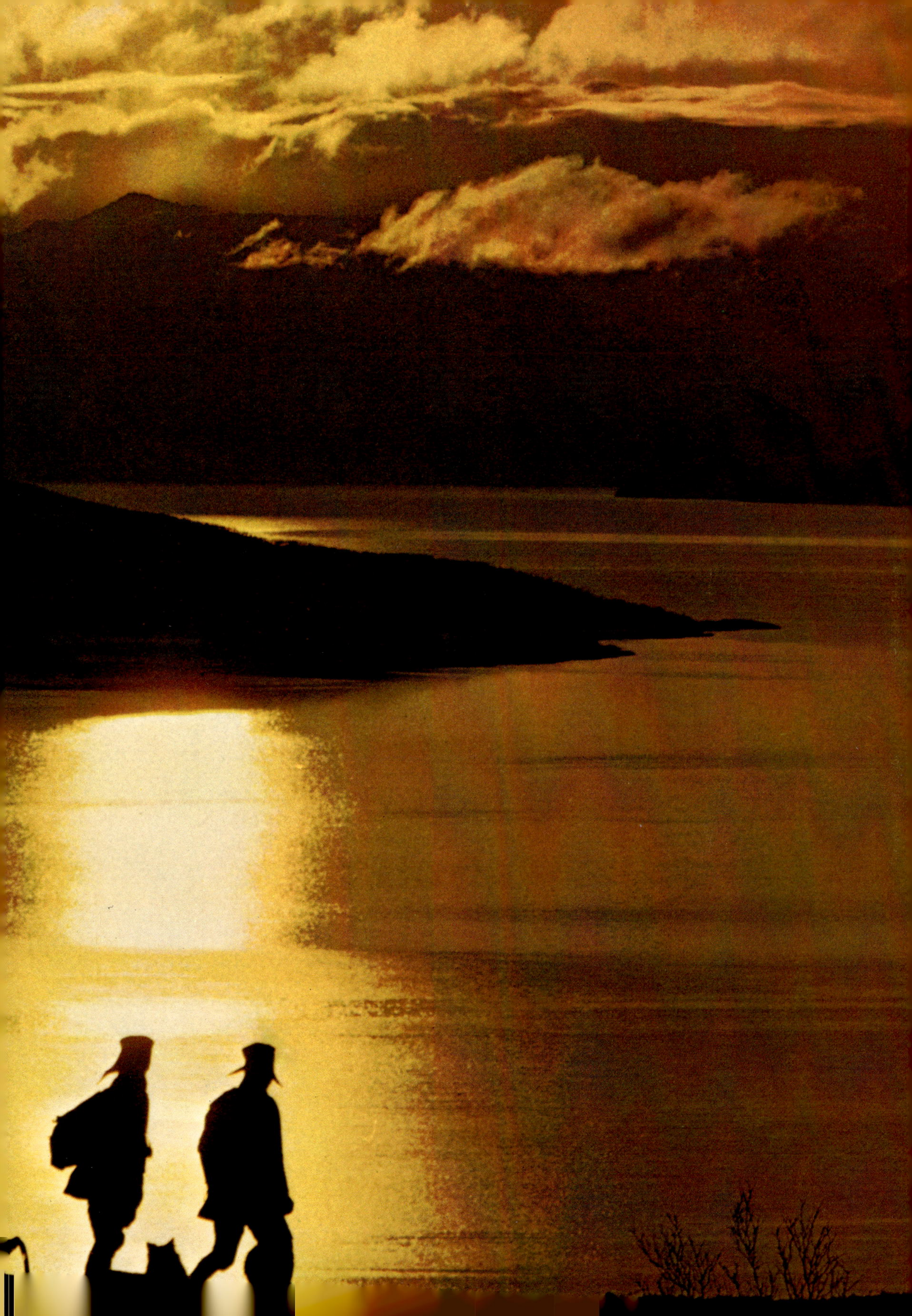

3

The Bushmen: Gentle Nomads Of Africa's Harsh Kalahari

By Elizabeth Marshall Thomas
Illustrations by the Marshall Kalahari Expeditions

Bushmen of the kalahari do not take a woman on a hunt. Hunting is *chi go*—male thing.

A woman may not touch arrows. If she embraces her husband before he sets out after big game, it brings bad luck. But the lean, short hunter named Gai thought that I, not a woman of his race, might be exempt from the taboo of his African homeland. One day Gai agreed to take me along, and my brother John Marshall also joined the hunt.

On a cool, fresh morning, we left the little Bushman camp and walked in single file into a land of wide horizons.

The Kalahari region, covering 583,000 square miles, smothers much of Botswana with its sandy soil and spills into South-West Africa, Angola, Zambia, Rhodesia, and South Africa. Once the Bushmen roamed a much larger area, the continent's southern quarter, as far as the Cape of Good Hope. But then, in the 17th century, they began to give way as larger, stronger Bantu people pushed south with their cattle, and European settlers moved north, fanning out from their Cape Colony, established in 1652. The Bushmen fought back in bloody battles, losing tens of thousands of their people. Fighting raged sporadically until the late 1800's. By then, the country they could call their own had shrunk to the arid Kalahari, where natural barriers—ferocious heat and lack of water—offered protection from their enemies.

Some Bushmen still lead the life of nomads there, neither planting crops nor domesticating animals. Women dig roots and gather melons, berries, and nuts. The men hunt.

We saw no game as we trekked in silence, Gai with arrows shouldered in a quiver made from a hollow root, his bow and spear in hand. At midmorning, weary and thirsty, we moved toward a forest of spindly thorn trees to rest. Semidesert, the Kalahari still receives enough seasonal rain to support lonely baobabs *Continued on page 64*

Strumming a five-stringed guashi, *a smiling Bushman matron expresses in music—sometimes gay, sometimes sad—the life of her people, nomads who wrest subsistence from southern Africa's harsh and arid Kalahari region. Soon, her family group will move to a new camp. Ostrich-eggshell beads hang from her hair. Her hunter-husband fashioned the hide armlets.*

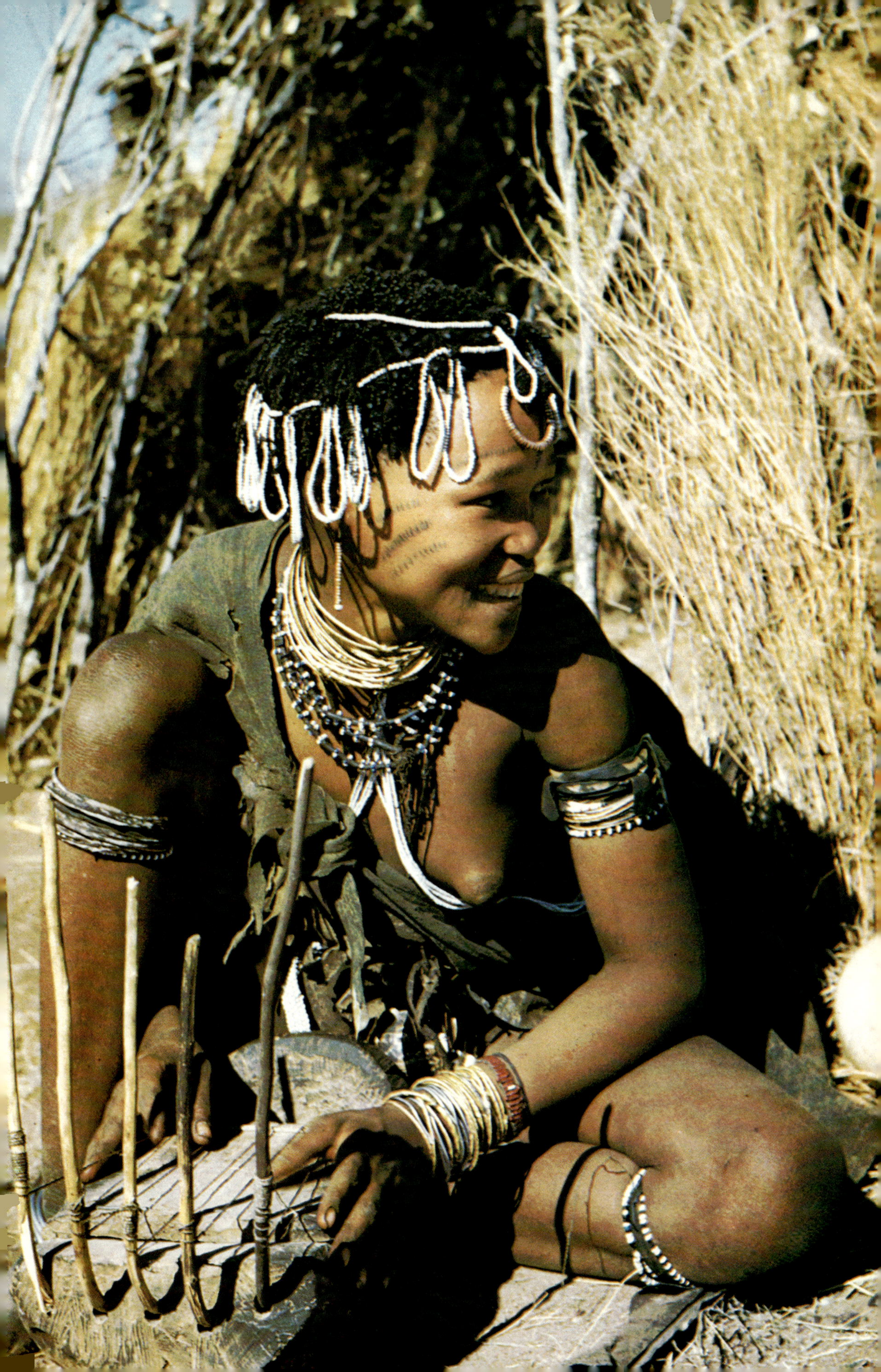

Bushmen crouched in tall grass stalk foraging wildebeest with skill and patience. The hunters, only their backs

Panicked by the first arrow, the beasts stampede, and the swift hunters begin the pursuit, shooting as they run.

Testing his sinew bowstring, a Bushman prepares for a hunt. With poisoned arrows, he kills kudu, hartebeest, springbok, and other game animals that range the Kalahari. The pupae of certain beetles yield the powerful poison; hunters crush the grubs and smear the juice on their arrows directly behind the points. None of the deadly substance goes on the sharp bone or metal heads—a single drop entering a man's bloodstream through an accidental cut or scratch would kill him within a day. When an arrow strikes an animal the section coated with poison remains embedded. Bushmen track their dying quarry closely to reach it before lions or

visible, creep slowly and quietly toward the herd, remaining downwind to avoid alarming their wary prey.

Bushmen often track wounded animals for days, carrying only their bows and spears, and living off the land.

leopards, hyenas or jackals can close in. At right, skinners begin butchering a gemsbok spread on a bed of leaves. Everyone in the camp will receive a share. Scrupulous division creates mutual obligation and lessens the fear of hunger. The poisoned meat causes no harm when eaten, for the toxin must enter the bloodstream directly to kill. Virtually nothing goes to waste. Hides become capes; hoofs serve as hones for sharpening knives. Aged members of the clan with poor teeth get the blood, brains, and heart. Birds and small animals—porcupines, partridges, ostriches—supplement the diet. Bushmen regard lizards and snakes as incidental delicacies.

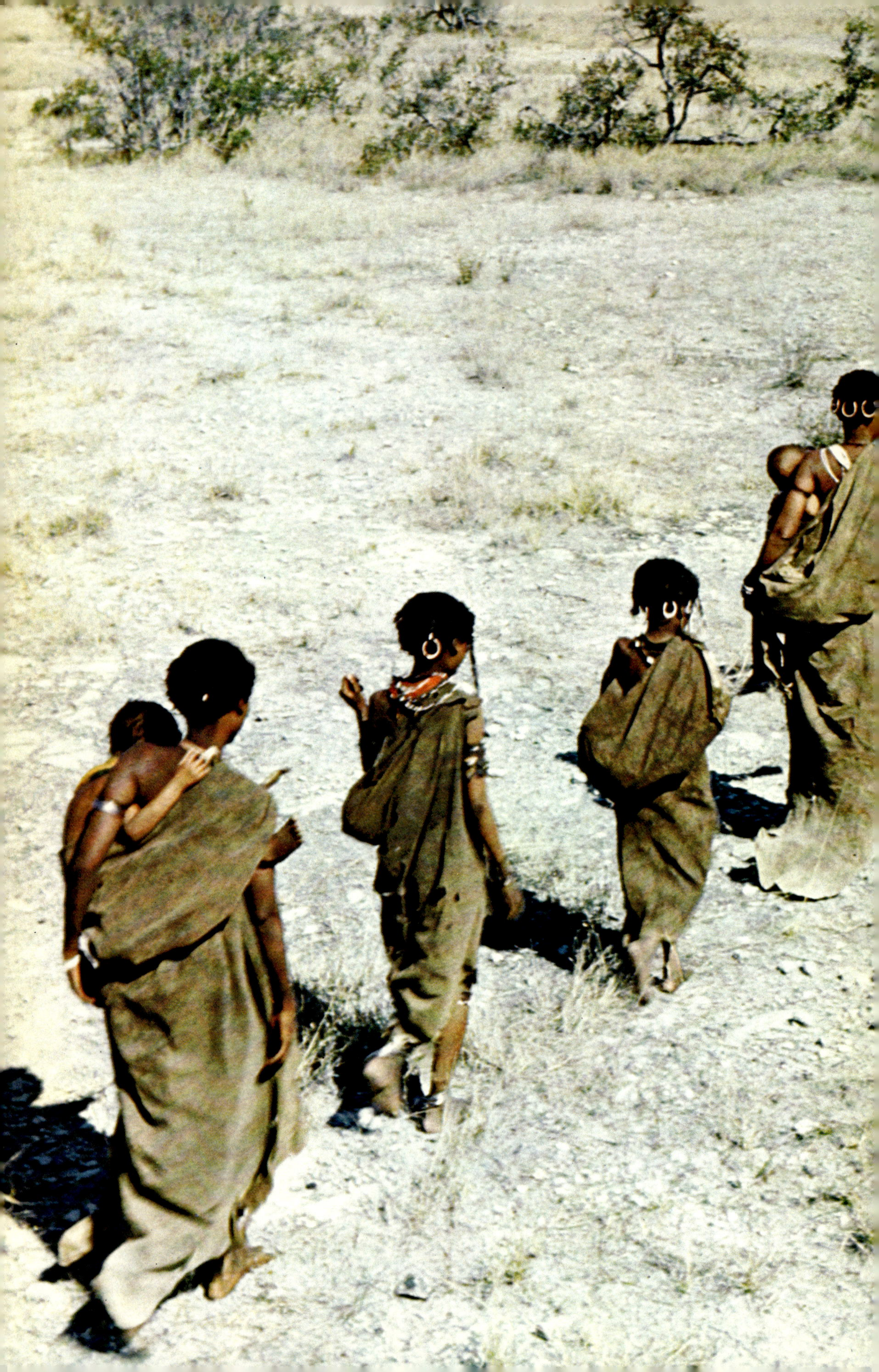

Lightly burdened Kung Bushmen take everything they own to a new camp after depleting the supply of fruits, nuts, roots, edible plants, and game around the old one. Such family bands may number fewer than a dozen persons or more than 50. The nomads limit their possessions—the more a man has, the more he must carry.

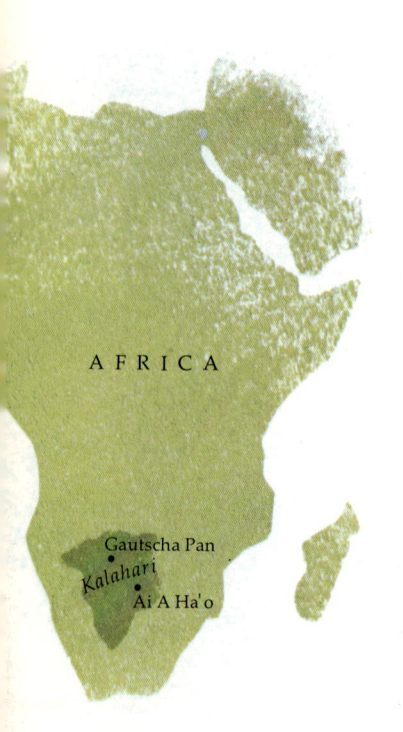

"*A hostile country of thirst and heat and thorns where the grass is harsh and often barbed and the stones hide scorpions.*" Author Elizabeth Marshall Thomas thus describes the sandy wastes of the Kalahari region, home to some 55,000 Bushmen, short-statured nomads who once freely roamed most of southern Africa. In the 17th century their domain began to shrink as Bantu tribes moved down from the north with their cattle and European settlers advanced from the south, squeezing the Bushman from his hunting grounds. Thousands of Bushmen died in fierce battles that raged for two hundred years. Others fell victim to diseases introduced by the outsiders. Virtually all Bushmen eventually disappeared from the fertile lands. Only those in the Kalahari—an area wanted neither by the Bantu nor the Europeans—survived. There they hunted and gathered food from the arid land, following the game and the seasons in an endless migration. Today, two out of every three Bushmen have abandoned nomadic life to work on farms and cattle posts and in the households of the Bantu and the Europeans. Encroaching civilization increasingly changes their culture. The author, in her account of these gentle hunters and food gatherers, records a vanishing way of life.

---

and cool groves of other drought-resistant trees. We had almost reached the forest when Gai raised one hand. We stopped. Like a wild creature, Gai slipped off among the trees, running in a crouch so his back would look like an animal's. At my feet I saw why: the heart-shaped tracks of a gemsbok, an antelope the size of a Shetland pony.

Gai halted, motionless, silent, knees bent, like a cat waiting for the moment to spring. A typical Bushman, he was a handsome sight, strong and lithe and built for running, with slender, lean-muscled legs. But he looked very frail contrasted with John and me. These hardy people are among the shortest in the world, averaging about five feet tall. Sun and soil darken their naturally golden-brown skin and their short, black hair spirals into peppercorn tufts. The Bushmen have rather triangular flat faces, wide noses, and often the Mongolian fold of skin on the eyelid that makes their eyes look slanted.

Gai raised his head slightly to see between white thorns. Something moved in a bush near us. I caught a glimpse of an oval ear outlined against the blue sky. The ear flicked, then vanished.

Crouching for a handful of dust, the hunter let it slip through his fingers to tell of the wind. His hand moved to the quiver on his shoulder, then dropped to his waist with four arrows. He eased the two-foot shafts into the leather waistband of his loincloth—the only garment he wore. The arrows fanned out like a pigeon's tail, easy to snatch with speed. He began to move quickly in a half circle to a place downwind of the gemsbok, only the length of his back showing above the grass. He wore nothing that could catch or tear or make a sound. I saw him carefully aim his arrow and heard a whir as he let it fly.

The gemsbok heaved a great snort. Branches splintered, and the animal bolted past me. Gai darted after it. He stopped, shot again, burst forward and let still another arrow fly. His stride lengthened as he and the gemsbok gained speed; Gai ran in wide, free leaps until both he and the antelope were gone.

Gai soon came back, picking up his arrow shafts as he walked. The arrows are fashioned in two parts—reed shafts and bone front sections.

The reeds easily fall away, leaving heads embedded, difficult to dislodge if the animal tries to shake them out or scrapes against a tree.

Drops of blood stained the shafts. Gai's shots were successful. Each foreshaft carried a coating of poison squeezed from the pupae of certain species of the *Diamphidia* or *Polyclada* beetles and parasites that live in them. The poison, for which no antidote is known, will kill a giraffe in less than a week, a man or an antelope within a day. We walked back to the camp; Gai planned to let the poison take effect while he got someone to join him in tracking down his quarry.

I F YOU WENT LOOKING for a Bushman camp in the vastness of the veld, you might never find one. On our first expedition in 1951, we searched a great expanse of land for many weeks before we found the Kung Bushmen in the Nyae Nyae region of South-West Africa. In a later trip we searched almost a month to find the more remote Gwikwe —Gai's language group—at Ai A Ha'o in what was then Bechuanaland. These people, by nature very shy, feared strangers for another reason as well. Bantu and European farmers often took them by force and made them work as servants or field hands, but now the practice is outlawed.

Our camp huddled under the branches of a tree at the edge of a plain. Usually, Bushmen build temporary shelters of sticks and grass. But Gai's band of eleven Gwikwe had simply scooped three shallow pits in the sandy ground so they could lie curled up for warmth as the cold night wind passed.

Winter temperatures in July can drop below freezing. The people huddle in their capes of animal skin and talk around their fires under the desert's brilliant, hard white moon. Fire, like hunting, is also a man's thing; women may not start, or "roll," a fire or even touch the sticks—one spun against another—that create it.

That night around the fire, Gai casually mentioned he had shot a steinbok, an antelope much smaller than the gemsbok already dying somewhere from the poison in her blood. It would bring bad luck to say exactly what he had shot. Gai spoke of his successful hunt only to get help with the tracking.

Mist rose from the veld before dawn as Gai prepared to set out. An old man named Ukwane, his skin hanging in the deep, loose wrinkles that Bushmen get with age, ate at Gai's side. Lacking water, they drank liquid squeezed from the green pulp of a tsama, a small round watermelon. Both took bows, spears, and quivers of arrows and walked off, relying on the veld to give them food.

Four days later Gai returned alone to tell the people of the gemsbok, leaving Ukwane to begin the butchering and to guard the meat from black-winged vultures that circled overhead. The antelope had wandered far in her death agony, but in a circle. Her tracks had led back to a spot not far from where she had been shot. Several of the men went with Gai to get the meat.

When they arrived they saw that Ukwane had found milk in the udder. The men approached him with outstretched palms for a squirt of it and licked at drops of the rank and gamy liquid. Using a gemsbok hoof as a hone, Gai sharpened a knife and helped Ukwane with the butchering.

Mongolian eye fold and flat, broad nose distinguish the Bushman. Like most of the Kalahari nomads, Kwi (below) stands about five feet tall. Desert grime and years of sun darken his golden-brown skin. The origin of his ancestors, as well as how and when they arrived in southern Africa, remains a mystery.

66

Pink lily blossoms garland girls of the Kung group; the one at left wears a woven ostrich-eggshell headband around her neck. Below, mothers shave their babies' heads. Bushmen believe the first such shaving protects the child's health. Razor blades reach the nomads through trade with other tribes and Europeans.

These people waste almost nothing. The blood, along with liquid from the stomach, would supply them with fluid for almost a week. The meat, cut into strips and dried in the sun, would last longer. Even the meat around the wound, blackened and full of poison, was edible, for the poison remains harmless unless it reaches the bloodstream directly through a cut in the skin or an ulceration.

The hide might make a cape, or straps for carrying empty ostrich eggshells used as water bottles, or perhaps small aprons that women wear as loincloths. Sometimes Bushmen roast a tough hide, then beat it to powder, licking the tasty brown dust from their hands. Many days later, the long bones, grayed by weather, offer marrow, a delicacy the people hungrily dig out with straws.

Bushmen share all big game. It is their law. And although we saw the Gwikwe give the hunter a larger share at first, in the end no person had more to eat than any other. Whoever owns the fatal arrow owns the beast. But "ownership" means nothing more than responsibility for the first round of giving.

The first distribution goes in great pieces. Then the men cut up the meat uncooked and share it even further, according to bonds of kinship. A final wave of sharing spreads portions wider. Even visitors from another band receive some. Sharing not only assures everyone's survival, it also brings members of a band closer, binding them by links of kindness and mutual obligation. In a Kung band we once recorded 63 gifts of raw meat from a single animal.

Bushmen share more than meat. All their possessions pass from hand to hand. "Look at him," you might hear by the fire one evening, "admiring his fine knife while we have nothing." The owner of the knife would begin feeling guilty, and likely as not give it away.

Trust, peace, and cooperation form the basis for Bushman social relations. All Bushmen fear ill feeling. We heard the Kung speak with awe of rare incidents of anger. Living in a wilderness where a man alone might die in days if luck goes bad, they cannot afford ill will and division. Dependent on one another, they find comfort and security in tightly knit bands. With miles of emptiness surrounding the camp, members of a group will crowd shoulder to shoulder around a fire.

Bushmen carefully avoid any show of belligerence in greeting strangers. Whenever we met nomads on the veld, they always came forward unarmed, leaving their arrows and spears in the grass whether the men of the other party were of Gai's Gwikwe group, or of the Naron, Auen, Ko, or Kung. Language differences divide Bushmen into more than a dozen groups or nations, each tongue unintelligible to the others.

The Kung and Gwikwe permit divorce and remarriage. A man may have two wives. If, however, they become jealous, decency demands self-control and silence so their feelings cannot spill among the others.

Theft is virtually unknown. After all, the people do not enhance their status by acquiring goods, and a person's footprints are as well known as his face. When Bushmen exhaust the land around a camp, they move on, some 20 miles a day, with all their possessions carried on their heads in great bundles or in skin bags. For a nomad, especially under the harsh conditions the Kalahari can impose, many possessions burden life.

In summer, sunlight pours down like molten brass and temperatures soar to 120° F. and higher. During the worst droughts the Gwikwe, whose desert domain can be waterless for nine months of the year, dig shallow holes under shade trees, then line the holes with root scrapings squeezed for juice. Later, during the hottest part of the day, they wet the scrapings with urine and lie in the holes cooled by the evaporating liquid.

In the Nyae Nyae countryside, which has permanent water holes, a band's land rights begin with use of the water and extend away in a particular direction from the hole. And all the plant food in a territory belongs strictly to the band. Raids on such food are as unknown as theft. Nor is there need for raiding. If a band finds food too short, some of its members, all relatives, trickle away across the low dunes and scrubby plains to find other bands where they have relatives or friends.

Towering storm promises replenished water holes. Rain in the Kalahari averages six to ten inches a year. Pools disappear quickly when the rains stop. Kung Bushmen live in an area of some 10,000 square miles, where just three water holes are permanent; four others, including the Tsumkwe (right), fail only in severe drought.

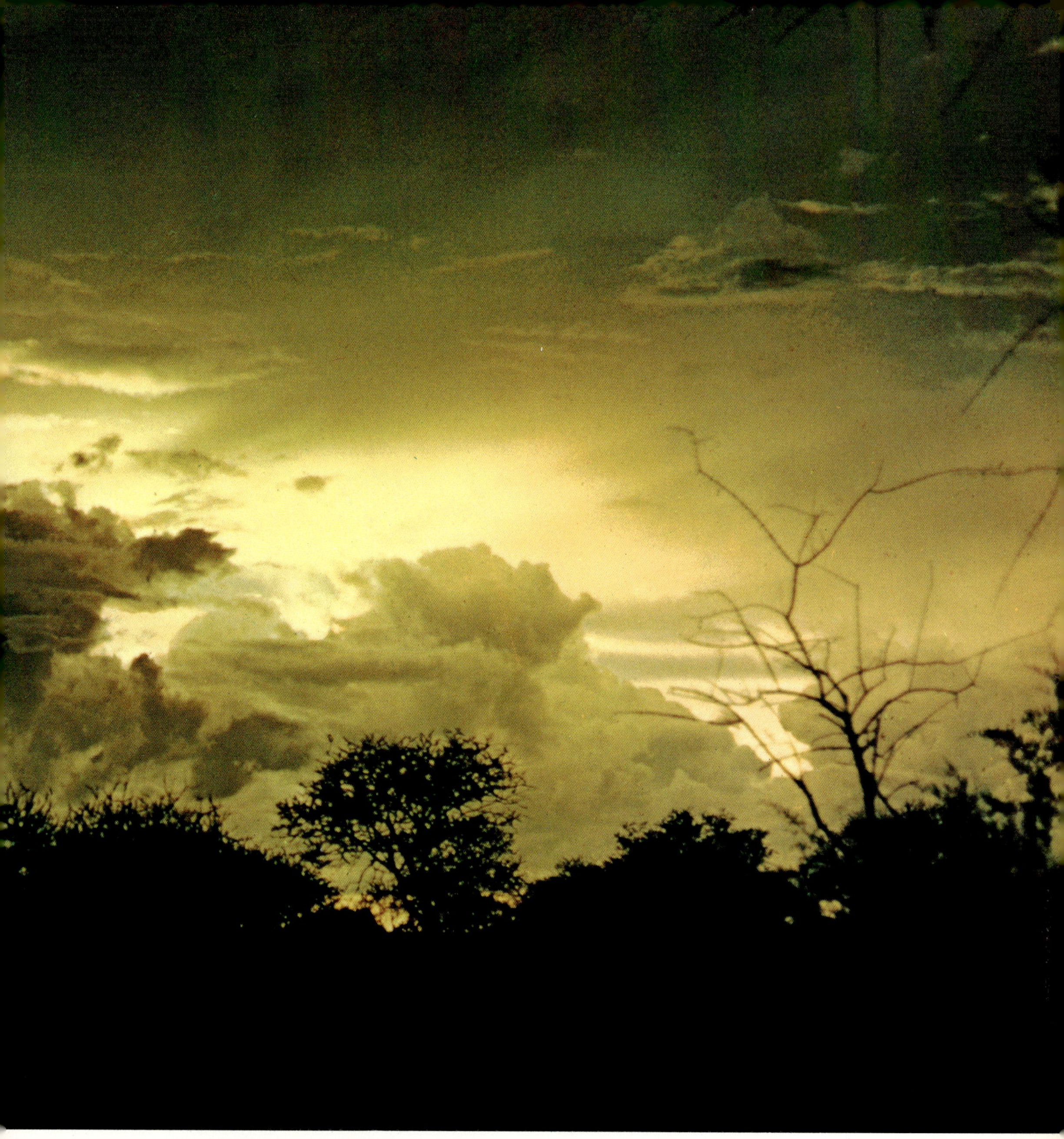

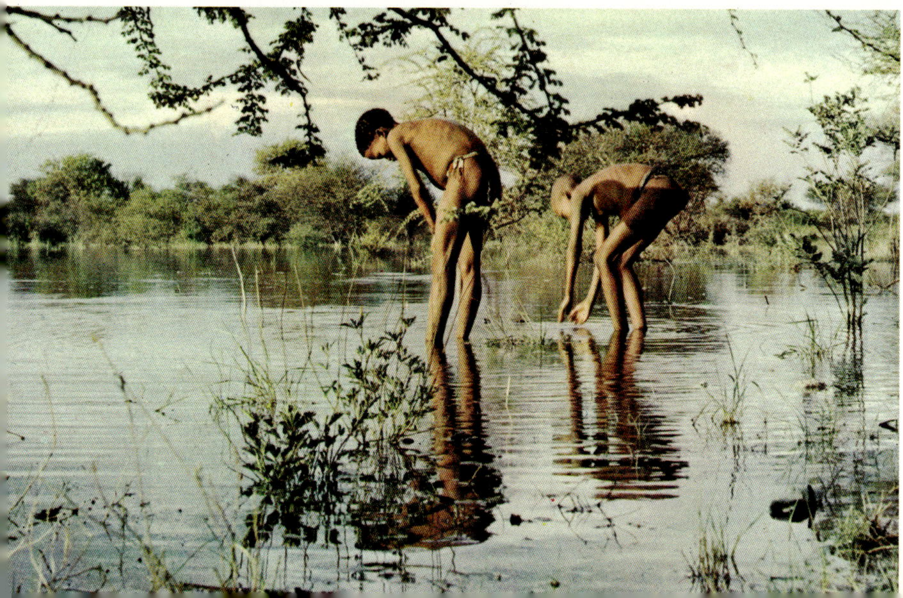

Every territory falls under the nominal ownership of band headmen. Ownership, however, does not mean the same thing to the Kung and Gwikwe that it does to us. A headman represents a claim not for himself, but for his entire band. He personifies the band's rights.

A headman leads by deciding when the people have taken enough from a patch of earth and directing them where to go next. Headmanship passes usually from father to eldest son. Sometimes a headman may abdicate, simply by leaving his water hole and going to live with another band. We were at the water hole at Gautscha Pan, an enormous dish-shaped depression dazzling white with salt, while Toma, a tireless hunter, served temporarily as leader. During our second visit, the old headman's crippled son, Lame Gao, took over.

Lame Gao's chances of becoming a leader had been slight. As a child, he told us, he had complained of a sore leg during a long trek. His family had refused to stop and suck the sore place, a Bushman manner of curing. The leg got worse, crippling him forever.

Lame Gao became his name. He received the nickname not in insult, but because Bushmen give relatively few proper names. "Lame" would distinguish him from Gao Feet; similarly, Lazy Kwi, a bad hunter, was distinguished from Crooked Kwi, who had a stooped shoulder.

Before Lame Gao could inherit the headmanship, or even marry, he needed initiation into manhood. And for that, he had to shoot a large animal. How could he chase after game on a crutch?

But he did. Many times he had hunted, with incredible effort and no success. Then one day he saw a kudu in a clump of bushes and silently hobbled toward it. Propped on his crutch, he shot. The arrow flew true and struck the animal. When the kudu was found and killed and eaten, it gave Lame Gao a passport to manhood, marriage, and the headmanship of his people.

D*URING OUR FIRST EXPEDITION*, we witnessed a Kung betrothal, and when we came back the next year we saw the wedding. A handsome boy named Gunda, 16 years of age, married Nai, 8.

The marriage, for the most part an agreement between parents, required little ceremony. The two mothers built a grass shelter for the couple and kindled a fire there with embers from their own households. That evening, Gunda's friends seized him by the wrists and led him to the shelter. Three little girls not much older than Nai carried the bride to him wrapped in a cape.

The people held neither feast nor dance, and sang no songs. Only a few little children joined the couple—and they left before darkness came. From then onward, the young people would live together, though they could not consummate the marriage until Nai reached puberty.

Before the wedding, Nai was a child, playing tossing games with her friends, using a melon for a ball. Bushmen have no schooling for their youngsters, and few responsibilities fell upon the girl. Sometimes her mother would urge her to go into the veld and dig wild roots with the women. But if Nai wished, she need not go and her mother would only say, "You are lazy."

When she awoke at the side of her husband, however, Nai could no longer behave like a child. Gunda arose and left on a hunt. He would

Women perform a ceremonial eland dance to celebrate a girl's entry into adulthood. Below, a rubbing on paper of a 200-year-old South African petroglyph mirrors the dancer's figure and a physical feature called steatopygia, an accumulation of fat on the buttocks.

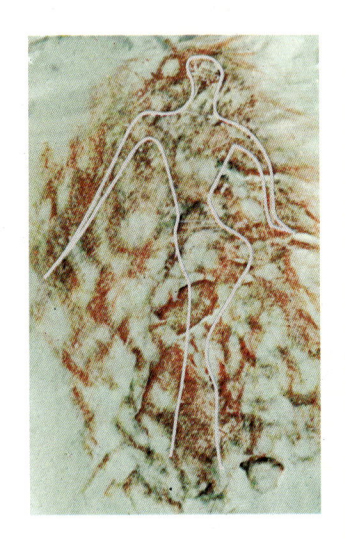

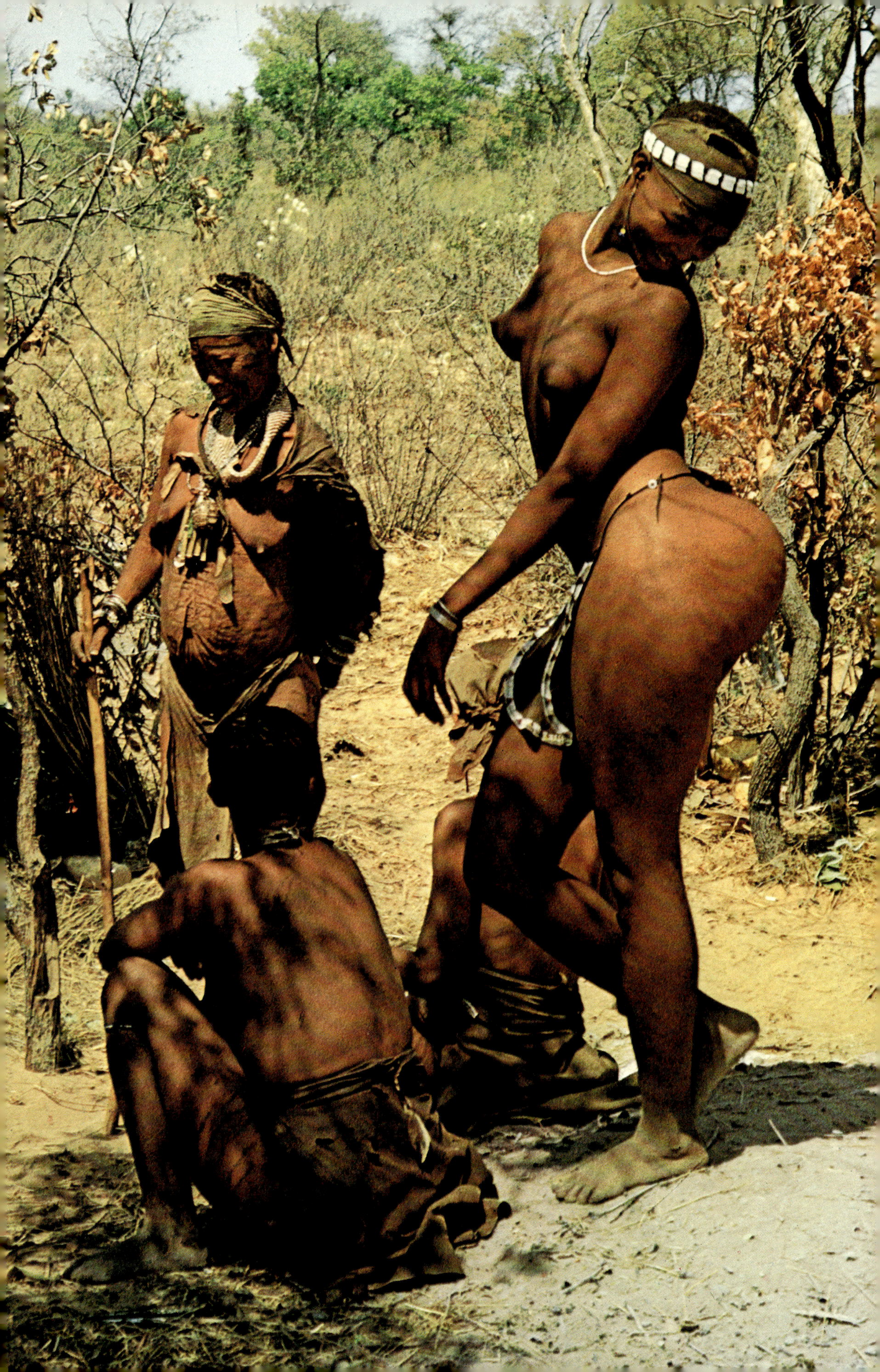

return hungry. So that morning Nai took a sharpened digging stick and walked into the veld for food.

Though the Kung, like all the Bushmen we met, greatly relish the big-game meat that hunters bring to the camp, women find as much as 80 percent of the food a band requires by fanning out as far as 15 miles from the campsite in a single day. The Kung search for more than a hundred different kinds of plants.

Tsama melons grow in patches, lying smooth, shiny, and green in the grass. A woman picks them with the efficiency of a machine, scooping one hand under the fruit, twisting her elbow, dropping the melon into a fold of her cape.

The succulent melons provide not only food but also water for drinking and cooking. When mixed with meat in a pot, the juicy pulp yields sufficient liquid for boiling. Bushmen roast the seeds and eat them or grind them into flour. Rinds make pots, mixing bowls, containers for loose objects, drums, or arrow targets for the children, as well as resonators for musical instruments.

Searching for food with the Gwikwe women from Ukwane's band, I watched them uncover a patch of spiny cucumbers, each less than three inches long with sweet watery green flesh. Poking at sandy ground with a digging stick, we unearthed a *ga* root, brownish-gray and warty as a toad. Despite its bitter taste, the root can mean life itself to Bushmen—it stays moist in the driest season. Only if rain comes in the dry season do ga roots wither, for then the plant starts to grow, giving up nourishment to its vines.

In the hot season from the end of August until December when the summer rains return, melons vanish and a fibrous, watery root called *bi* becomes the mainstay of the Bushmen's diet. My brother and I asked Gai to show us such a root. He could not remember where a bi root grew. We told Gai that we would not eat it; the roots are not abundant, and if we took one the people would not have it when the heat came. At last Gai remembered.

We set off in that direction and came to the place, not quite so far as Gai had said, an hour later. In the center of a broad plain with no bushes, trees, or other landmarks, Gai stopped and pointed with his toe. We saw no more than a wisp of vine curled around a lone blade of grass. During the last rainy season months before, Gai had walked by and seen the vine still green. He knew the bi root would be here, for if someone else had taken it he would have heard. Bushmen speak about such things.

Gai decided to dig it up. He found the root two feet down and tore it from the earth. With a tassel of small roots bristling from the bottom and the vine poking from the top, the bi had a shape like a huge beet, gray and hairy with a crust as hard as bark. What nice water it would give, Gai said.

As the women wandered home with a heavy load of food and firewood, the sun sank small and red, making the distant trees look black and very lonely. Presently, the stars appeared. Gai told me they were dead people's eyes.

Bushmen sometimes reach into the world beyond with their only art forms—music and dance. Their music combines intricacy of rhythm

Resourceful and good-natured, Bushmen placidly accept the rigors of their life. At left, young Gishay holds a guinea fowl he bagged with one shot. A child (right) drinks from an ostrich-eggshell canteen held by his sister. Below, a Bushman's family—including one or two wives, and often in-laws and elderly parents—drinks the juice from tsama melons after mashing the pulp. The small, round watermelons provide a vital source of liquid in a land of thirst. Later, as darkness comes, the family will crowd around the fire and tell stories.

with melodies sweet and sad. In his hunting bag Gai's elder son carried a *te k'na*, a flat, square piece of wood about the size of his hand. From it protruded 11 metal prongs. In the pale light of evening when the veld turned peaceful and breezes rippled the grass he borrowed a dry tsama rind. Placing the te k'na on top of it, he began to pluck the prongs, producing a pure, delicate sound.

One evening Ukwane, who composed songs, played "Bitter Melons," tapping on the taut string of his hunting bow with a reed. The song expresses the feelings of a Bushman who finds that the melons he has counted on for water have become dried and yellow. Peering at the embers of the fire, he played "A Song of Shouting," the story of a man lost on the veld. In such songs Bushmen lament the dangers and difficulties of their lives.

Saddened by the music, an old woman suddenly spoke up, "To die is bad, but in the end we all die anyway." And Ukwane said he did not expect to live another season. Once, he added, his band had many people, but in a single horrifying time of drought when the ground turned too hot to walk upon many died of thirst and others in a smallpox epidemic. Bushmen believe, however, that many of their songs have curing power when sung at special medicine dances.

K UNG BUSHMEN fear spirits of the dead, for they bring death, hunger, and disease. Many times while we lived at Gautscha we saw the Bushmen dance and sing to drive the spirits away. One night when the moon had risen dusty red and full, we heard a few women singing, and then the sound of clapping. We found them in the camp around a special fire, backs lighted by the moon, crowded as tightly as roosting birds. Behind them in a circle, the men danced. Strings of dried cocoons full of ostrich-eggshell fragments, the only instrument used in the ceremony, rattled at their ankles.

All Kung and Gwikwe men believe they can cure illness by exorcising evil. But some have greater power than others. Once, after midnight, a medicine man of renown began to shudder in a trance. He fell to the ground, then stood up and staggered to a woman of the band. Leaning down, he placed his hands, trembling like bird wings, on her back and chest, drawing out illness and evil with his moans and shrieking them away to the darkness where the spirits waited.

Beyond the camps waits a more tangible threat to these Bushmen as they are today—encroaching civilization. In 1951, we once traveled eight arduous days through trackless, waterless land. Now you can drive the same route on a well-cleared track in a day.

Contrary to reports of decades past, the people of the Kalahari are not vanishing as a racial group. A recent count listed about 55,000 Bushmen spread widely over arid wilderness and farmlands of southern Africa. Many of them work as laborers on European ranches or in Bantu villages. Others still live as hunters and food gatherers, though their numbers are dwindling.

The Bushmen we knew in the deeper Kalahari will probably live out their lives in the wilds of the veld. Men will hunt for meat and women will gather food, and in the evening they will walk toward the camp to share what they have found and talk softly by the fire.

Cradling her nursing son, a mother returns to the family, a fold of her antelope-hide cape bulging with hard-shelled mangetti *nuts. Over the centuries, her people have learned well the lessons of survival in their hostile domain—where to find food and water, when to move on. Today, many Bushmen work on farms and cattle posts, their children learning little of the Kalahari or the skills demanded of those who make it their home.*

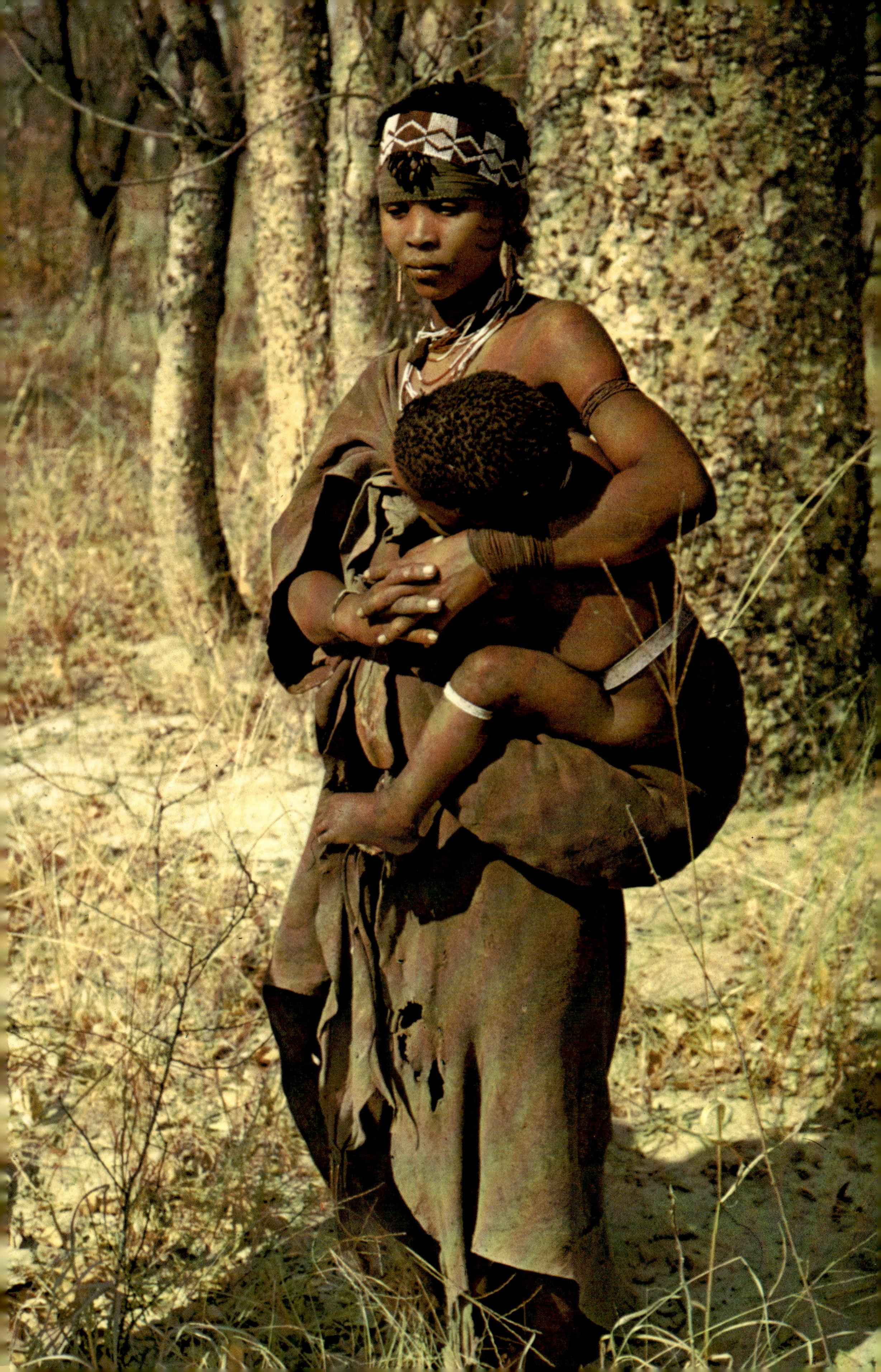

4

Nilgiri Peoples of India: An End to Old Ties

By David G. Mandelbaum, Ph.D.
Illustrations by Albert Moldvay,
National Geographic Photographer

IN THE HALF DARKNESS, I waited to hear the call of the first bird of the morning. With me the Toda tribesmen, swathed in their embroidered cloaks against the predawn chill, listened intently too. We could not begin the ceremony—the first public showing of an infant's face—until a bird announced the dawn. The ritual would formally introduce the child to nature and the Toda world. I shivered a bit as a breeze rustled through the forest around us. Though we stood only 11 degrees above the Equator, we also stood some 7,000 feet above sea level in the Nilgiri Hills, near the southern tip of India.

I could barely make out the arch of the temple in front of us, shaped somewhat like a Quonset hut. The priest inside lit a lamp for the ceremony and prepared for his regular duty—churning milk of the sacred buffalo. The Todas center their religion and their lives on the large-horned animals. Temples serve as dairies, priests as dairymen.

Much time passed, it seemed, but still no bird sang. I thought I heard a few murmurs from the women, also wrapped in their cloaks and sitting huddled together a short distance away. They could only watch the ceremony, for according to Toda custom women may take little active part in rituals. The men alone deal with the buffalo, with their sacred milk, and with all other sacred things.

Suddenly the trill of a bird split the silence. Then the eldest clansman, who held the three-month-old infant in his cloak, exposed the baby's face publicly for the first time.

Gently the old man knelt to hold the baby boy inside the low entrance to the temple and said to him, "See the temple light and the sacred things." He stood up and coaxed the child to look at the sky, the birds, the trees. The other men laughed softly when the elder added, "See my moustache."

Then he bent over, carefully lowered the baby almost to the ground,

In the Nilgiri Hills of south India, Toda women pause before a wood-and-thatch dwelling. Tattoos mark their arms and shoulders; their hair hangs in tight ringlets dressed with ghee, a type of butter tribesmen make from buffalo milk. Enveloping civilization has destroyed an interdependence between Todas and other Nilgiri peoples—the Kotas, Badagas, and Kurumbas.

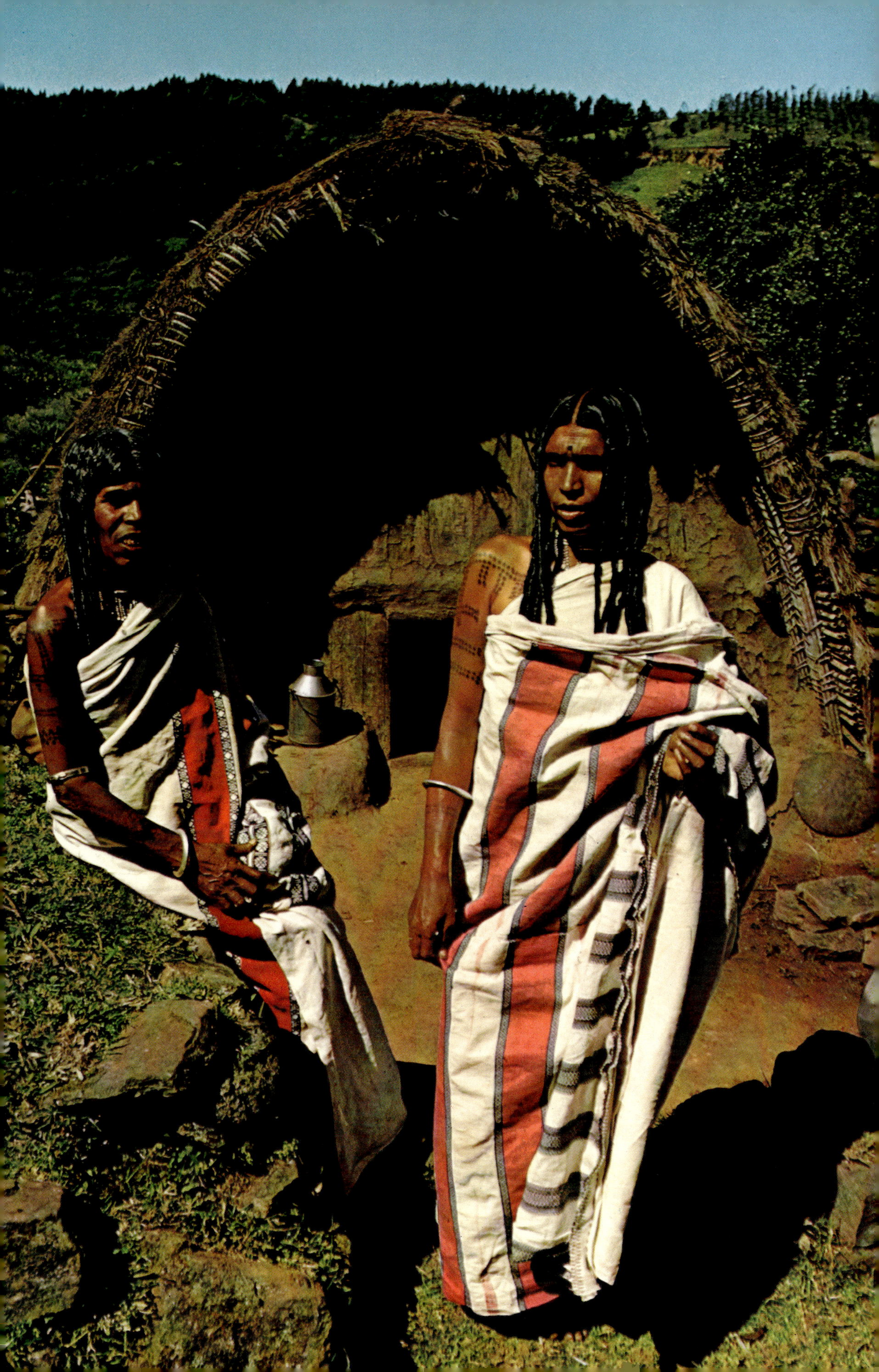

Terraced hillsides around the Badaga village of Tuneri yield potatoes for sale in city markets. Once the Badagas shared their crops with other Nilgiri tribes, but the old network of exchange among the mountain people has disappeared. A herdsman (right) tends part of the Todas' 3,000 buffalo. His tribe now sells its dairy products at town bazaars.

and held him for a moment at the feet of one of the men of his mother's clan. He repeated the action before all those assembled for the ritual. With this introduction, a child takes his place with the proud Todas to grow up secure in his knowledge that he lives among the most superior people in the world. After the elder had shown the infant to the men and the women, he proudly brought him to me. I patted and admired the baby after the fashion of my own people, as a final, incidental addition to the rite of introduction.

Afterward, as my jeep bounced over the steep road past dense forests and tea plantations toward the town of Ootacamund, I felt as exhilarated to be among the Nilgiri people as I had when first I met them more than 30 years ago. In 1937, I had come up to the plateau, an area of hills and glades and rolling downs, to recuperate from a fever contracted while studying tribes in the dank lower jungles. Now, in 1968, arriving from Madras at its hottest season before the monsoon, I enjoyed the cool, bracing air and the heady views with all the old zest.

The aboriginal tribes had attracted the attention of Europeans as early as 1602, when a Portuguese Jesuit ventured up the jungle slopes. He found not only a different climate, but also a very different people from those of the surrounding plains of south India. The steep, arduous climb and the unaccustomed cold of the Nilgiri nights had discouraged the plains people from settling on the plateau.

Through centuries, four Nilgiri groups lived on a strip of land about 35 miles long and up to 15 miles in width. Each spoke its own language and peacefully followed its own customs and traditions, but every group had a role to play, a function to fulfill in the culture and life of the others. The pastoral Todas supplied ghee, or clarified butter. The enterprising Kotas provided tools and music. The shy Kurumbas, who lived scattered through the surrounding jungle, appeared at the settlements from time to time to perform feats of sorcery as well as to supply honey and wood. The Badagas cultivated grain and beans for all.

An intricate network of exchange closely linked a family in one group with a family in each of the other three. I once saw a Badaga frantically searching through a Kota village for the musician with whom he always dealt. The Badaga's father-in-law had just died, the cremation had to be performed quickly, and Kota music was needed for the funeral ceremony. The Badaga found his Kota deeply engaged in an important council session, but prevailed upon him to gather a band of musicians and to leave at once for the funeral. A tip always helped in such times of persuasion, whether in the emergency of a funeral or in the repair of a suddenly broken plow, but the Kota's main payment came when he appeared at the Badaga's field at harvest time and received a share of the crop. Cash purchases and markets have replaced the traditional exchanges; however some families still have strong ties with their old friends.

The Badagas came to the Nilgiri Hills after the Todas, Kotas, and Kurumbas, around the 14th century. Though late-comers and more numerous than the others, the Badagas settled among them, and adopted some of the customs of the Nilgiri tribes.

As I revisited my old friends, I saw signs of change in many of those customs, particularly in the Kota villages and the Toda settlements where I concentrated my study. Let me sketch here the modern Todas and Kotas. For the Badagas, who increased from 20,000 in 1871 to about 85,000 in 1961, have spread far beyond the plateau. They have abandoned many old ways and no longer identify with the tribal society. The Kurumbas remain so withdrawn in their jungles that I scarcely know them. But the Todas and Kotas are anything but withdrawn. The Todas, especially, stride through the streets of Ootacamund, the main Nilgiri town, as if it were one of their tribal settlements.

In 1820 one of the first Englishmen to write about the Todas, Lt. Evans Macpherson, described the typical tribesman as "fair and handsome, with a fine expressive countenance, an intelligent eye, and an aquiline nose; his appearance is manly, being tall, strong-built, and

One of the few Todas educated beyond her Nilgiri home, head nurse Evam Piljain studied in England and today travels among her people in a mobile medical unit. Before Evam began her work, almost half the tribe's babies died in infancy; since 1963 all have survived.

well set up; his limbs muscular and finely proportioned." Other Europeans since have written about the striking appearance of the Todas, though the people themselves have their own, rather different standards of beauty, especially female beauty. The crowning feature of a woman's loveliness, they believe, is the hair on her face. The more facial hair, the more attractive the woman.

By Toda standards, a truly handsome woman should also have narrow feet. When a famous Indian film star once came to the Nilgiris on location, the Toda men studied the renowned beauty. One of them said to another, "She is not so beautiful. She has such broad and ugly feet."

Each Toda woman wraps herself in a simple cloaklike garment adorned with embroidery. She twists her hair in long ringlets, using ghee to enhance its gloss and curl. All women once wore blue tattooing on their arms, shoulders, and feet, but the younger ones have given up the old tribal fashion.

Much as Toda men appreciate beauty in women, they are just as interested, sometimes even more so, in the beauty of their buffalo. A man knows each buffalo in his family's herd by name and temperament. He also knows buffalo of other herds as individuals, and often can identify in photographs many of the Todas' 3,000 animals.

During the 19th century, buffalo provided the Todas with their entire livelihood. The tribesmen consume great quantities of ghee, curds, and a type of buttermilk, and have traditionally exchanged ghee for grain and utensils with the other Nilgiri peoples. But now the Todas receive income from the sale of dairy products and from the lease of some of their lands, so the tribesmen buy their grain and other goods at markets. In recent years the women have earned money for the first time; they embroider cloaks, shawls, and table napkins sold in town bazaars. Members of the tribe do not eat buffalo meat or make any material use of their beloved animals except for their milk and milk products.

Todas believe that everything connected with the care of their buffalo is sacred, and that everything sacred has to do with buffalo. The tribe holds certain herds descended from a special bloodline as particularly sacrosanct, and only priests tend them. During the months or years when a Toda takes his turn serving as a priest, he keeps apart from others and leads an ascetic life to maintain a ritual purity. He lives alone in the temple-dairy, he wears a small black loincloth and shawl, and he may not cut his hair or nails or shave. He must not wear anything of foreign origin, not even dentures.

Only Toda men may go within the stone fence around the temple. When the Papal Nuncio to India visited a Toda settlement, his hosts showed him around with the respect they give all men of religion. But when some of the Nuncio's party wanted to go inside the temple, the Todas politely barred the way. "But you can go anywhere in *our* church," the Nuncio's aides objected. "That is *your* church," came the reply; "this is a Toda temple."

Only when men rethatch a temple roof can outsiders see the two simple rooms—one where the priest lives and the other where he keeps the clan's sacred lamp, churns, and utensils for making clarified butter.

Toda woman winds yarn she will use to embroider cotton putkulis, *the simple, one-piece cloaks worn by both men and women.*

In a gesture of respect, a woman crouches before an elder. She guides his upraised right foot, then his left, toward her head, a greeting common among Todas.

81

Kotas in ceremonial dress whirl to the rhythm of trumpets and drums. The tribe's musicians once played for Nilgiri religious events, but now perform mainly at their own rites.

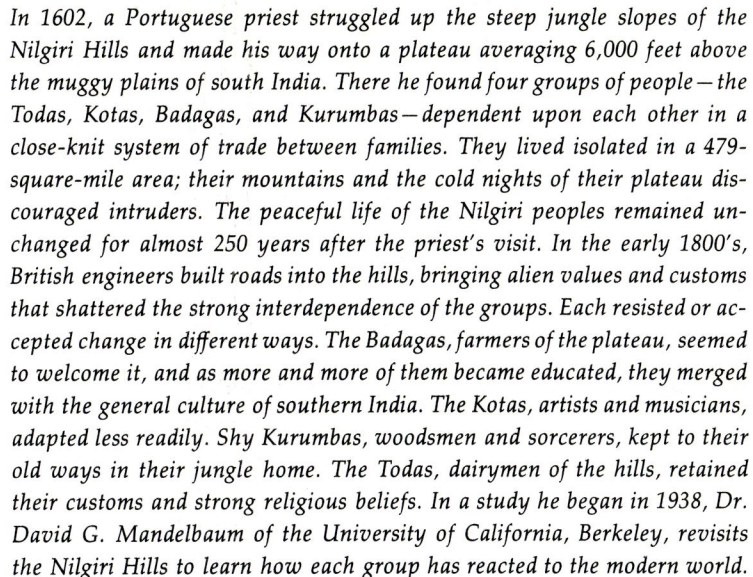

In 1602, a Portuguese priest struggled up the steep jungle slopes of the Nilgiri Hills and made his way onto a plateau averaging 6,000 feet above the muggy plains of south India. There he found four groups of people—the Todas, Kotas, Badagas, and Kurumbas—dependent upon each other in a close-knit system of trade between families. They lived isolated in a 479-square-mile area; their mountains and the cold nights of their plateau discouraged intruders. The peaceful life of the Nilgiri peoples remained unchanged for almost 250 years after the priest's visit. In the early 1800's, British engineers built roads into the hills, bringing alien values and customs that shattered the strong interdependence of the groups. Each resisted or accepted change in different ways. The Badagas, farmers of the plateau, seemed to welcome it, and as more and more of them became educated, they merged with the general culture of southern India. The Kotas, artists and musicians, adapted less readily. Shy Kurumbas, woodsmen and sorcerers, kept to their old ways in their jungle home. The Todas, dairymen of the hills, retained their customs and strong religious beliefs. In a study he began in 1938, Dr. David G. Mandelbaum of the University of California, Berkeley, revisits the Nilgiri Hills to learn how each group has reacted to the modern world.

Each temple belongs to one of the 16 Toda clans, but all of the tribesmen gather to celebrate the rethatching, or renewal, of a temple. The visiting clansmen assemble on the road leading to the scene of the ceremony. There they link arms and enter in formation, shouting a cadence of "o hau hau" in a kind of throaty bark. The men of the host clan run toward their guests and bow to the ground in front of them, expressing their appreciation for the visit and their unity as fellow tribesmen.

Later, all the women greet their elders and relatives among the men: Each woman crouches and guides the man's upraised foot toward her head—a gesture of respect and solidarity, not at all of servility. Not long ago, a Toda woman near death from an abscessed liver illustrated how meaningful the Todas consider this custom. The medical-van driver taking the woman to a hospital in Ootacamund stopped to pick up two Toda men walking along the way. As the elders clambered into the van, the sick woman, her eyes glazed but her spirit firm, struggled up from her stretcher, brushed aside the nurse's objections, and bowed respectfully to the men.

When the Todas celebrate a temple renewal, dancing plays a significant part in the observance, as it does in all major ceremonies. Only the men dance; they move in a circle, their arms tightly linked, their tempo marked by shouts. Inside the ring, a poet composes verses as he dances and calls out a line between the men's shouts. Sometimes subtle, sometimes vivid, these poems always evoke the mood of the occasion whether the poet creates them for a funeral, a paternity rite, or some other important event.

In marriage, the Todas still follow their old custom of polyandry. A girl's parents arrange for her betrothal as soon as she is born. When she is about 15 years old, she moves to the boy's home. There she becomes the wife, not only of the boy, but also of his younger brothers as well. Later, with her husbands' consent, she may take a lover from within the Toda tribe.

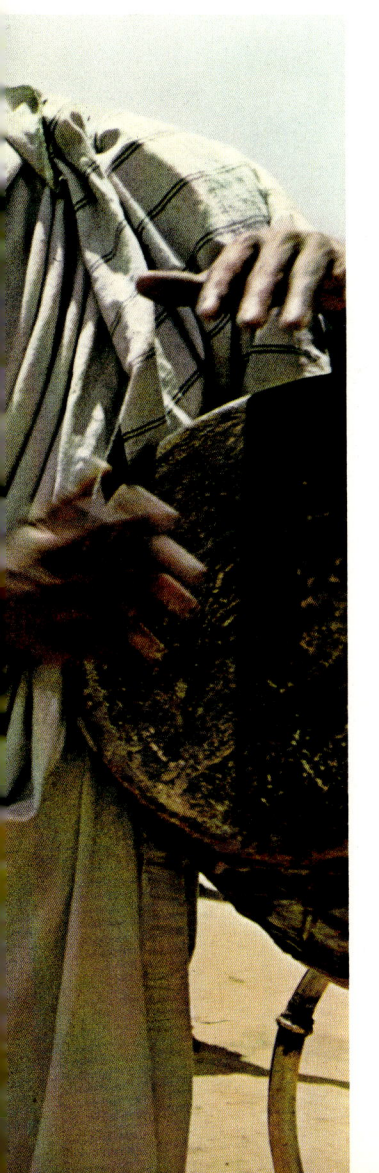

Two months before a young wife's first child is born, one of her husbands, usually the eldest brother, performs a paternity ceremony amid a gathering of Todas, presenting her with a symbolic bow and arrow to proclaim himself official father of the child. He continues to be the legal father of all her future children unless some other man subsequently performs the bow ceremony with her. Who the actual father of a child may be, in Toda eyes, is unimportant.

Todas assemble often, whether for a happy occasion like a bow-giving or for the sad event of a funeral. If two men or two families quarrel, they promptly take their dispute to a council of elders and readily accept its decision. In this way the Todas have remained immune to prolonged bickering.

Unfortunately, they lacked immunity to diseases introduced in the first half of the 19th century, and for a time their population steadily decreased. They numbered 805 in the census of 1901 but only 630 in 1941. Then His Royal Highness Prince Peter of Greece and Denmark, an anthropologist, went to the Nilgiris to study the Todas. He determined to do something about the danger of the tribe's extinction and persuaded the Madras state government to provide a mobile medical unit for the Todas and the other three Nilgiri peoples. An Ootacamund civic club provided funds for a ward in the district hospital.

The action produced quick and dramatic results. Previously, almost half the babies died in their first year, but all infants born since 1963 have survived. Toda men and women now also recover from illnesses that once meant death.

The work of a remarkable Toda woman, Evam Piljain, helped in large part to make the medical unit effective. Evam—the Toda word for gift—once played the role of Florence Nightingale in a school drama and, in a moment of self-discovery, knew that she wanted to become a nurse. She worked hard during her initial training, and went to England to complete her studies. In London, Evam thoroughly enjoyed her new life and her work. She probably would have remained there if a friend had not sent her a copy of Prince Peter's alarming report on the decline of the Toda population. The news stunned her. For days, as she later wrote, she could not eat or sleep. Within two weeks she resigned her position and left for home.

BUT BACK IN THE NILGIRIS she found that the new mobile medical dispensary had begun operation without any provision for a nurse. Evam became a voluntary assistant and worked without pay for a year and a half, living on money she had earned in England. She had almost exhausted her savings when help came unexpectedly.

At a political meeting in Madras, she met the Prime Minister of India, the late Jawaharlal Nehru, and told him that she had taken the advice he repeatedly urged on educated young people—to work in the countryside—but that she could not get a paid position. Within a short time Evam Piljain received an appointment as the head nurse in charge of the mobile dispensary.

The Prime Minister did not forget the Toda nurse. Several years later, he came to the Nilgiris on vacation and asked to meet her again. They talked about the Todas, and finally Nehru delicately brought up a subject that troubled him. "What are you doing," he asked with

GOTTFRIED KLAUS

Tribesmen struggle to subdue a buffalo during a Toda funeral ceremony for an elder clansman. They will sacrifice the animal, and it will accompany the dead man to Amnodr, the Toda afterworld, to supply him with milk.

obvious reference to Toda love life, "about their marriage customs?" "Nothing, sir," Evam replied. "Why not?" countered the Prime Minister. "Because," Evam said, "they are only doing openly what many so-called civilized people do in secret. They are more honest. Why should I try to make them dishonest?"

Nehru thought for a moment, then broke into a wide grin, and without another word, thrust out his hand. With that handshake, they affirmed their confidence and respect for each other.

The confidence and respect of her fellow tribesmen came gradually. Todas at first had little faith in modern medicine, preferring treatment

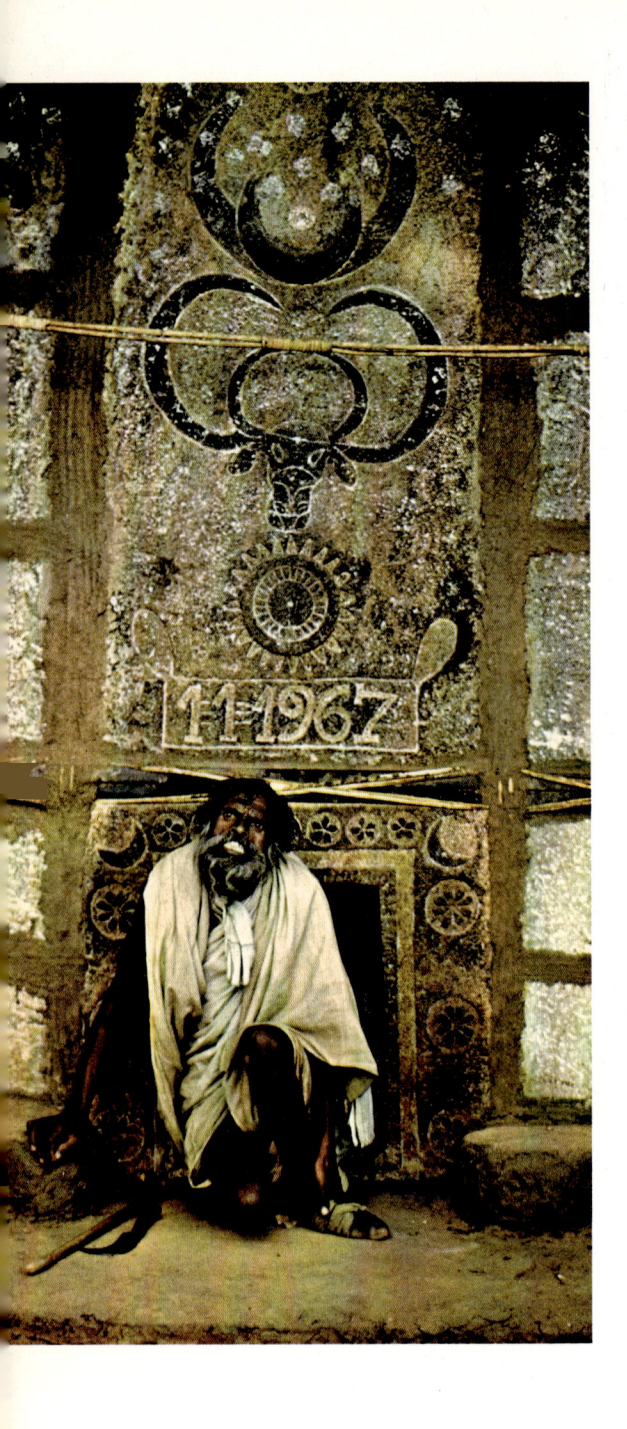

Toda life and religion center on herds of sacred buffalo: Temples serve as dairies and priests as dairymen. Tribesmen from several clans (right) dance at the completion of a temple-thatching ceremony. A priest (left) kneels as he leaves the low square doorway of a temple where he must live alone. Every morning and evening he milks the buffalo and prepares ghee, curds, and a type of buttermilk. Hindu stonecutters, commissioned by the Todas, carved the temple wall and decorated it with images of the sun, the moon, and a four-horned buffalo. Below, a priest carries a bamboo milk container and churn paddle as he moves to another buffalo pasture lower in the Nilgiris.

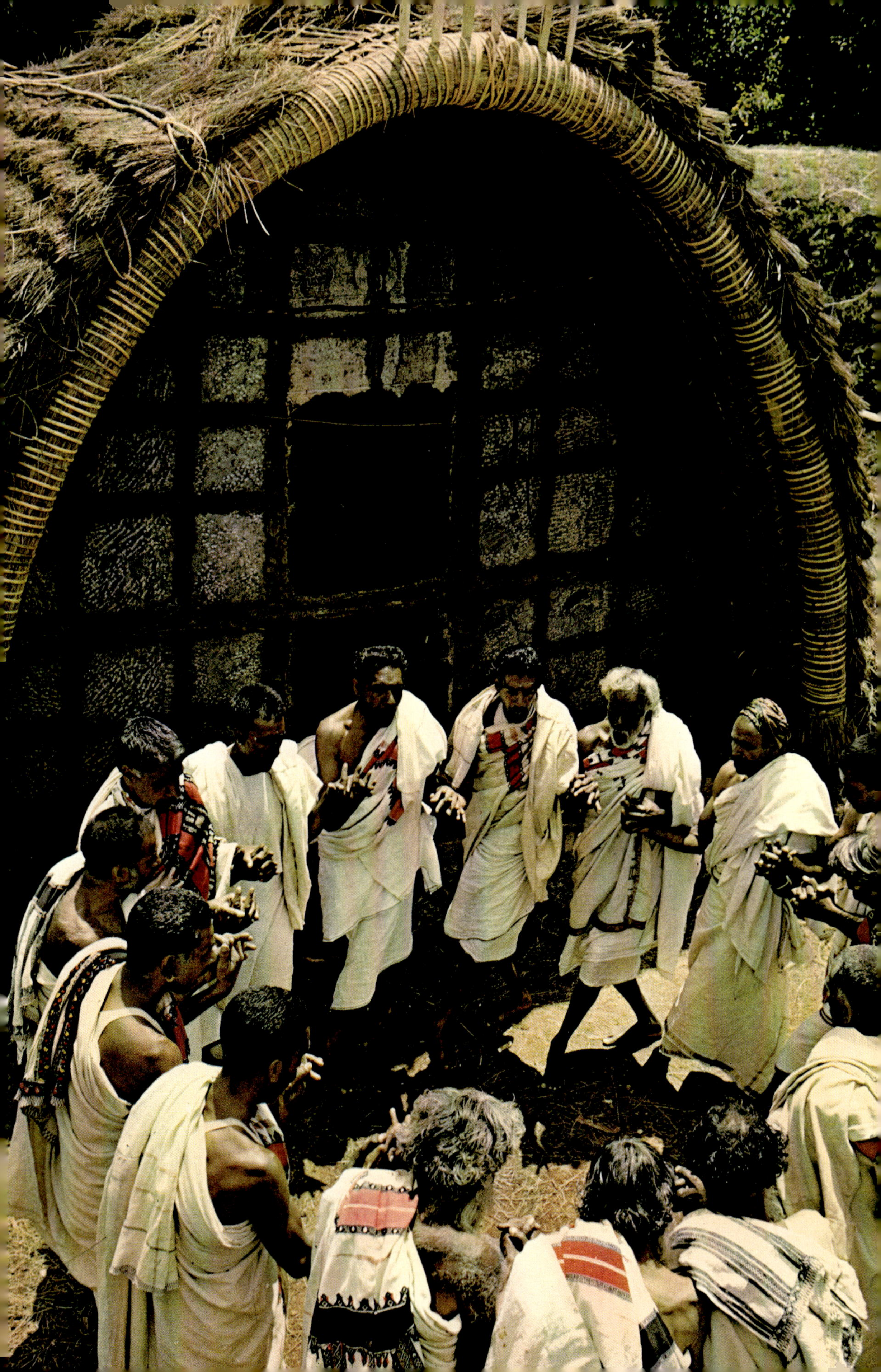

with amulets, charms, and local herb remedies. A turning point occurred when one of the nurse's cousins—Evam's sister by Toda reckoning—became seriously ill as the time approached for the birth of her child. Evam rushed her to the hospital and gave her own blood in an emergency transfusion. That night the woman's husband came to the nurse's home, furious that she had taken his wife away. In his rage, he smashed windows and demanded that the woman come back to his house where, if she had to die, she could die in dignity.

Evam refused, and he finally strode away angrily. But in a few hours she learned that she would have to go after him, for doctors urgently needed the husband's permission for an operation. Evam quickly went to his home, hiking over a dark forest trail. In Toda belief, the forest at night holds many dangers—both animal and supernatural—and Evam's courage and determination so impressed the husband that he gave his consent to the doctors' request. Next morning, when the man saw his wife and new infant son alive and well, he quickly spread the news through all the tribe that Evam had rescued two Toda lives, even with her own blood.

T ODAS NOW CLUSTER around the medical van when it comes to their settlements. Ordinarily, women do not participate in a council, but when a knotty problem arises the elders often ask Evam Piljain for her views. Toda women may not step inside the temple grounds. Yet when a man fell into a coma inside one of the shrines, his clansmen summoned Evam there to give him first aid.

Evam also has helped her people in a continuing struggle to protect their lands. Though they have lost part of their old pastures to agriculture and reforestation, they still have enough to support the cherished buffalo. So long as Toda herds remain intact as the basis of the people's livelihood and the center of their fond devotion, Toda culture probably will remain intact and retain its vitality.

But the close interdependence among the Nilgiri peoples has vanished. The breaking of old ties has affected the Kotas more than the Todas, for they can no longer make their living by providing tools and music. Some Kotas now journey beyond their homes for jobs. Many have learned to cultivate potatoes, introduced by British administrators in the 19th century, and have come to depend on cash payments from their crops. A new economy, an influx of plains people, and new customs divided the villages into conservative and reform factions. But now the Kotas want to hold fast to as much of their tradition as their changing life will allow.

Funerals remain among the most important Kota ceremonies, taking place in two stages: the "green" and the "dry" observances. At a green funeral, performed immediately after a death when the loss is fresh like a green plant, the Kotas cremate the body. At a dry funeral, the villagers commemorate all the departed of the previous year in a final, tremendous burst of mourning, ritually cremating parts of skulls saved from earlier ceremonies. Except the priests, who must not contaminate their sacredness by contact with mourners, Kotas from all villages attend the second funeral.

I saw a heated argument break out at one dry ritual. A man who

Tears streaming down their faces, two young Toda women (below, right) gaze steadily at a lamp symbolizing new life. Without blinking, they must stare at the flame until it flickers out, during a ritual held two months before the birth of their first offspring. Each woman has received a bow and arrow fashioned of leaves and twigs and carried to the ceremony by one of her several husbands (opposite) who has proclaimed himself father of the unborn child.

89

had opposed sacrificing buffalo at funerals because the custom was unprogressive had a change of heart at his own father's funeral. He then wanted to observe fully the old way of showing respect for the dead man and of providing him with animals in the afterworld. Long debate ensued; the elders finally compromised and allowed the sacrifice of one buffalo as a special concession.

WHEN I WENT to a salt-giving ceremony in a village near the town of Kotagiri, I saw how Kotas combine the old and the new. As I made the steep descent to the village, I talked with a young man who had come to escort me to the rite. He is one of two Kotas who now have a college education.

As we trudged down the path to the village, we met several men on their way to work. One, in much-used coveralls, supervised a crew of mechanics. Others, also in work clothes, operated a metal-working shop not far from the site of an old Kota smithy. Another, neatly dressed in a tweed jacket, white shirt, and tie, worked in an office. All of the men—attired much differently—had participated in the ceremony that would last through the morning.

In the village we found others still dressed in the costume of worship, the traditional waistcloth and cloak. Men who still followed the old style and let their hair grow long had tied it into a chignon with a sacred cord. Those who had cut their hair wore the cord as a necklace.

I watched the men ritually pay respect to the creatures that help them make a living. In the ceremony, the owners reward their buffalo and cattle, leading them to a trough filled with salt water where the animals eagerly lap up the liquid they need and like. The Todas and Badagas perform a similar rite.

Sulli, the man who taught me most about Kota life and ways, was the first of his people to get a high-school education. He became a teacher and waged campaigns throughout the rest of his life to raise Kota standards and to defend their rights. By the force of his personality, Sulli persuaded his people to abandon the customs that degraded the status of the Kotas in the eyes of their neighbors. Kotas no longer will haul away dead cattle and butcher the carcasses for meat. Nor are they on call to drop all other work and hurry to play music at funerals. The younger people have taken his advice to reach out beyond their own villages for education and jobs. But all of them adhere faithfully to their traditional religion, speak the Kota language, and many still perform the centuries-old ceremonies.

The Kotas, who number only about 1,000, have faced a new threat in recent years: The incidence of tuberculosis among the people has risen to epidemic proportions. But the Kotas, like the Todas, now have access to modern medical facilities and to educated men and women who can help guide them through the complexities of modern life.

Both the Kotas and the Todas are grappling with problems like those perplexing thousands of others in tribes and villages throughout the world. They know that they must give up some part of their old ways, and many of their people want much of the new. But they do not want to lose their identity and merely dissolve into the nondescript mass of the population.

In late afternoon shadows, Toda boys stroll through a patch of lush forest near their home. These groves—called sholas—lie scattered across the rolling countryside where herds of buffalo graze. The Todas' tight-knit culture has survived more than 100 years of exposure to outside influences; it probably will endure as long as nothing threatens the sacred buffalo, foundation of the tribal society.

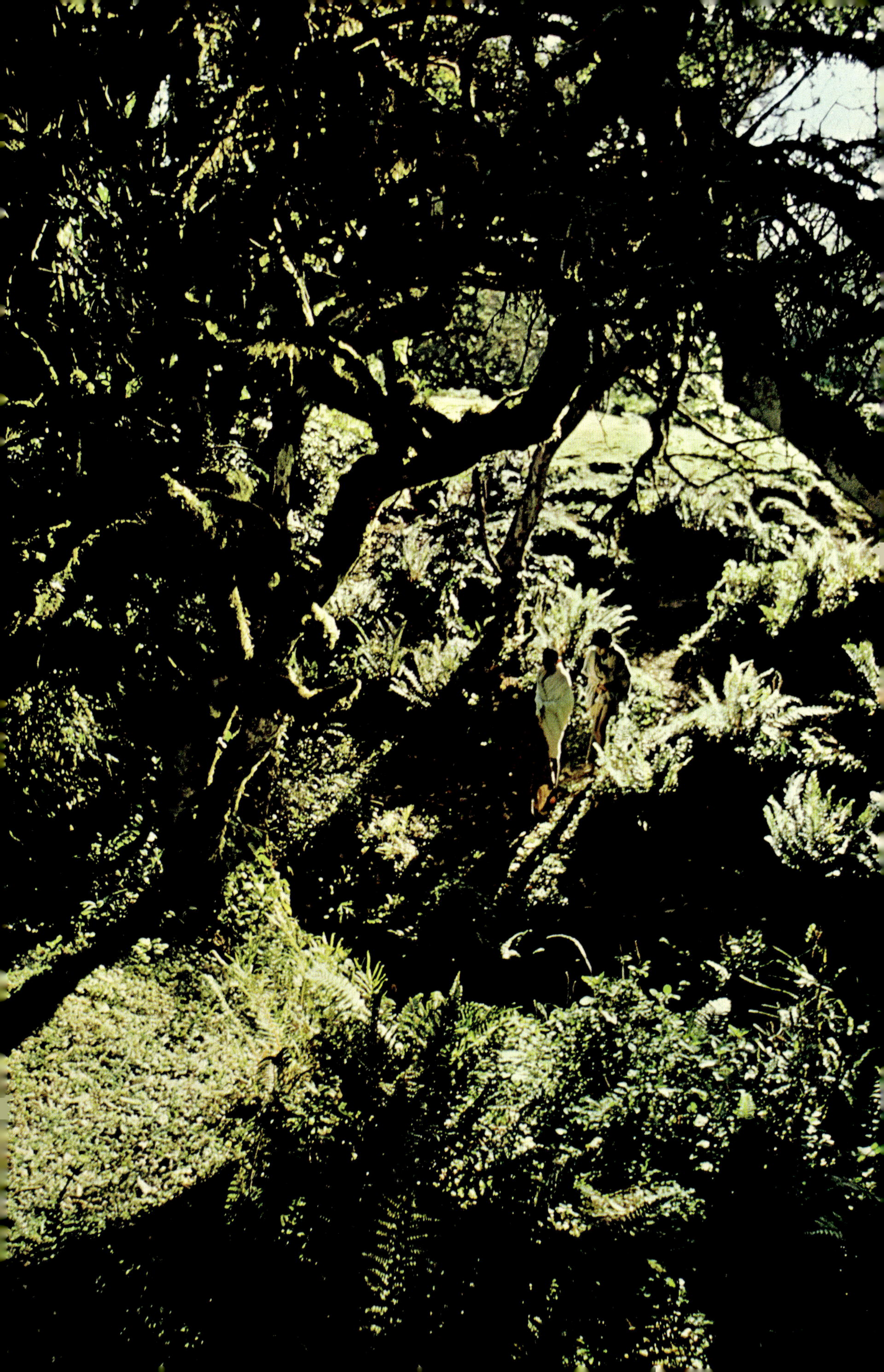

5

Mysterious "Sky People": Japan's Dwindling Ainu

By Sister Mary Inez Hilger, Ph.D.
Illustrations by Eiji Miyazawa, Black Star

"WE PERFORM THIS CEREMONY in good faith—we do not slight the spirits," began the old man who led the ritual that formally welcomed me to the home of Japan's vanishing Ainu. Wearing a richly embroidered robe and a crown of braided vine with a small carved bear's head in front, the white-bearded *ekashi,* or elder, raised his arms three times, then picked up a black-lacquered bowl filled with rice wine. Using a delicately carved stick, he dipped into the bowl and sprinkled the hearth while offering prayers to the spirit of the fire. He slowly sipped from the bowl, then passed it on to me.

A Benedictine nun from St. Joseph, Minnesota, I had come more than 5,000 miles to the island of Hokkaido to gather information about these people, already dwindling in number, before they dissolve completely into the Japanese culture.

A research grant from the National Geographic Society enabled me to undertake the longtime dream. I enlisted the aid of two American-educated Japanese women, Chiye Sano, who received her doctorate in anthropology from the Catholic University of America in Washington, D. C., and Midori Yamaha, who earned her master's degree in sociology from Loyola University in Chicago. Both assisted with the research and served as my interpreters.

Only a few of the people continue the old Ainu customs that I planned to record. All of us sitting around the open hearth in the traditional one-room house had witnessed at least half a century of rapid change. All of us knew time was short for the Ainu way of life, and as the welcoming ritual ended, I could feel our bonds of friendship growing stronger.

These aborigines of Japan, with their round, dark-brown eyes, curling eyelashes, wavy hair, and full beards and moustaches, have mystified anthropologists and travelers for years. Who are the Ainu, whose

Quiver slung from his forehead, a bearded Ainu bowman of the 1600's wears a tunic of woven bark in this Japanese silk-scroll painting. The barefoot hunter stalked game on Hokkaido, the northernmost island of the Japanese Archipelago. By intermarriage and cultural blending, the Japanese have nearly absorbed the Ainu— once a proud and powerful people. Today about 300 full-blooded Ainu survive.

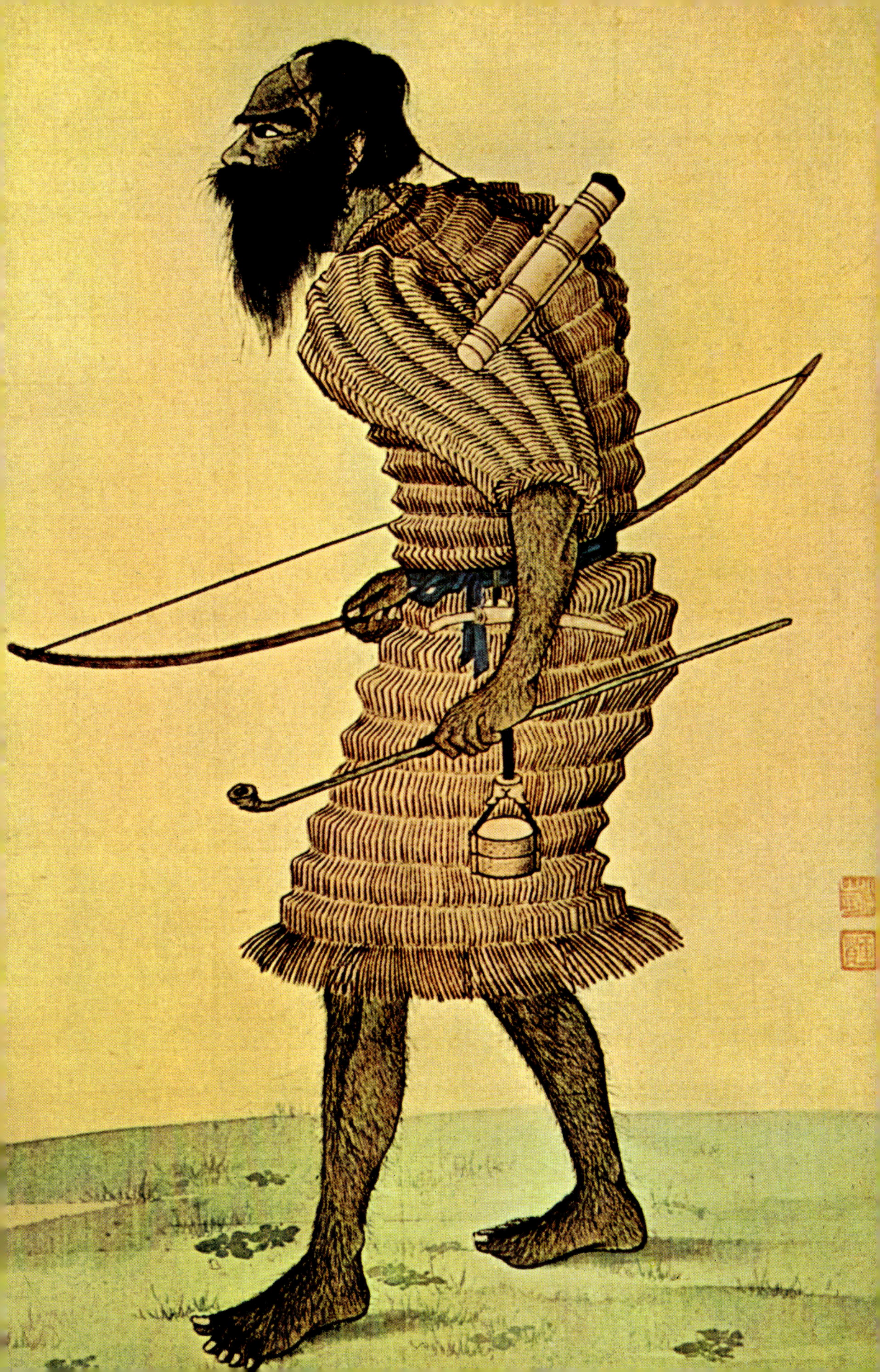

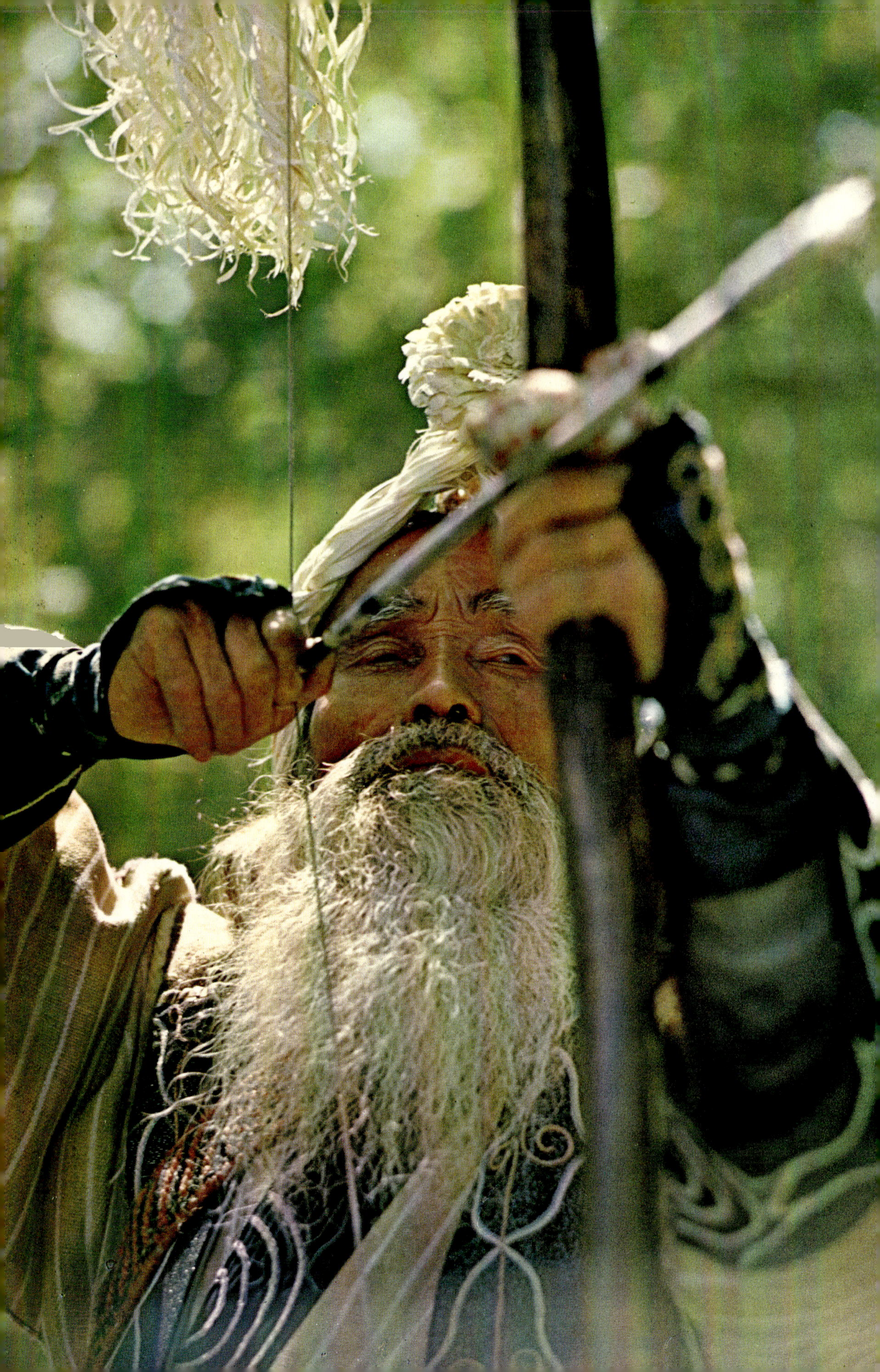

appearance, language, and culture differ so completely from those of the Japanese who dominate the islands today?

The Caucasian-like features of the Ainu persuaded many scholars in the past to believe that the people had a common origin with Europoids and that they slowly drifted across Siberia and Sakhalin Island to the Japanese Archipelago. Other scientists have held that they came from Indonesia or are related to the Australian Aborigines. Anthropologists today tend to view the Ainu as a separate race, a surviving remnant of the ancient population of the area now known as Japan before the great expansion of Mongoloid peoples. Recent archeological discoveries suggest that the Ainu lived in the northeastern half of Hokkaido as long as 7,000 years ago.

We made our headquarters in Tomakomai along the southern coast, where most Ainu now live. One day I received a telephone call from a Japanese man: "Are you the holy lady from America here to learn about the Ainu?" I showed immediate interest, and he assured me he knew where the Ainu had originated. "They came from the skies. Yes, from the skies! Their ancestors were space people—the same who still live in the clouds and send those flying saucers to earth."

About the size of Ireland, jagged Hokkaido rises from the sea as the northernmost island of the archipelago and constitutes nearly one-fourth the total area of Japan. A backbone of volcanic mountains and rich forests slices through the island's fertile plains like a shark's fin. Cold ocean currents sweeping down from the Bering Sea give Hokkaido severe winter weather. Here the Ainu lived for ages, hunting and fishing, until Japanese settlers overran the island, changing the economy to agriculture.

Of the island's population of more than five million, only 300 full-blooded Ainu remain. Many of the thousand or more mixed-bloods who consider themselves Ainu show Mongoloid characteristics after centuries of intermarriage with the Japanese. As I looked at the quiet eyes and wrinkled hands of an elderly, tattooed grandmother, I realized that with the passing of her generation, the Ainu as a separate people will disappear. Younger Ainu parents want to fit in with their Japanese neighbors, teen-agers scorn the customs of their grandparents as quaint superstitions, and children are almost unaware of their heritage.

THE OLDER AINU, saddened by this generation gap, carry on alone. Tsurukichi Seki and his wife Riyo invited me to their home in the Mukawa Valley to meet some of the older women in the community. A single bulb hung from an electric cord, casting a dim yellow glow throughout the room.

"Electricity has not come to part of the valley," Tsurukichi said, "but in our home we have generated it ourselves by windmill power since 1959, and we store the excess in batteries. Until recently four bulbs burned in this room; now we use only one because our batteries are low and growing old."

"Just as *we* are," added Riyo.

The women greeted me Ainu fashion, clasping both my hands while they uttered muted whines and moans of welcome. They felt the muscles in my forearm and asked me my age.

Gruesome bear skull in a tree fork forms a sacred altar in Nibutani. Opposite, bow and arrow poised, an Ainu elder enacts the solemn Dance of the Bow to keep evil spirits from interfering with a hunt.

Ainu punished criminals with shutu—*heavy clubs of wood or bone. A misdemeanor such as stealing brought a severe beating by villagers. This club, about 200 years old, measures two feet in length.*

"Unbelievable!" they cried when I told them 73. "You have the strength of a much younger woman." Sitting around the stove, we drank tea while we talked. Broad blue tattoos outlining the mouth confirmed the age of the women, since I knew the Japanese had outlawed the Ainu custom more than 60 years ago.

From these Ainu women I learned about the religious world of their grandparents. The Ainu religion holds that invisible spiritual beings called *kamui* live in another world and occasionally visit the villages disguised as animals. The Ainu also believe the kamui reside in the trees and mountains. Spirits range from the very good to the very bad, with mischievous, lazy, negligent, destructive, and clumsy ones in between. Kamui and the people's reactions to them govern the day-to-day life of the Ainu. They communicate with the spirits through prayer, usually thanking and petitioning the favorable ones for good fortune and threatening the bad ones for evildoings.

I remembered how the ekashi sprinkled the hearth with the wine called saki before he drank, and I understood the supreme importance of *Abe-fuji-kamui*, the spirit of fire. On an island where winter can often bring up to five feet of snow and temperatures well below zero, Ainu women have always looked after the fire—and do so even to this day.

One of the women I met in the Seki home told me the names of some of the good kamui: *Nupri-koro-kamui* of the mountains, *Nutaph-ushi-pet-kamui* of the valleys, *Pet-koro-kamui* of the oceans. Rivers, trees, even the tiniest creatures, have kamui. "It is sad that the paved roads have no kamui so we could pray to them to stop car accidents," she lamented.

I later met the grandfather of a young woman who had been killed on the road, and he told me how much he had wanted to do something about the tragedy.

"At the time it occurred, my wife and I intended to give warning with a ceremony just in case there might be an evil spirit who lingers on the road causing such accidents," he said, "but we feared ridicule from the younger Ainu and Japanese who had gathered in the crowd."

Only the older Ainu believe in the supernatural powers of the kamui. An elder in Chikabumi explained that when a man drowned at sea, all the men in his *kotan*, or village, put on ceremonial robes, and with swords in hand marched along the beach shouting threats to the evil spirit. If a house burned, the villagers marched around the ashes in the same way.

To contact the world of spirits, the Ainu use their *inau*, hand-carved prayer sticks, as sacred to them as the cross is to Christians. We saw inau in every house, always at the entrance and often in a corner of the fireplace.

Only men make the prayer sticks. I watched Kashiko Kaizawa, a wood carver in Nibutani, first strip the outer bark of a willow stem with his thumbnail. Then he shaved the surface with a blade to make a paper-thin curl, leaving a ring of these delicate spirals on the stem. Inau vary according to the spirit they petition. For a special curative ceremony, Kashiko made an inau with a vertical slash in the stem, then wedged into the slit a piece of charcoal, representing the heart.

Ainu legend recalls that long ago a giant bear came from his realm in

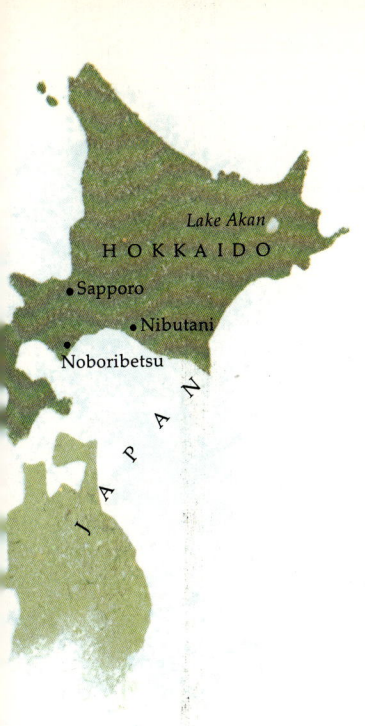

The Japanese Archipelago rises out of the waters off the Asian mainland, dividing the Sea of Japan from the Pacific. At the northern head of the chain lies Hokkaido, second largest of Japan's major islands, with 30,309 square miles of mountains, forests, and valley farmlands. Its harsh terrain and severe winters make it the most sparsely populated island in the country. This is the retreat, the last outpost, of a dying culture — the Ainu. Because of their Caucasian-like features and characteristics, the Ainu — and their origin — have never been fully understood by anthropologists. Their presence on Hokkaido dates from about 5000 B.C., and a few of the people remain today on the Kuril and Sakhalin Islands north of Japan. About 300 full-blooded Ainu survive, and they face total assimilation into the Japanese culture as the young embrace new customs. Sister Mary Inez Hilger, a Benedictine nun from St. Joseph, Minnesota, and a distinguished ethnologist, has conducted extensive research among Indian tribes of the Americas and has lived among the Ainu to record what remains of their ancient way of life.

the skies to rescue the people from a terrible famine. Every spring the Ainu celebrated their deliverance in a three-day ceremony called *iomande*. By sacrificing the Hokkaido bear in their ritual, the Ainu sent the animal's spirit, laden with gifts and honors, back to the world in the sky.

In preparation for iomande, men whittled special inau, and women baked cakes and dumplings for the feast. Everybody dressed in his heavily embroidered ceremonial robe. As soon as the men led the bear into the village center, the women danced around it, clapping their hands in rhythm while the elders prayed: "Oh most honorable bear! You are good to us. Your fur keeps us warm. You give us meat to eat. We dance for you. We send you back to your home in the spirit world with gifts for the other kamui."

The women continued to dance, and young men bombarded the bear with blunt ceremonial arrows. Then an elder shot the bear with a special arrow, and finally the men strangled the animal between two logs.

The rejoicing people feasted on the meat while the bear's head and skin rested between special inau for all to see. Dumplings, persimmons, walnuts, and sweets surrounded the bear to make it happy in the other world. Eventually the skull formed part of an altar when the Ainu fastened it into the crotch of a forked pole; from there it carried messages to and from the land of spirits.

Men still hunt the big brown bear in the mountains of Hokkaido, eating the meat, drying the liver and gall bladder for medicine, and selling the skin. I found that the older Ainu still revere the bear. In Chikabumi I met a man with a bear tooth hanging from a black and white string around his neck. An old woman told me that her husband made a similar talisman for her son when he went away to World War II, and he came back unharmed.

A U. S. Army sergeant stationed on Hokkaido witnessed iomande in 1952 and told me that "one participant was a young girl, very attractive, proudly wearing a fancy ceremonial robe — but under it she wore a canary-yellow turtleneck sweater, brown slacks, high-heeled shoes, and she chewed gum furiously!" Today the young people, especially those with Ainu features, perform in the Bear   *Continued on page 103*

NATIONAL GEOGRAPHIC PHOTOGRAPHER ALBERT MOLDVAY (ABOVE AND LEFT)

98

Mimicking graceful cranes, Ainu women perform a slow, stately dance in Akan National Park on eastern Hokkaido. The dancers form wings with shawls fluttering from outstretched arms. At left, a woman purses her lips to hold a mukkuri — *a musical instrument of bamboo. By jerking the string, the 78-year-old matron vibrates a reed, producing a twanging sound. A gigantic leaf of butterbur (far left) shades a young spectator from the sun. Unlike the Japanese, the Ainu have round eyes and wavy hair. This similarity to Caucasians led some early anthropologists to believe that the Ainu migrated to Japan from the northwest by way of Siberia. Others speculate about a southern origin in Indonesia or a relationship to the Australian Aborigines. A third group suggests that the Ainu represent the remnant of a prehistoric people who inhabited Hokkaido at least 7,000 years ago. Legend contributes a fourth theory: The Ainu forebears descended from the sky.*

Autumn-hued hills of southern Hokkaido rise above traditional Ainu dwellings of wood and thatch, re-created to exemplify and preserve a disappearing way of life. Broiling fish over a sunken hearth, an Ainu woman prepares dinner for her husband, Ichitaro Nitani. A sacred prayer stick, or inau, made of a peeled willow stem with curled shavings, brings blessings to the fire pit. Below, a mother nurses her child in a shinta—a wooden cradle suspended from the ceiling.

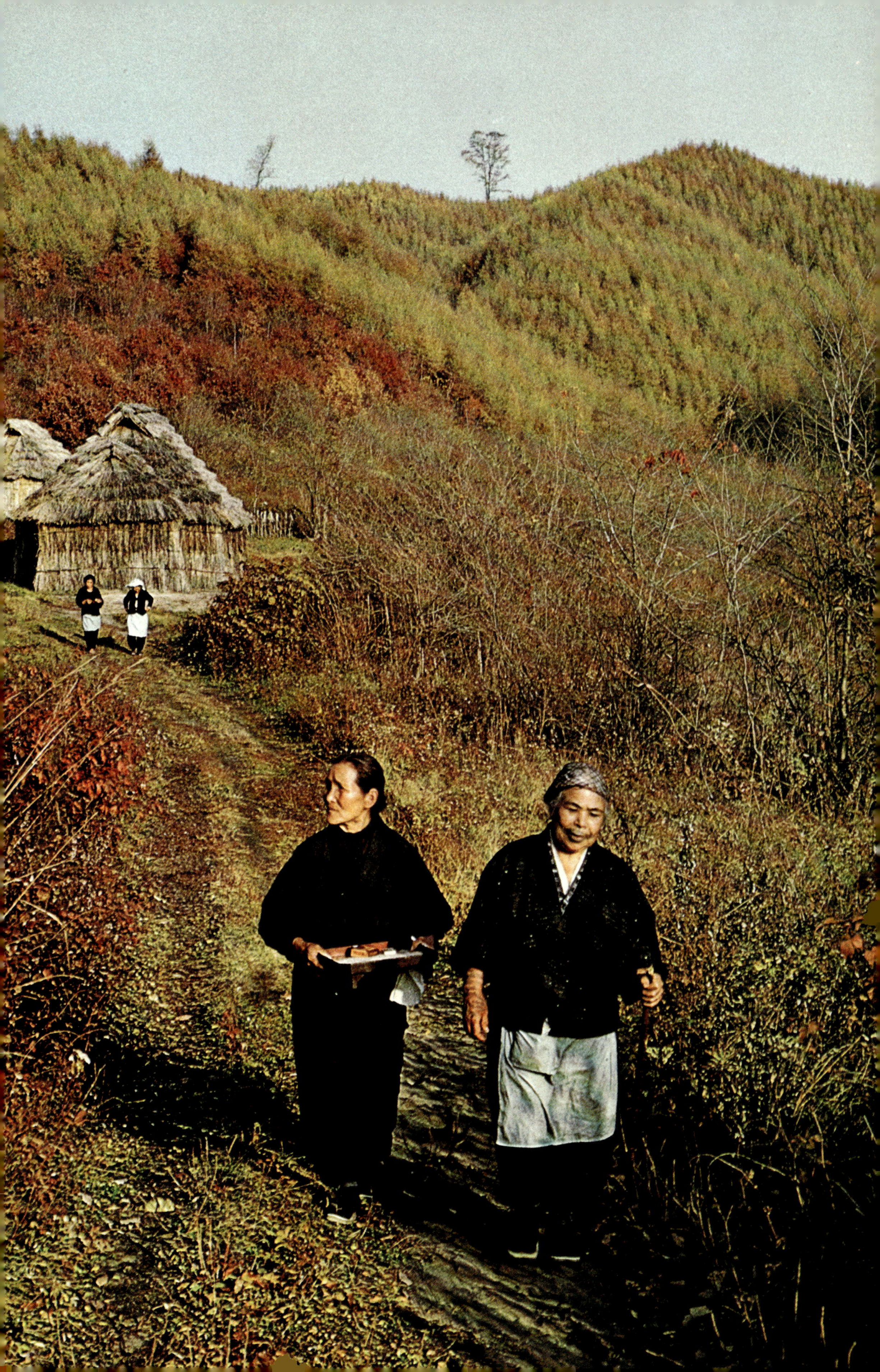

Village elders offer saki, a rice wine, and millet cakes to a slaughtered bear in a Japanese painting of the sacred Ainu ceremony—iomande. The Ainu believed that centuries ago, during a prolonged famine, a giant bear came to earth to give its meat as food. Left, using a carved libation wand, Matsuji Kaizawa offers drops of wine to an inau before drinking from the ceremonial bowl. The foot-long wand on the lacquered bowl (right) keeps his moustache out of the drink.

THAMES AND HUDSON, LTD.

NATIONAL GEOGRAPHIC PHOTOGRAPHER
ALBERT MOLDVAY

Festival, which is staged for tourists as a substitute for iomande, but the youngsters do not believe.

Fifty years ago the gum-chewing girl he described would have worn a broad blue tattoo around her mouth. Grandmothers and maternal aunts usually tattooed the girls in three stages; each time they darkened and broadened the mark.

After washing the lips with a solution of boiled birchbark, the women pricked the outline of the tattoo with a flake of volcanic glass or the point of a very thin knife. They wiped away the blood with a cloth saturated with the solution and rubbed birchbark soot into the cuts to give the design its blue color.

Although the Japanese prohibited the practice late in the 19th century, the Ainu ignored the law, my friend Toroshino, aged 75, explained. "The Japanese thought the custom cruel. Maybe it was, but our men thought us more beautiful with tattoos. Besides, a completed tattoo showed that we were marriageable. I got my finished tattoo at 17 and found a husband right away."

In Noboribetsu I talked with 40-year-old Shigeru Kayano, one of the younger full-blooded Ainu. He and his friends are trying to preserve the best of their culture. Some of the older people resent the commercializing of their customs, but at Noboribetsu the tourist center is doing much to tell visitors about Ainu culture. Here they watch the old dances, the weaving of *attush*, a cloth made from the inner bark of the elm, and the carving of bear figures.

I saw the traditional Ainu house, called a *chisei*. Grass, bulrush, and bark covered the one-room dwelling, and a window, with special religious significance, opened to the east. Inau guarded the open fire pit in the center of the packed dirt floor, kettles and pans hung over the hot charcoal, and wicks burned in clamshells filled with fish oil to provide more light. Here I could well imagine the life of the ancient Ainu and their world of good and bad kamui.

In addition to accidents, I learned, evil spirits can cause bad character, which, like some diseases, is contagious. Parents warn children not to kiss a bad person for fear of catching the evil. Bad kamui also cause convulsions, neuralgia, hysteria, rheumatism, crippled limbs, and insanity. The Ainu have rituals to exorcise these afflictions.

I watched as a woman from Nibutani was treated for a facial tic. The ekashi led the ceremony wearing his crown. His attendants, four women and another man, wore ceremonial robes that once would have been the soft attush, but these were made of cotton. The patient, her neck bound with strips of bark, dressed more somberly.

The group began the rite at the outdoor altar—a row of forked poles that cradled the hoary skulls of bear, deer, fox, and squirrel, whose spirits carry messages between this world and the other. All prayed for the solemn woman, her face twitching every few minutes.

Then the group marched across the tangled field to an oak tree, "well-shaped and leaning to the east," as dictated by custom. A belt of curled inau shavings girded the trunk. Drawing his long gilded sword, the ekashi stamped around the tree flailing the air as if he were actually striking the evil spirit that caused the tic. His attendants prayed and tapped their feet in time to their rhythmic mumblings while the ekashi

103

circled the tree six times. Then he sheathed his sword, took the lacquered bowl containing the rice wine, and with the libation wand sprinkled the saki on the ground.

The afflicted woman stood very still. The ekashi pulled her lips apart with little forked twigs while the women severed the bands of bark around her neck. Finally, they picked up leafy mugwort branches and gently flogged the patient to drive out the evil spirit. I don't know whether this ritual cured the woman—I never saw her again.

For more conventional cures, the Ainu search the fields and forests for home remedies. To help children with stomach-aches, mothers rely on a combination of sweet flag and celandine. It works so well that mothers call it "doctor killer." Adults mix the bear's powdered gall bladder with clear water for pains and colds. When men go hunting in the mountains, they nibble pieces of dried bear meat in the belief that it gives them special protection against the terrible Hokkaido winter.

Lily roots are supposed to check diarrhea, powdered bones stop buzzing in the ears, and in Chikabumi I heard that some Ainu drink a concoction of jack-in-the-pulpit, hoping to develop an immunity to cancer. The Ainu had no resistance to the strange diseases, such as tuberculosis, that appeared when the Japanese spread over Hokkaido in great numbers, and many fell victim to the new maladies.

"We were healthy," an old Ainu told me. "We ate much meat and could stand cold winters. Then it all changed. When my father was small, his father gathered his family and fled to the woods high in the mountains to escape a smallpox epidemic. Many of our people died because we had no cure for it."

I ONCE ASKED TAKEICHI MORITAKE, an elder who has a little shop in the Ainu village near Shiraoi, to tell me about their belief in life after death. "All Ainu go to another world where they live very much as they have on earth," he replied. "The world after death is a world of souls, the dead body an empty shell—useless. So we Ainu say, 'Toss it away.' But the souls are very much alive, and we never forget them. When we old Ainu eat or drink, we throw an offering into the fire to share it with the dead."

Only the grandparents practicing the ancient ways still speak the Ainu language; it has no written form except as its sounds are transposed into Japanese characters. Prayers, history, literature, and lore are passed down orally from generation to generation. The famous Ainu epic called *Yukar* follows a definite poetic form, and my old friend Tsurukichi persuaded his wife Riyo to recite some of it for me.

Yukar literally means "to imitate," and it tells the legends of the Ainu immersed in their world of spirits and animals. Often a story centers on the fatal flaw of human beings and animals who dared to play the part of deities; sometimes the Yukar relates adventures of kamui who came to earth in disguise.

As I listened to Riyo recite the Yukar, she changed her voice from

Harvest from the sea: An Ainu woman on the Pacific Ocean shore carries a tangled mass of kelp. Processed into soup stock, relish, and iodine, the sea plant yields a seasonal income to many coastal dwellers.

NATIONAL GEOGRAPHIC PHOTOGRAPHER ALBERT MOLDVAY

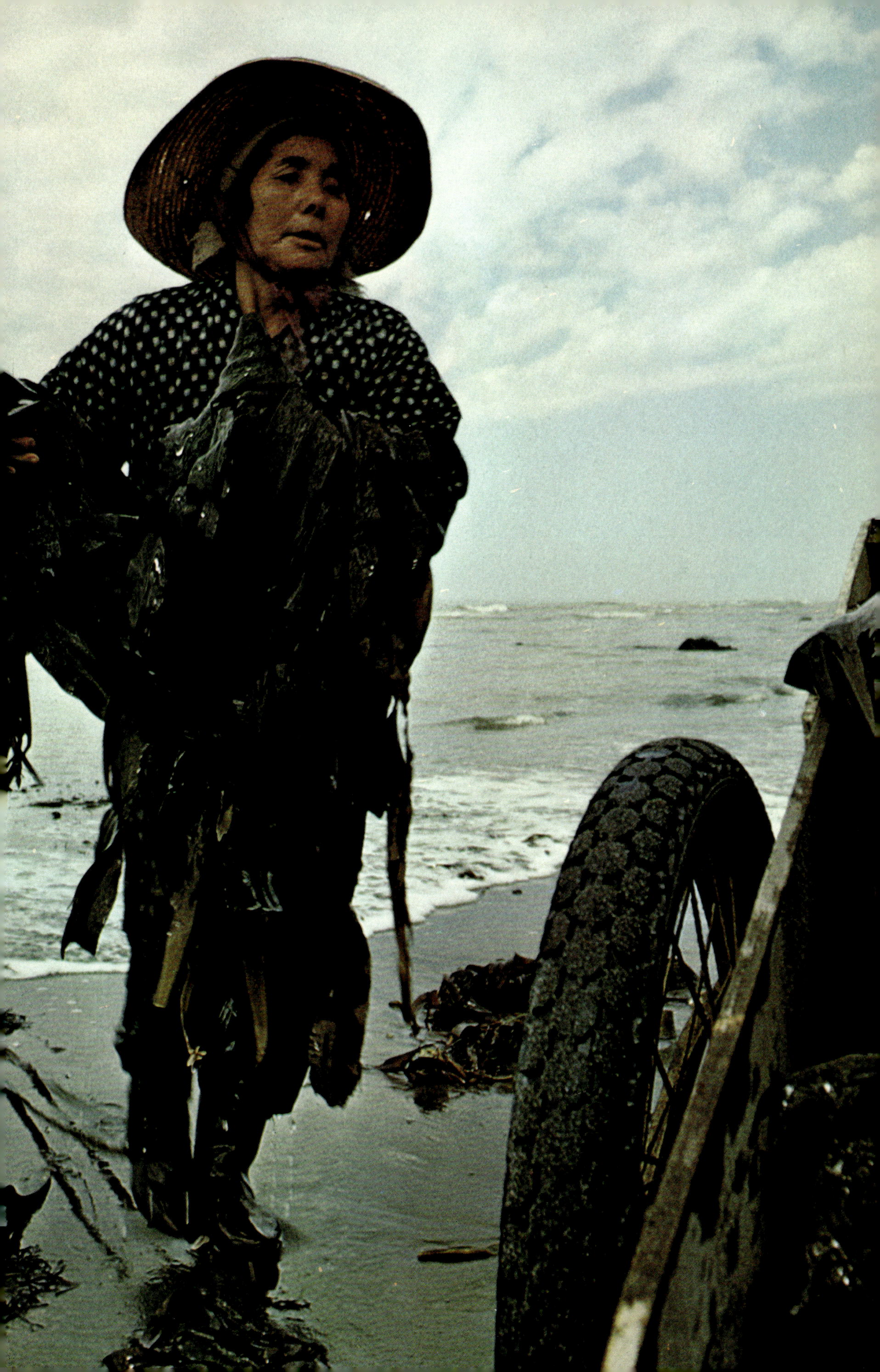

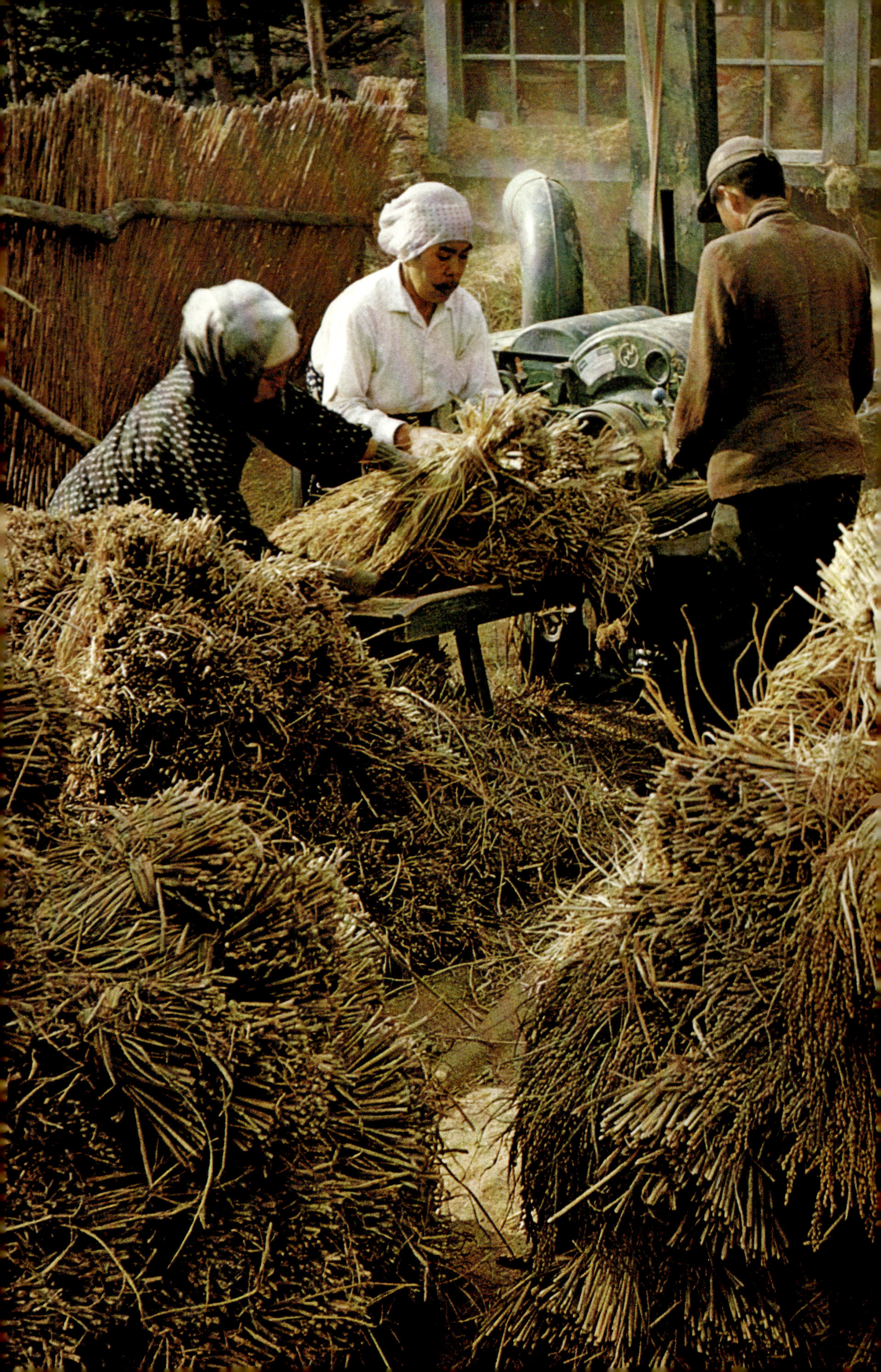

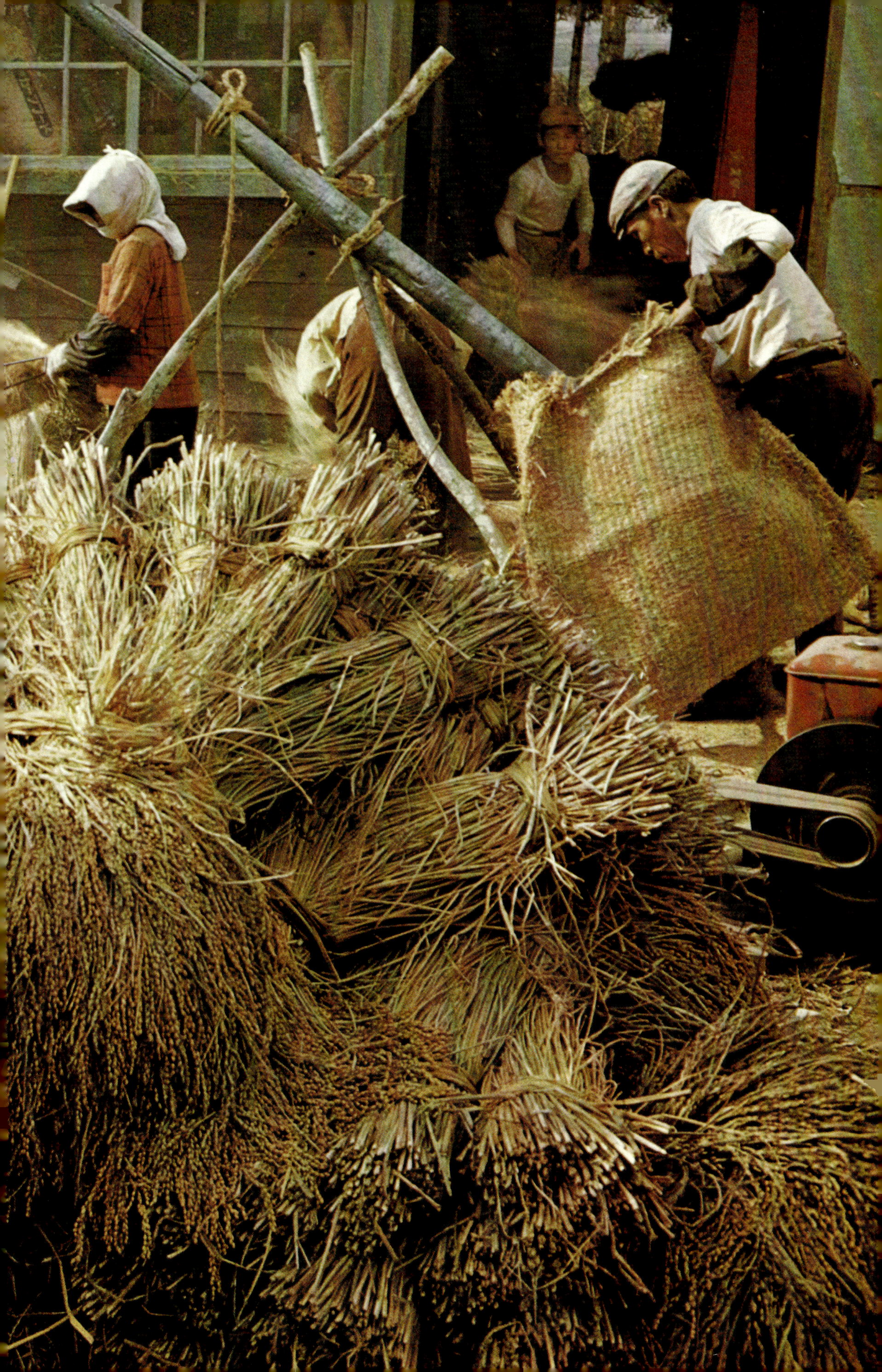

high-pitched angry phrases to playful tunes, staccato dialogues, dramatic passages, subdued chants, even groans. We had to ask the enthusiastic Riyo to stop after 40 minutes, but I'm sure she could have gone on for several hours. In the old days, or even in the days before radio and television, the family gathered around the hearth in the evening to listen to Ainu lore and legend. Little children particularly loved the *Uwepekere,* tales comparable to Aesop's fables, which always end with a moral.

I recorded many Ainu poems, chants, love songs—even tongue-twisters. I especially liked the lullabies. Ainu babies go to sleep in their *shinta,* a hammock-cradle hung from an overhead beam, while listening to the songs and swinging back and forth gently, as if riding waves of air.

In addition to listening to the old songs and tales in the evenings, the children learned by observing and imitating their parents and grandparents. Kaneto Kawamura remembers how his grandfather taught him all about the food plants—where they grew, when they yielded fruit.

"Boys were encouraged to be active and industrious. Besides acquiring the skills of hunting and fishing, they learned to debate," Kayano said. "Children often argued about nonessentials. In this way they improved their power of reasoning and ability to speak out."

Girls stayed with the mothers, first to watch, then to help with the cooking, sewing, embroidery, weaving, and food gathering. All girls learned to weave fiber into cloth and to stitch the distinctive Ainu designs onto ceremonial robes.

Today the young learn not only from their parents and grandparents, but also from teachers in Japanese schools. I watched Ainu and Japanese children playing together in harmony and teachers conducting classes without distinction between the two groups.

Ainu teen-agers seem embarrassed to talk about the old ways of their grandparents. Although they feel distressed because the young people have departed from tradition, the elders carry on their customs as best they can, sadly accepting the change.

The Japanese edged north from the island of Honshu in the 17th century, and their trade with the Ainu developed rapidly. The Ainu bartered furs and fish for rice, tobacco, swords, and lacquerware. Along with other people on the island, the Ainu soon found themselves involved in an intense commerce with the Japanese. Unfortunately, what began as trade ended as exploitation. In time the Ainu, like others on the island, became vassals to the feudal lord merchants of the Japanese Matsumae clan.

During the 19th century the Japanese Government took control of Hokkaido, breaking the power of the Matsumaes. In 1899 the Hokkaido Natives Protection Law partitioned land and gave tools to the Ainu and encouraged them to engage in agriculture. The Ainu had always lived by hunting and fishing, and they believed that the seas, rivers, and forests belonged to everyone.

Overleaf: Ainu and Japanese work together in a farmyard near the town of Shizunai, threshing their crop of rice. Only a frost-resistant variety of the grain can mature during Hokkaido's short growing season.

PRINT COURTESY TOMAKOMAI CITY LIBRARY
Offering tributes, bearded Ainu bow submissively before a Japanese overlord in this 1751 woodblock print. Ainu then controlled Hokkaido, but Japan's Matsumae clan regulated fishing and trading rights and exacted heavy taxes. Today Japanese tourists don Ainu ceremonial dress and pose for picture-mementos.

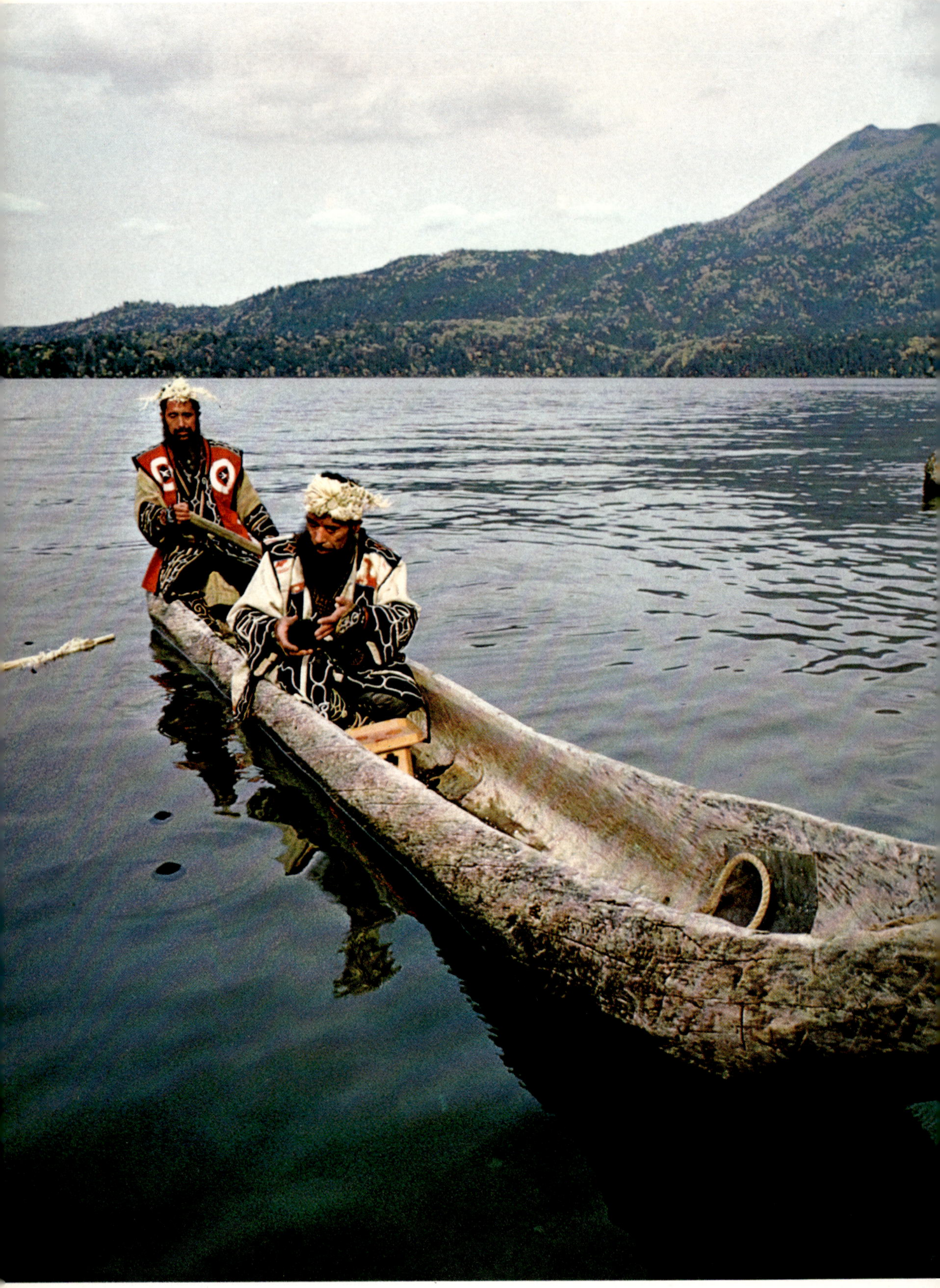

Ainu lore tells that spirits, or **kamui**, powerful
enough to grant blessings or inflict misfortune,
exist throughout the world in the form of animals,
plants, mountains, fire, and water. Elaborate rituals
seek to please the benevolent spirits and exorcise the
evil ones. A festival held on Lake Akan annually
honors the spirit of **marimo**, a rare algae. Floating
in a dugout, Ainu elders ceremonially return balls
shaped from the water plant to the placid waters.
Near the village of Nibutani, a woman receives
treatment for a facial tic supposedly caused by a
wicked spirit. Ainu "physicians" gently flog their
patient with leafy mugwort branches, hoping
to drive the evil being from her.

As an increasing number of Japanese came to settle on Hokkaido, they occupied more and more of the tillable land. The Ainu, who knew nothing of agriculture, continued their life of hunting, but as farms spread across Hokkaido, the once-abundant game grew scarce. The government resolved the conflict between established communal hunting grounds and private land ownership by decreeing that the Ainu could keep his land if he worked it.

Legislation also required Ainu children to attend schools and to study Japanese customs, history, and language. Compulsory classroom integration began in 1937. During World War II Japanese and Ainu soldiers fought side by side, further weakening the barrier between the two groups. Soon children of both cultures mixed freely at play and at school.

TODAY AINU AND JAPANESE live and work together. They belong to the same fishing cooperatives, pooling their resources for modern boats and equipment. The trout, salmon, herring, flounder, squid, and crabs, which Ainu in dugout canoes used to catch with spears and nets, still flourish in the waters off Hokkaido and provide the island with a major source of revenue.

As the Ainu people blend into the Japanese scene, their culture attracts more and more attention. Anthropologists will always wonder who they were and from whence they came.

When the old shopkeeper Moritake wondered about the future of his people, he jotted down this poetic reflection:

> Long pipe leans against ekashi's cheek
>   Smoke of tampaku (tobacco) quietly wavering
> Tampaku went out... one more Ainu gone
>   Ekashi's grandchild born tomorrow
> He may grow up Shisham (Japanese)
>   But his blood and flesh always Ainu

Aging Ainu grandmother reflects the serenity of her people as their distinctive way of life draws slowly but inevitably to a close. Today ancient rituals and customs —like lip tattooing—die with the older Ainu. Teen-agers, embarrassed by the old traditions, seek roles in Japanese society. An Ainu schoolboy symbolizes the new life —he studies the Japanese language and culture in a Japanese schoolroom.

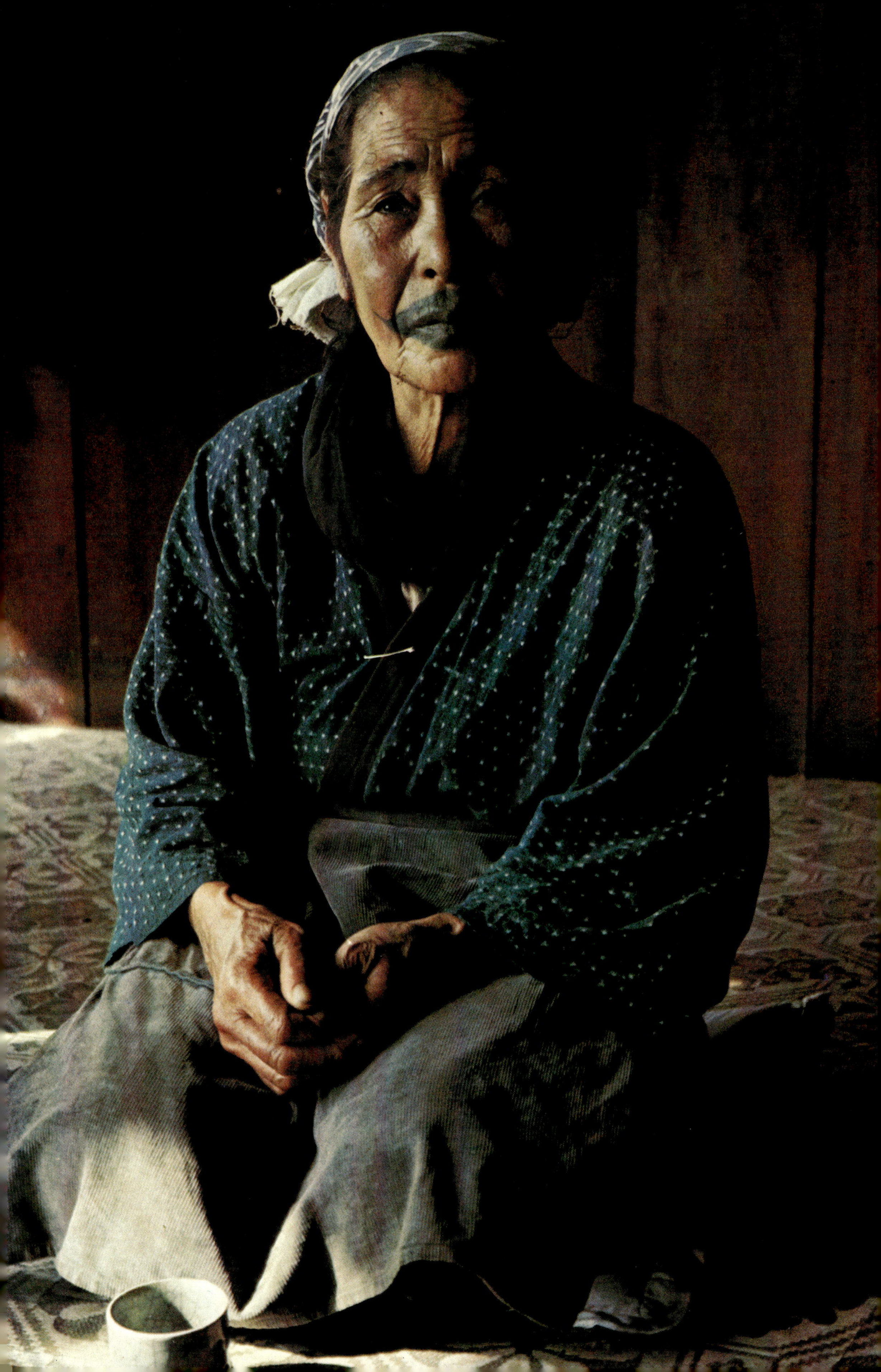

6

Australian Aborigines: Blending Past and Present

By CATHERINE H. BERNDT, Ph.D.
and RONALD M. BERNDT, Ph.D.

RETURNING to Elcho Island in May 1968, we found the once-secret ritual boards looking shabbier than ever, their yellow, red, and black patterns faded by ten years of monsoon rains and tropical sun in Australia's Northern Territory.

Weeds grew in clumps at the bases of the narrow planks, some short and some six feet tall, standing in a cluster by the beach. On the low fence around them, cotton frocks hung drying in the breeze. If we had not known otherwise, my husband Ron and I would hardly have guessed that the boards had stirred such great excitement a decade before when they were first put on permanent display.

Buramara, one of the Aboriginal leaders, had said to us then, "These are our most precious possessions. Surely if we reveal them and share them with the *balanda*, the white man, he will give us something special in return—schools, jobs, money."

I had looked at them in the beginning only out of the corner of my eye, like the Aboriginal women. Since long before the first English settlement on the continent in 1788, the penalty had been death for women who even by accident saw the religious boards that the men held so secret.

In 1946, during our earliest visit to Yirkalla on Cape Arnhem and to Elcho Island in the Arafura Sea, the men had allowed Ron to see the secret dances in which the Aborigines used the boards. Men, their bodies patterned with paint, held the sacred planks and chanted songs appealing for fertility—major theme of all their religious rites. Some boards represented spirit beings and objects such as trees and hollow logs, associated with spirits in myths of the Dreamtime, or Creation. Other planks stood for game—snakes, quail, fork-tongued lizard, and many more. The men imitated the creatures with movements and postures as formal as a ballet.

Towheaded Aboriginal youngsters of Ernabella Mission, South Australia, crowd a water hole dug in a dry creek bed. Light hair, peculiar to people of the central and western deserts, darkens with age. While many Aboriginal customs persist, government policy stresses preparing young people for a full part in Australian life.

DAVID MOORE, BLACK ST

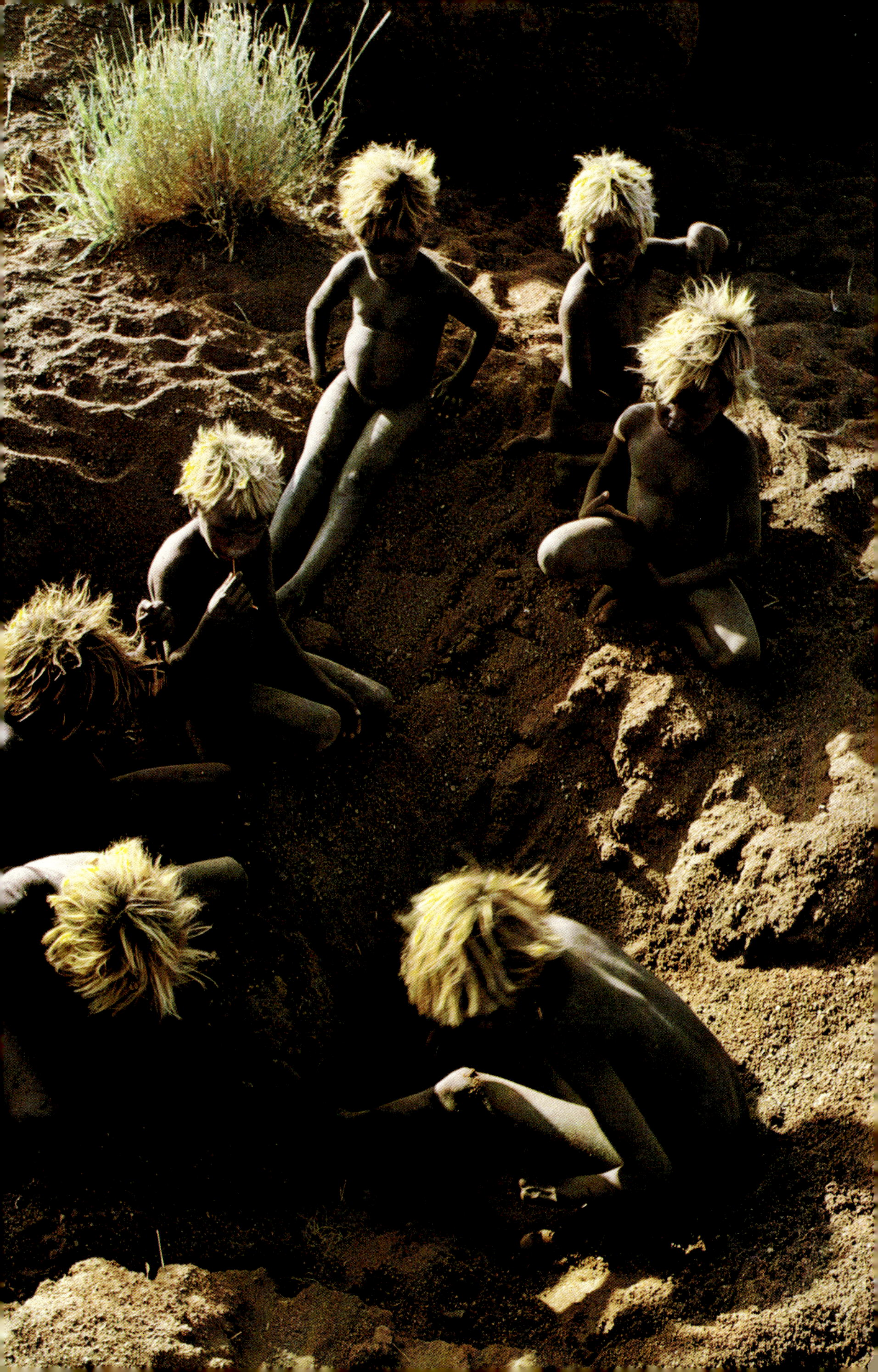

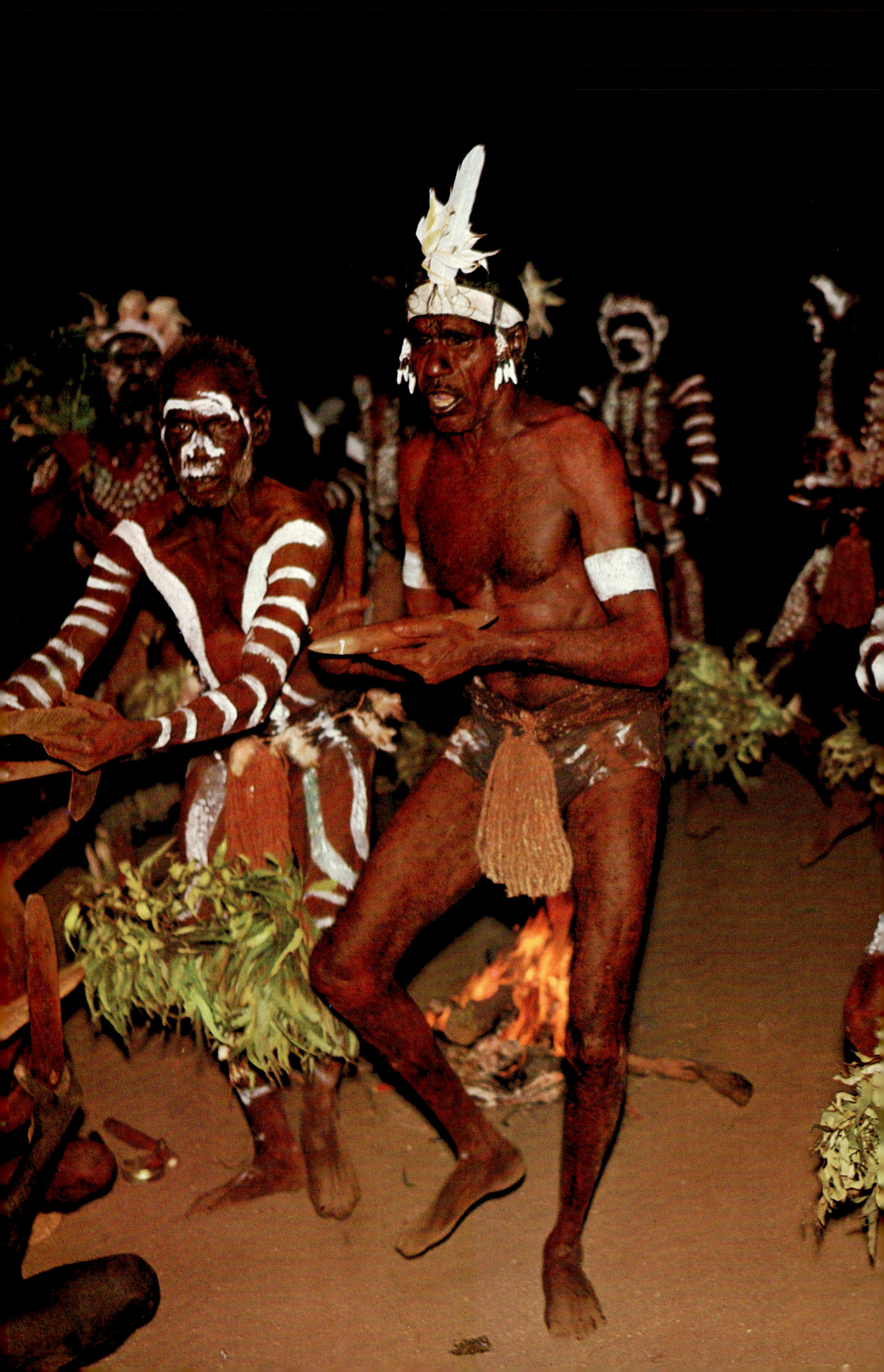

DOUGLAS BAGLIN (LEFT) AND ROBERT EDWARDS

To the staccato sounds of boomerangs and clapping sticks, Lardil tribesmen of Mornington Island in the Gulf of Carpentaria stamp and chant at a corroboree, a series of dances and songs that lasts for hours. Eucalyptus leaves on the legs of the men rustle with every motion; feathers and body paint gleam in the firelight. Ceremonies still play a crucial role in Aboriginal culture, expressing the beliefs, hopes, fears, and pleasures of the people. In religious rituals, dancers re-enact myths; in others they mimic animals and mirror their own everyday life. An ancient painting (above), recently discovered in an abandoned rock shelter near Katherine, Northern Territory, may portray Lightning Brother, a mythical figure.

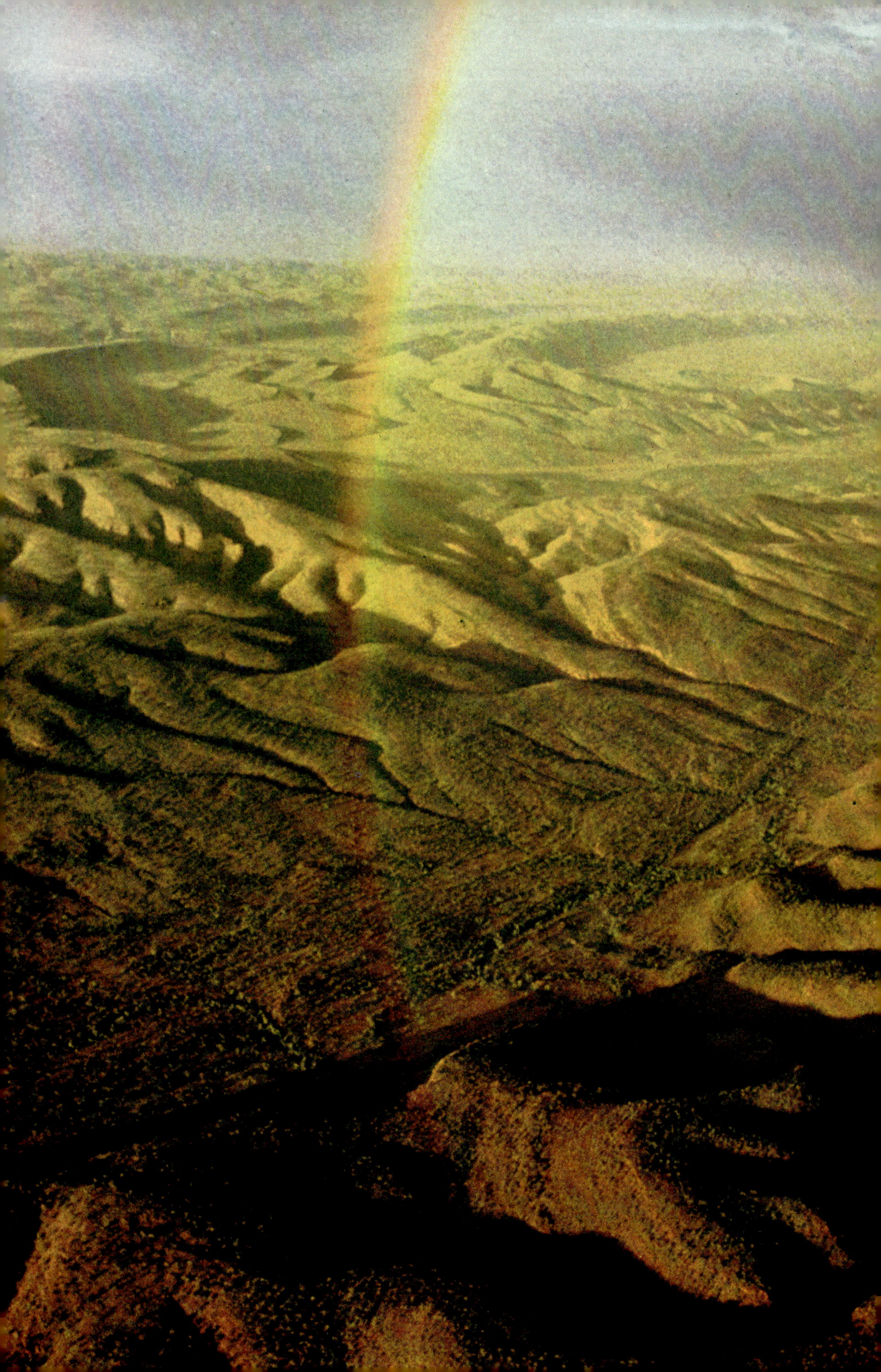

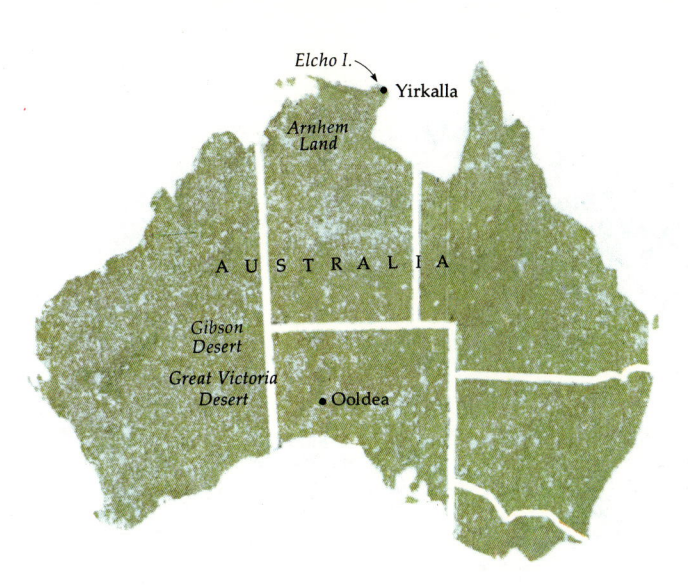

The first Australians, dark-brown people who may have migrated from Asia perhaps 10,000 years ago, did not know the wheel, had no written languages, and no implements except spears and throwers, wooden sticks, stone axes, and boomerangs. Adapting superbly to the land, the Aborigines hunted and gathered food along the verdant coast and in the arid regions across the continent. Life for each of the 500 or so groups centered on religious ceremonies based on stories about mythical creators. From the late 1700's when Europeans began killing the nomads and displacing them from the land, the Aboriginal population dropped from an estimated 300,000 to 46,000 full-bloods by 1947. Today their numbers are growing, and full- and half-bloods total about 80,000. The Aboriginal life of hunting and foraging has almost died; only vestiges of their culture remain. Dr. Catherine H. Berndt and her husband Dr. Ronald M. Berndt are anthropologists at the University of Western Australia. She tells about Aboriginal camp life they saw in the 1940's in tropical Arnhem Land and the Great Victoria Desert. Her account also deals with changes that have come since then and with the efforts of the Aborigines to hold on to their lands and to remnants of their religion.

These ceremonies retelling the sacred myths were the focus, the heart, of Aboriginal society. The stories explained everything—the workings of nature, origin of the people and of every detail of the landscape. From the myths came patterns for family and community life. The rituals ensured that animals and people would bear young, seeds would sprout, and seasons would arrive at the proper time.

Everyone knew the main myths, even though the men kept a tight grip on the secrets of the more intricate symbols. I first heard the most important story, that of the Djanggau Sisters, from Kamal, a thin young woman with short, black, wavy hair. She was a daughter-in-law of clan leader Wonggu, a hot-tempered old man who had 15 wives or more.

"The two Djanggau Sisters came across the water," Kamal told me, "traveling on the path of the rising sun from an island away to the

Arcing rainbow trails a storm across the Krichauff Range in Australia's Centre. Through dry wastes carved by ancient rivers and scarred by eons of sandstorms and rain, Aboriginal hunters stalked kangaroos and emus as the nomadic families moved from one water hole to another.

DAVID MOORE, BLACK STAR

Carrying spears, spear-thrower, and a lighted fire stick, Minmara, an Aboriginal hunter, leads his family through Western Australia's Gibson Desert. After furious digging (left), he captures a rabbit bandicoot, a rare marsupial that burrows deep to elude predators. Before his death in 1967, Minmara lived at Warburton Mission but occasionally returned to the bush and his old nomadic life.

ROBERT TONKINSON

northeast. They made the first people. They made the water holes and the sacred ritual sites.

"At first the sisters possessed all the most secret sacred objects, the most sacred rites. Men had nothing. And so men stole them. But the sisters said, 'Oh, let them keep those things. Now men can do this work, looking after those things for everybody.'"

Thus, the men made the boards like those on the Elcho beach, working long hours to paint them with great care and to decorate their own chocolate-colored bodies with red and yellow ocher designs or fluffy down stuck in streaks of blood. On the ceremonial grounds they performed dances for days and sometimes weeks at a time.

Living in a land well endowed with water and food, the men of tropical Elcho Island, Yirkalla, and coastal Arnhem Land had more time to devote to art and drama than the several hundred small groups of their kinsmen who roamed the arid country to the south and west. Still, people living off a well-stocked land must move about to take advantage of seasonal food supplies.

Even after Methodist missionaries made staple foods available, the Aborigines continued to hunt and collect food as they always had and settled only intermittently in the camps by the mission stations. During our 1946 visit to Elcho Island and Yirkalla, Ron and I met numerous families and took part in their daily routine, one that Aborigines had followed for centuries.

The division of labor between men and women extended through the activities of daily living, as well as the religious ceremonies. Ron would accompany the men while I stayed with the women. When they scattered over the beaches or nearby countryside, I walked with one of the groups of chattering, gossiping women and helped them collect food. They gathered wild yams and fruit from the scrub and jungle, shellfish and turtle eggs at the water's edge, seagull eggs from rocky nesting places, roots from the swamps, and lily stems and roots from quiet pools, or billabongs. Children ran among the women, playing, carrying baskets, and helping to dig. In late afternoon the men returned with fish and stingray they had speared in the low surf, turtles they had caught from seagoing canoes, or kangaroos and wallabies they had chased and killed with their long spears.

In camp, after the evening meal, a songman often would take up his clapping sticks and begin to sing while the women gathered to dance. From a long, hollow, wooden tube, the didgeridoo, a musician blew a droning sound.

OCCASIONALLY a sacred ritual, such as the actual surgical operation in the weeks-long circumcision ceremony—a major event then and now in the lives of Elcho and Yirkalla Aboriginal boys—took place in the main camp. The men gathered in such a tight circle around the six- and seven-year-old initiates that the women could not see what was happening. Noise of beating sticks, chants of the songman, and ritual calls of the dancing women drowned out any cries the boys might have made.

During these all-important rites the men, noted for being excitable and impulsive, easily became annoyed. I found out one evening just how irritable they can get. I was standing with a little knot of women getting ready for a precircumcision rite. According to the rules the women should have been skipping in a circle, calling out, and starting to weave in a long line across the clearing. They hadn't begun to move, even though they could hear the ritual cries of the men approaching from their ceremonial ground. Suddenly a spear swished by us and thudded into the soft earth. "You women! Get moving or there'll be more!" shouted bearded Mawulan. Clearly he took his responsibilities as a ritual leader quite seriously.

With such dramatic evidence of the men's strong feelings about their religion, I was utterly astonished to hear in 1958 at Yirkalla that long-secret ritual boards now stood by the Elcho Island beach on public display. Ron and I couldn't believe it, but when we flew the hundred

Only a few people of the desert still depend on age-old skills for survival:

A boy practices throwing a toy spear, and a mother winnows grass seed, an important food resource. She will grind the grain, mix it with water, and bake flat cakes in hot ashes. A hunter plucks an emu he speared at a water hole. At night, family members sleep between small fires that ward off the chill.

IAN DUNLOP

Poised in a dugout, a Tiwi fisherman (opposite) aims a pronged spear into the mangrove-lined waters of Melville Island's Snake Bay. Below, a boy on Groote Eylandt launches his toy craft in a creek that flows into the blue Gulf of Carpentaria.

HOWELL WALKER, N.G.S. STAFF (BELOW) AND TOR EIGELAND, BLACK STAR

miles to Elcho, we found the story was true. A new chapter of Arnhem Land's history had begun.

The Aborigines wanted to share the white man's material world and were offering to share the best of their material world in exchange, even though it meant giving up a custom sacred to them for centuries. How much of the white man's world would the Elcho Islanders gain, Ron and I wondered, and how much more of their own would they have to give up?

In 1958 about 200 people lived fairly permanently in small houses and shacks, spreading inland from the Elcho mission church. Most of the people wore clothing, and several spoke English. In May 1968 we found an elementary school, a more advanced grade school with manual-skill classes, and a preschool. A third of Elcho's growing population of 900 are children, and they must go to school until the age of 15. For them and their families a beautiful new hospital, a well-stocked store with plate glass windows, and timber and asbestos homes have been built.

More than half the families live in the new, low-rent houses, which have electricity and running water. The tenants sleep in beds, cook on stoves, and eat at tables often covered with bright tablecloths. Each house has a toilet, shower, and a laundry room. The older and smaller houses on the shore offer few facilities, but they are rent-free and their location by the sea appeals to many families.

Down at the beach we saw men storing fish and other seafood in a big refrigerated room. Many of the men earn money by fishing, cutting timber, or working in the mission sawmill or garden. A few gather pearl shells; several paint Aboriginal designs on sheets of eucalyptus bark and carve wood figures to sell to tourists and collectors. Women weave baskets and mats of pandanus fiber, which the mission—now with a staff of more than 40—sells in Darwin and other cities.

Like other Arnhem Land stations, Elcho now has its own Village Council. Members include younger Aborigines of both sexes, not just the old men. The Council decides on a wide variety of community questions: "Shall we ban child betrothals?" Girls soon after birth customarily were promised in marriage to mature men or young boys. "What shall we do about the sale of alcohol?" "How can we keep this country, this island, for ourselves, and not have a lot of balanda coming here to use it up?"

Elcho has reason for anxiety about the last question, for at neighboring Yirkalla the government has leased portions of Aboriginal reserve lands to mineral companies. The government and the companies had agreed to protect sacred places and to pay royalties, but still the Aborigines were disturbed, and disputes made national headlines. On our way to Elcho we had seen some of the excitement and confusion.

A new town will be built near Yirkalla to house 3,000 whites who soon will be working in the area. Older Aborigines felt apprehensive, but younger members of the mission welcomed the news. "There'll be work for us," they said, "and we'll have money to buy motor cars, transistor radios, bicycles, and new clothes."

To prepare the teen-agers for the new way of living, the mission store now serves as a milk bar at night. One Saturday evening, we had

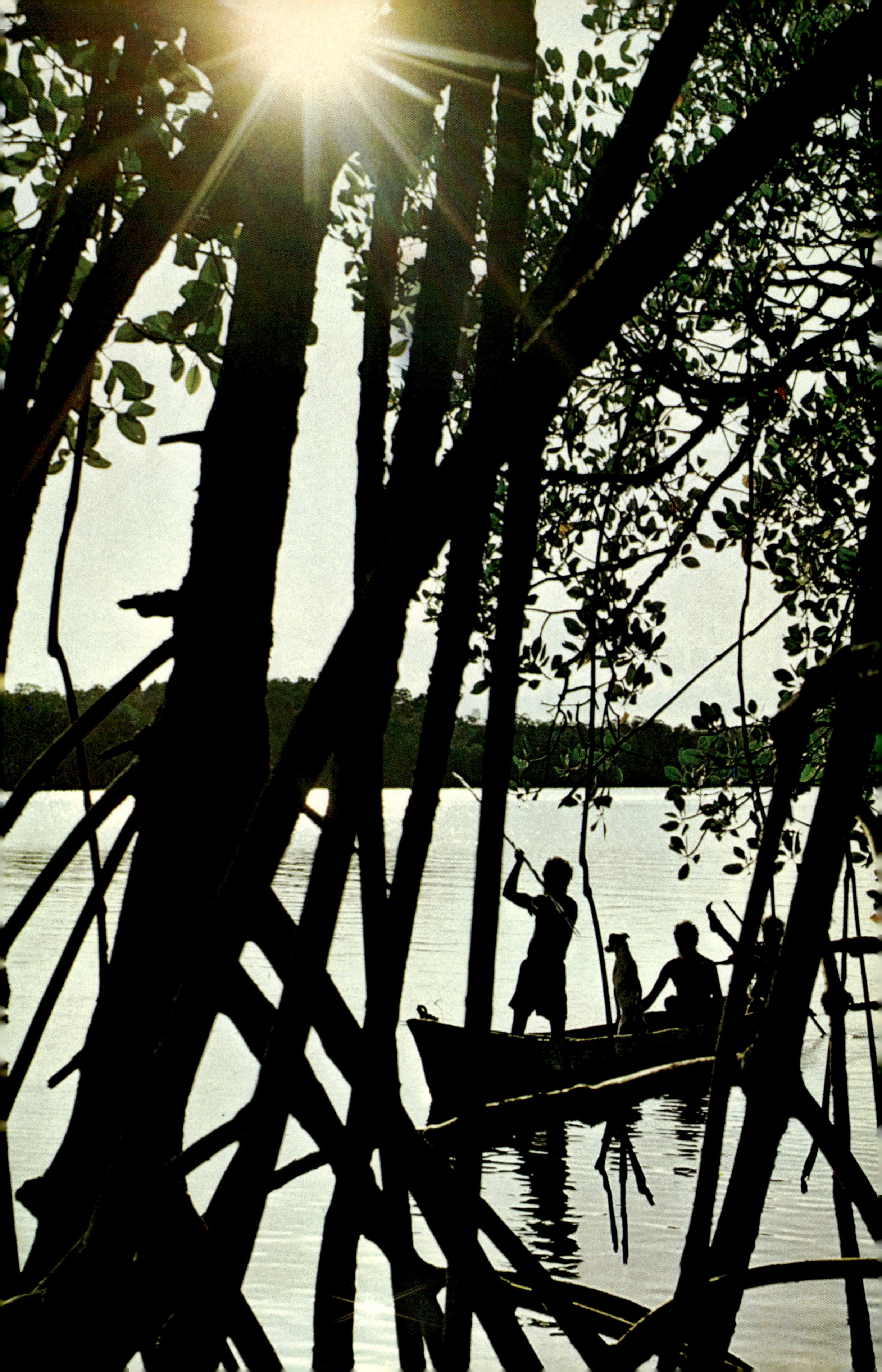

Fancifully carved and painted posts, gifts to the dead, surround the grave of a Tiwi man buried three months earlier. Climaxing a two-day ritual, part of the pukamani, *or final rites, mourners perform the basket dance, symbolically offering yams to the dead man. Later, in a hysteria of grief, men will slash their heads with knives and wailing women will thrash themselves with sticks. At right, an Arnhem Land Aboriginal decorates a hollow-log drum, or* ubar, *beaten with the stump of a root during initiation ceremonies.*

HOWELL WALKER, N.G.S. STAFF (ABOVE) AND JANE GOODALE

126

to elbow our way through a laughing, shouting crowd of young people dancing to the pop songs of a guitar-playing "Yirkalla Band."

Despite the changes during the past few decades, however, the Elcho Islanders and Yirkalla people have retained much of their myth-centered religion. They have preserved their language, their pride, and a great deal of independence. The mission's policy of building on, not destroying, local traditions has helped to make Arnhem Land a great reservoir of Aboriginal art, dance, and song. Nonsacred corroborees—joyous dancing and singing about myths and events of Aboriginal life—still go on nearly every night. Sacred ceremonies have been shortened, however, and they now are held at seasons and hours convenient for men with jobs.

In the dry lands stretching across the continent, Aboriginal tribes or clans have not fared so well as their Arnhem Land cousins. Most of their social organization and much of the religion that gave meaning and interest to their difficult life have been lost. Until the government recently increased its educational and welfare programs, many desert Aborigines lived as beggars with little chance of learning how to become sharers in the Australian society. Turning away from the constant quest for food and water in the land they knew, they were beginning in the 1920's to converge family by family on missions, small railroad towns, and large cattle stations looking for handouts. They divided their time between foraging on the fringes of the desert and begging from white Australians.

In the early 1940's Ron and I saw many Aborigines as they came to Ooldea Mission at the edge of the Great Victoria Desert in South Australia. We often watched drifts of smoke move closer and closer across the desert, marking the route of other families coming to join the 200 people already camping there. When a group drew near, we could see eager, excited faces. Skinny men with long, thin arms and legs came lightly laden with boomerangs, spears, and spear-throwers. Behind the men followed wives with digging sticks and wooden dishes, a child or two, and always a couple of dogs. Hastily the mission would send out a bundle of secondhand clothes to cover the nakedness of the new arrivals, who would squat on the ground and turn the garments this way and that, giggling at the armholes and legholes.

Why had they come? They told us they had heard reports of strange and wonderful foods and things, new experiences, an easy life—and they were curious. Once they came, they stayed. Like other Aborigines, they were deeply attached to their own country; they knew every water hole, every bush, every stone and patch of grass. Yet, they liked flour and sugar, tea and bully beef, goat's meat, canned fruit—so much easier to get than desert foods. I have seen Aboriginal hunters come back to camp dusty and hot, their faces drawn with fatigue, carrying only their spears and maybe a lizard or small ratlike bandicoot—all they had to show for a long day's trek across burning sand and through prickly spinifex.

I sometimes went out gathering food with the women, but I could scarcely keep pace with their long strides; their stamina amazed me. Mundja, a lame woman in her late twenties, became my frequent companion. As we walked along in the cool of early morning or late afternoon, she watched the sand around us, quick to notice anything that might spell food. From Mundja, I learned how much effort went into the making of a small, flat cake of grass seeds.

Sometimes it took two hours or more just to collect a cupful of seeds. There were many varieties, but none of them grew much bigger than the head of a pin. Some we got by shaking the grass stems; some we picked up laboriously from the ground. But one kind came easy. "See?" said Mundja as she bent down and parted the coarse spikes of a patch of spinifex grass. I looked to see a company of small black ants scurrying around a heap of dark seeds. Mundja laughed at my surprise. "The ants collect the seeds for us. We just wait until they've brought enough," she said, as she shoveled the seeds into her dish. "Now they can go after some more."

Back in camp, we tossed the seeds in large, wooden dishes to winnow sand, husks, and rubbish. "This kind we pound," Mundja said, banging away with a heavy stone. "These softer ones we grind," and she gave the stone a sideways motion. Then she mixed the coarse seed-flour with water and shaped the dough into small cakes that she baked in hot ashes at the edge of the campfire. "And this kind we eat raw," she said once, handing me a piece of moist, brownish substance. I ate it and managed a smile.

Mundja blamed her lameness on her first husband, an old man. It had been a "proper" marriage arranged by her family, and she had gone to him as a young girl. "He was always jealous," she said, looking at me through the curtain of shoulder-length, straight, dark hair that was always falling over her eyes. After he injured her with a spear thrust, she left him to his other wives and married a quiet, mild man. Even-tempered he needed to be, for soft-voiced, brown-eyed Mundja could fly into violent rages.

Yet, she was soft wax in the hands of her youngest son, three-year-old Djambidjin. He would come running to her from a group of playmates and grab her breast, staring at me with dark antagonistic eyes as he drank. To him I was an intruder, distracting his mother's attention. All conversation stopped as she cuddled him. Even when we gathered for one of the women's secret ceremonies, he tried to monopolize her, tracing with his finger the red-ochered lines on her body and legs, begging her not to join the dancers but to "stay here with me."

Mundja's life, like the other women's, was a series of small, inescapable tasks—collecting food, walking to the water hole, carrying firewood, cooking. But she had her small excitements, too: chasing and catching a goanna, digging out a marsupial mole or bandicoot, and best of all, on infrequent occasions, welcoming her husband when he returned to camp with a kangaroo slung around his shoulders.

At night at the Ooldea camp, the low, desert sandhills echoed with a vibrant pulse of boomerangs pounding on the sand, women slapping their thighs, and men's voices rising and falling. Ron sat with the singers, and I sat in the tightly packed cluster of women and children. The steady rhythm, combined with the sweet-smelling smoke of mulga and sandalwood from flickering fires, had an almost hypnotic effect. If one of the mythical song-characters had suddenly appeared out of the shadows, no one would have batted an eye.

Carved figure of Bremer Island's mythical Turtle Man wears a portrait of himself on his stomach. Aborigines send their art to growing markets around the world.

Elaborate bark painting from Yirkalla portrays a major myth of the Dreamtime, or Creation: The Djanggau Sisters bear swarms of children—ancestors of northeastern Arnhem Land Aborigines (second panel)—and cover them with mats (bottom). The Sisters appear with their brother and with trees they created (third panel). At top left, they stand by a sacred spring. Artist Mawulan, who died in 1967, pictures himself (top right) chanting the Djanggau story. Patterns on the wood carving below resemble those that Melville Island mourners paint on their bodies.

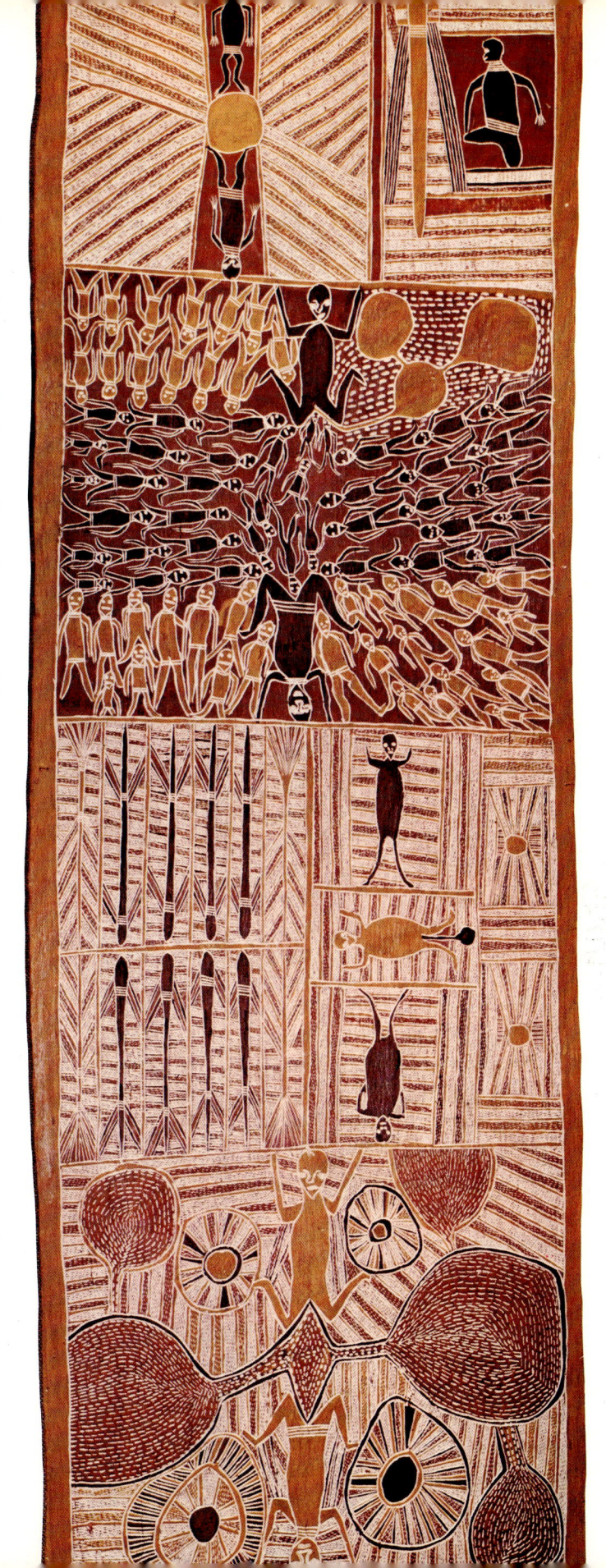

Beyond the firelight stood family shelters, windbreaks of green branches. Each had its own fire, and nearby a few dark shapes lay asleep. Dogs huddled against their feet and against their backs, providing warmth during the chilly desert night. People were close but as private and distant as they wanted to be. Nobody could feel lonely. I thought to myself, it's not surprising that they don't take kindly to living in houses.

At first, living a settled life did not affect the ceremonies re-enacting the myths, which have basically the same themes and characteristics among all Aborigines. Many older people had anticipated only a short stay away from the desert; they planned to return again when the time came to go to sacred sites and to perform the required rituals. Sometimes I saw them cry, and I heard talk about "my dear country," but those who went back did not stay long. As time passed, the lively ceremonies became shorter or were dropped entirely when missionaries and the police frowned on them, or when activities of the Aborigines' new life interfered. Young people learned less and less about rituals and pulled away from the authority of the elders.

T HOSE WHO GATHERED at Ooldea scattered after the mission closed in 1952. Many went to other missions. Some drifted to cattle stations and mines where the men could make a little money. Others camped outside small towns. A very few of the more daring tried their luck in the city. Gradually, welfare benefits increased, distributed through missions partly subsidized by the government. But only since the late 1950's has the official policy of integrating the Aborigines into the economic life of Australia been seriously pushed forward with new schools, job opportunities, and antidiscrimination laws.

During 1966 and 1967, Aborigines throughout the continent benefited from the national interest aroused by the Yirkalla protest over the loss of reserve land and by the Aboriginal wage strike at Wave Hill pastoral station in the Northern Territory. Federal social welfare benefits already had been extended to Aborigines. A national referendum in 1967 paved the way for the transfer of Aboriginal affairs from state to federal control.

Aborigines still assemble at convenient meeting places in the bush or at several hundred mission stations and government settlements to perform modified ceremonies of a waning way of life. For English-speaking, educated young people with jobs, the old stories and rituals inevitably will lose their meaning. Perhaps after a generation or so the imaginative variations of dance and song and art of hundreds of tribes will merge into a common pool labeled "Aboriginal Culture," acknowledged with pride but practiced only now and then in staged performances.

Aborigines speak proudly of their heritage and make a point of identifying themselves as Aborigines. At a crowded meeting in Perth recently, I heard a man almost light enough to pass for white exclaim, "Why shouldn't I call myself Aboriginal if I want to?"

Everywhere today we hear echoes of the sentiments so strongly expressed at Yirkalla: "We want to share with the balanda, but we are not balanda. We are *yulngu*—ourselves."

Elderly Walbiri tribesman on a government reserve in the Northern Territory squints to shut out the desert sun. By 1955, some 1,200 members of his tribe, one of 500 or so Aboriginal groups, had abandoned their nomadic ways. About two-thirds of Australia's estimated 80,000 half- and full-blooded Aborigines now live on reserves; the others stay on cattle stations or camp on the outskirts of small towns.

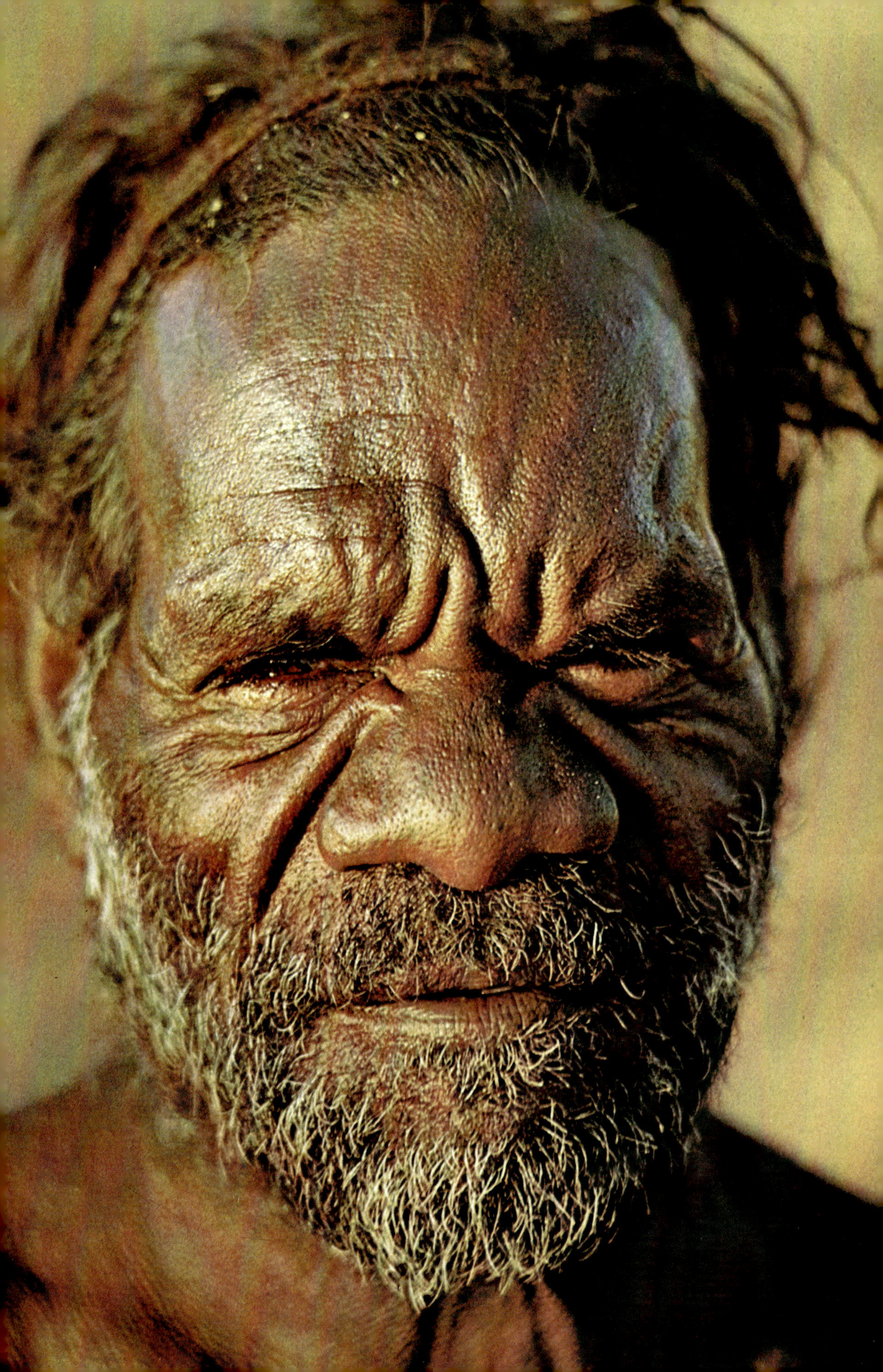

7

The Indomitable Eskimo: Master of a Frozen World

By Frederick A. Milan, Ph.D.

"In the old days hunters didn't start after walrus until a lookout man on the roof shouted '*Nunavaitch!*'" said Wesley Ekak as we finished our breakfast of coffee and dough fried in seal oil. "Nunavaitch means 'herd of walrus sitting on an ice cake.' Nowadays we don't wait at home for the animals to come to us. We go out in our motorboat to find them."

We walked down to the rough, stony beach to join the other members of our hunting party who waited beside the 30-foot-long *umiak*, a boat made of tough sealskin stretched over a wooden frame six feet wide.

At 5:30, with the August sun already well above the northeast horizon, we pushed away from the shores of the Eskimo village of Wainwright on Alaska's northern coast.

The outboard motor sputtered, then droned as we headed northwest across the cold expanse of the Arctic Ocean dotted with islands of floating ice. In bright calico parkas, women and children waving to us from the beach soon became tiny patches of color against the deep blue sky.

The owner of the umiak, Robert James, directed the helmsman with hand signals as his dark, slanted eyes scanned the polar sea for floe ice and signs of walrus or bearded seal.

Suddenly the helmsman cut the outboard motor. Game! In the distance, I could see several black lumps on the ice. Wesley took the helm, and three of us started paddling quietly. As we eased closer, we could see six huge walrus sleeping, sprawled on a large cake of ice.

We stopped for a moment, and Robert bowed his head to lead the crew in a short Christian prayer. Then one Eskimo and I took .306-caliber rifles and moved to the bow. With only a boat length separating us from our target, the nearest walrus, we fired, then fired again. Blood streaked the ice as the wounded creature struggled in vain to follow the other walrus into the water.

Dressed in caribou-skin clothing of his father's day, a Netsilik Eskimo warms himself inside a snowhouse after a day-long seal hunt on the ice of Pelly Bay, in northern Canada; his quarry lies at his feet. During the early 1960's, Netsiliks, in authentic re-enactments, showed anthropologists how the Eskimos lived before they began to use modern weapons and tools.

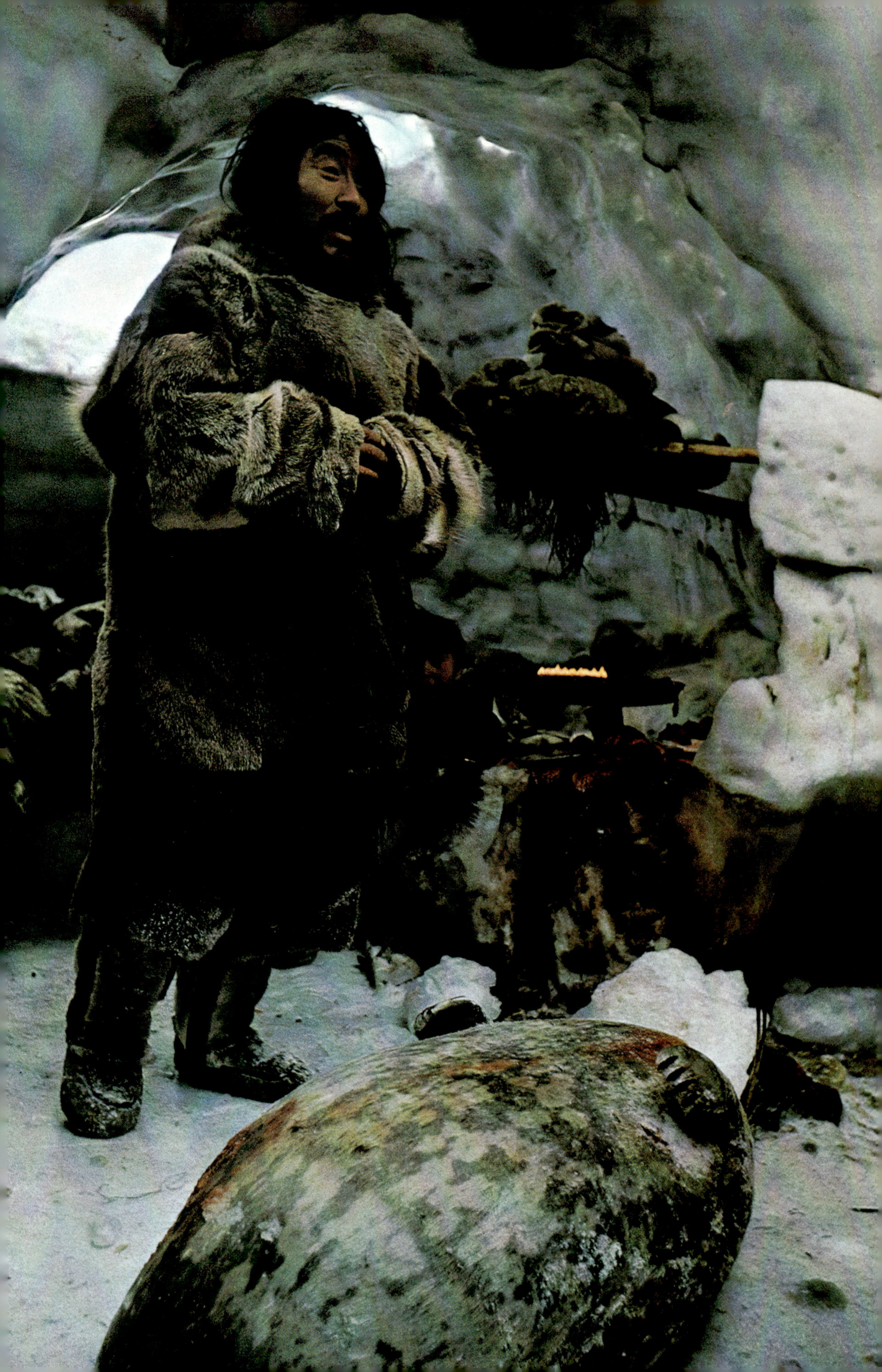

Wesley quickly leaped onto the ice and drove a harpoon into the grunting animal to keep it from sliding into the sea. Fastened to a line of walrus skin, the harpoon's brass head separated from its handle. As Wesley tugged on the line, the deeply embedded point turned sideways and the barb hooked firmly into the flesh.

All of us except the helmsman jumped onto the ice and held tightly to the harpoon line until Wesley fired a final bullet into the walrus' head. Quickly we set to work cutting the one-ton carcass into 20-pound chunks and loading them into the umiak. The boat sank lower and lower until the water stood within inches of the gunwales.

The Eskimos make use of almost every part of the walrus. Sections of hide would be cut into long, thin spirals for harpoon lines, the membrane around the liver would be used for drumheads, the jawbone for harpoon foreshafts, and the tusks for carvings. The red meat provides food for all the people and dogs in the village.

Before we headed homeward, Wesley threw a piece of meat into the sea, muttering, "*Qunnikun, qunnikun*"—"give us smooth water."

"For the souls of the seal creatures," Wesley explained. "Now we will have a good trip home."

"Do animals have souls?" I asked.

"We believe so. My father taught me always to honor animals. They were sent down here to us, and if I did not honor them, I would have bad luck hunting. 'Always cut their heads off,' he said, 'so that the creatures can come to life again.' Even as a boy I learned to pour fresh water into the mouth of every seal I killed because they grow thirsty from the salty sea."

For thousands of years the Eskimo has taxed his strength and turned his mind to surviving in an icy, windy wasteland beside an ocean frozen to a depth of 6 to 12 feet eight months of the year. Scattered along 4,000 miles of coastline stretching from the northeast corner of Siberia across Alaska, Canada, and Greenland, the Eskimo found a way to live in the northernmost regions of the earth. His knowledge of the Arctic gave him the ability to survive temperatures as low as −50° F. His genius created a rich material culture from bone, hide, ivory, sinew, and stone.

THOMAS J. ABERCROMBIE, NATIONAL GEOGRAPHIC STAFF

Sculptured by violent waves, the fan-shaped peninsula of Point Hope, Alaska, juts into an ice-studded Chukchi Sea. Eskimos have inhabited the cape for more than 2,000 years, living largely off animal life the cold waters yield. At left, whale bones form a ten-foot-high fence around the Point Hope cemetery. A towering jawbone with a painted cross marks the grave of an Eskimo whaler.

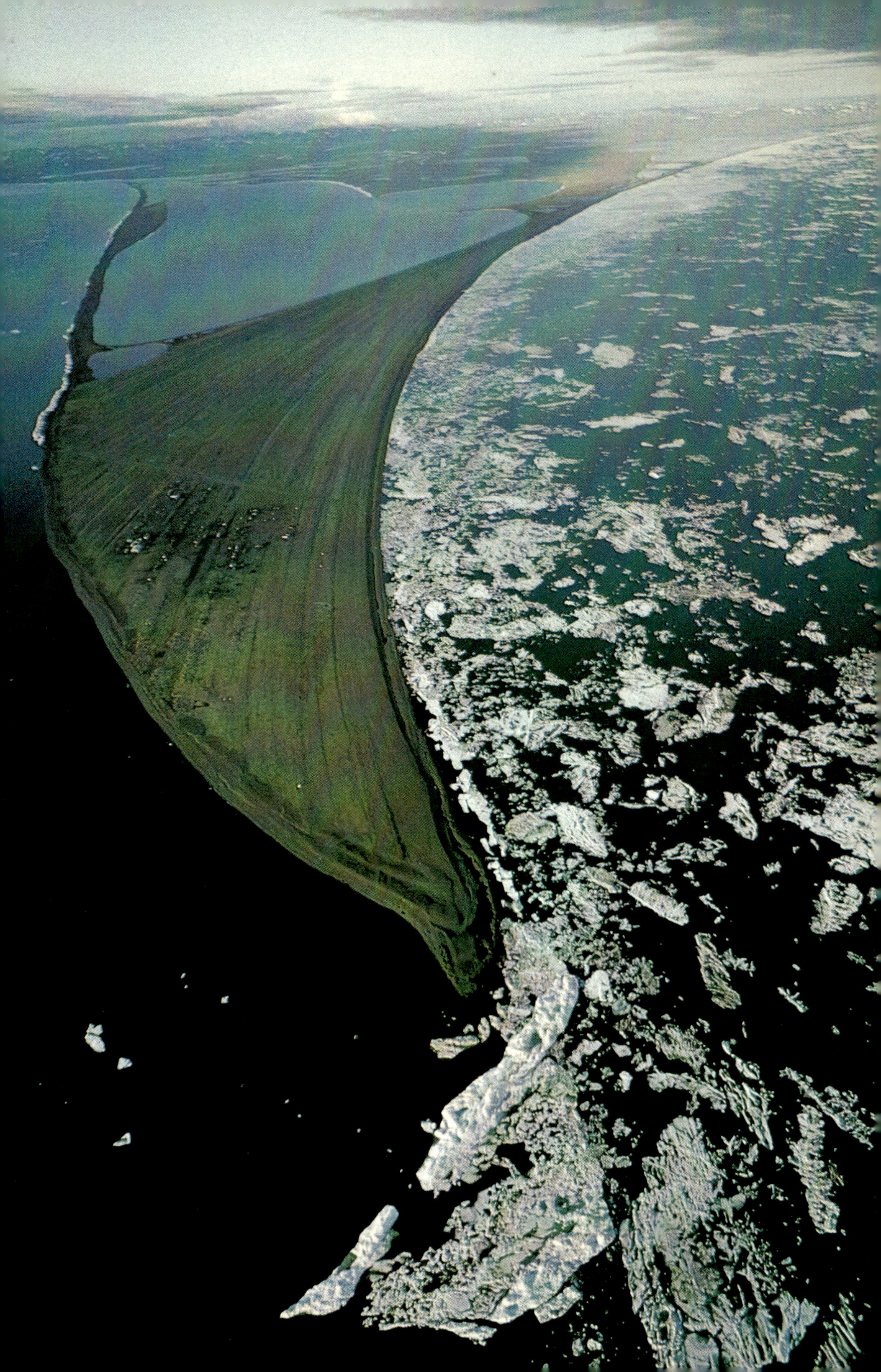

Bering Strait ice floe becomes a butcher's block for hunters who dress three freshly killed walrus. The huge mammals provide meat for food, ivory and bone for tools, and skin for boats. The severed heads of two animals rest on 15-inch tusks.

THOMAS J. ABERCROMBIE, NATIONAL GEOGRAPHIC STAFF

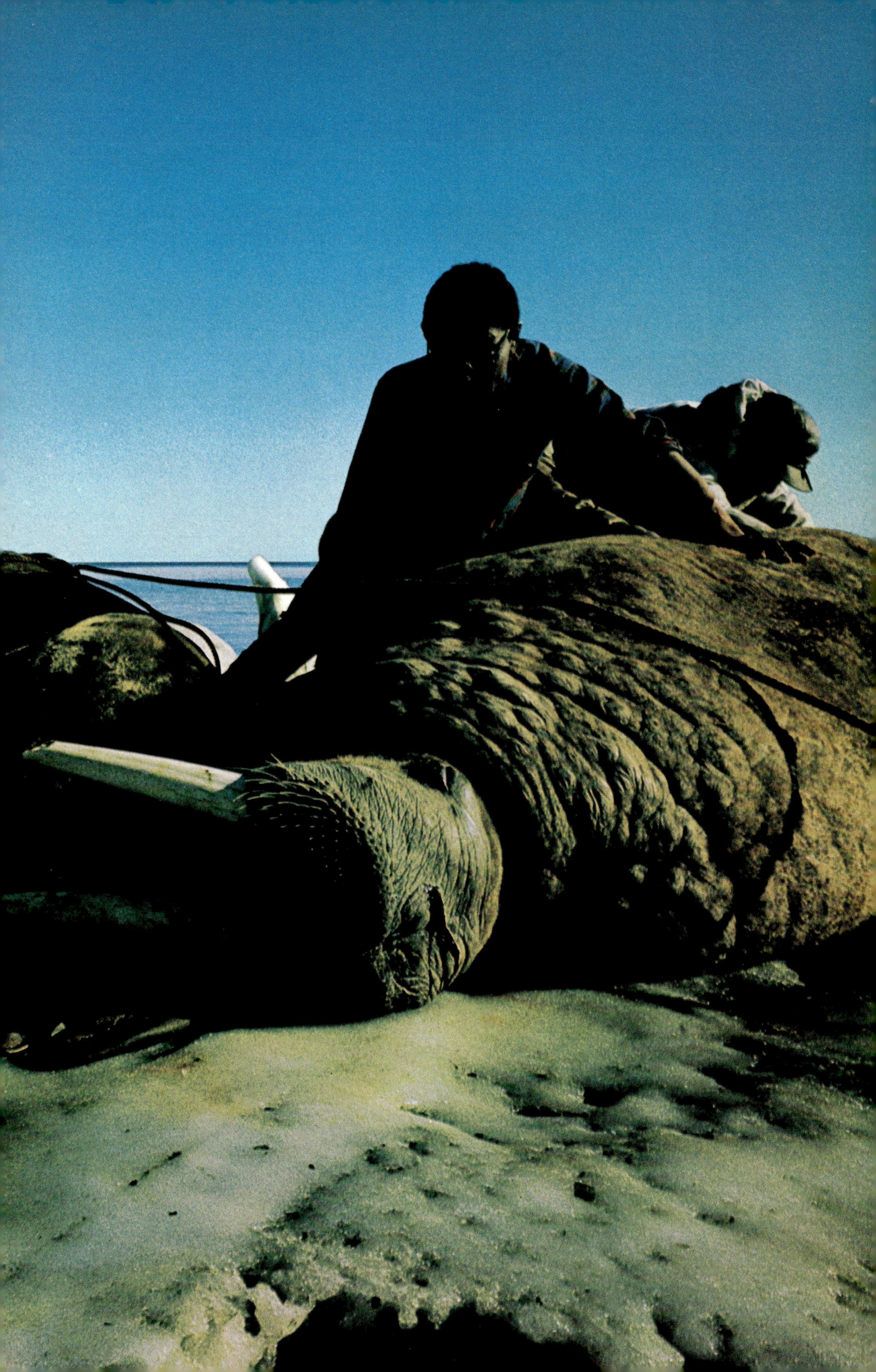

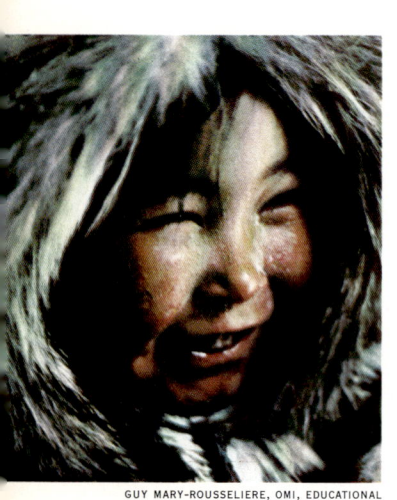

GUY MARY-ROUSSELIERE, OMI, EDUCATIONAL
DEVELOPMENT CENTER (ABOVE AND OPPOSITE LOWER)

Rosy-cheeked Pelly Bay girl peeks from a parka hood trimmed with wolverine fur, a pelt that doesn't mat from frost or breath. Their population increasing, some 70,000 Eskimos make their homes across the top of the Western Hemisphere, where temperatures plummet lower than −50° F.

I believe the Eskimo fashioned his implements and weapons more cleverly than any other primitive people. He traveled in skin boats, or on driftwood dogsleds with whalebone runners. From ivory or bone he made harpoon heads, ice chisels, fishhooks, needles, and knife handles. Knife blades he ground from slate or chipped from stone. He carved soapstone into bowls, which he filled with seal or whale oil to cook his food, and heat and light his home.

He kept warm outdoors in bitter cold and driving snow, wearing clothes of his own ingenious design. An inner garment of caribou skin, loosely fitted with the fur against his body, and an outer layer with the fur exposed, effectively insulated the Eskimo.

People who live in the Arctic have told me that nothing duplicates the warmth, flexibility, comfort, and light weight of caribou-skin clothing. When I first wore an Eskimo parka, I found that air warmed by my body rose within the garment and escaped through the hood, keeping my cheeks and nose warm. My feet stayed warm and dry in bearded sealskin or caribou-fur boots—now called *mukluks*—and socks of dogskin or caribou.

With the cool, fleeting summer comes a brief respite from the snow and sub-zero cold. The tundra blossoms with yellow and white poppies, buttercups, tiny blue forget-me-nots, white saxifrages, and pink campion. Patches of blueberries, cranberries, and salmonberries grow wild on a mosquito-plagued land carpeted with mosses, lichens, and hundreds of kinds of grasses and sedges. In years past, the berries added a touch of variety to the Eskimo's diet. The people never planted crops because of the cool, short growing season and lived entirely on meat—frozen, boiled, dried, or raw. In the language of Canada's Abnaki Indians, the word Eskimo meant "one who eats raw meat." Blubber was the Eskimo's candy, the back fat of the caribou his ice cream, and over-ripe walrus flippers his delicacy.

THE ESKIMO has always depended completely on the animals of the land and sea and has paid tribute to their souls in ceremonies and celebrations. A number of these rites persist today.

The Spring Whale Festival—*Naluqataq*—takes place only at the end of a successful season and expresses the gratitude of everyone in the village to the spirit of the slain creature.

"It makes everybody happy and maybe helps us to catch another whale next year," Wesley told me.

I saw my first Naluqataq in Wainwright in June of 1955. Weir Negovanna, *umailik*, or captain, of the boat that caught the whale, sponsored the festivity, which began before noon and lasted until four o'clock the next morning. The entire village of about 230 Eskimos gathered on the high bank overlooking the ocean and took turns getting tossed in a walrus-skin blanket. Twenty people, holding the rope handgrips sewn around the edge of the blanket, bounced each person into the air. To those who went 20 and 30 feet high and landed upright, the crowd shouted, "Aazigaa! Aazigaa!"—"Good! Good!"

Weir distributed chunks of *muktuk*, a delicacy of the bowhead whale's black skin and layer of fat. It tastes somewhat like walnuts and requires plenty of chewing. Each family also received slabs of whale

Moustached seal hunter displays the physical features of the hardy Eskimo. Flat faces, narrow-bridged noses, and sturdy bodies typify these lively but patient people.

THOMAS J. ABERCROMBIE, N.G.S. STAFF

Hunched over a breathing hole used by seals, a Pelly Bay Eskimo watches a small black bobber that moves when his prey nears the surface. The hunter then harpoons the seal, and chops the hole larger to land it.

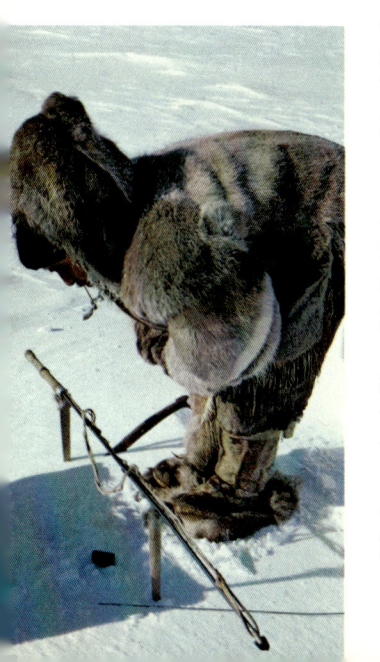

meat, which they carried away in buckets. By this formal sharing and generosity, the umailik acquires prominence and social prestige.

In the late afternoon Weir, his wife, and crew assembled on a temporary platform as five drummers beat on circular wooden hoops covered with tightly stretched, walrus-liver membrane. A chorus of women sang. Dancers, their faces contorted, waved their arms, leaped, and stamped their feet to pantomime a whale hunt, from the first sighting to the final thrust of the harpoon. Around ten o'clock, when the sun, a deep glowing red, hung just above the horizon, everyone danced—even the very old women with tattoo lines on their chins in the style of the past century. It was still daylight six hours later when the villagers began to leave for home.

Since my first visit in 1955, I have returned nearly every year to Wainwright to study how the Eskimos live and how they have adapted—physically, culturally, and psychologically—to life in the empty frozen spaces of the North.

Over the years I have struck up valued friendships with Wesley Ekak and Weir Negovanna. Wesley, a widower past 70 now, used to live in a house built of clumps of sod packed around a driftwood frame. Recently he moved to the modern but weathered frame dwelling of one of his sons.

Weir had only a rifle and a blanket when he married 30 years ago. His skill as a young herder of reindeer, his more recent success as a hunter, and his mechanical inventiveness have made him the Horatio Alger of the Eskimo world. Today he captains his own umiak and lives in a comfortable, two-story frame house heated by a coal-burning kitchen stove. He has a voice in the Village Council that governs Wainwright, and recently members of the congregation elected him an elder in the Presbyterian Church.

I have often watched Roseanne, Weir's cheerful wife, sew a mukluk with dental floss, a modern substitute for hard-to-prepare sinew, or neatly dissect a seal with an *ulu,* the half-moon-shaped knife that Eskimo women use.

Today the Negovannas order underwear, stockings, and summer clothing from mail-order catalogues. Jeans, plaid shirts, calico, and rabbitskin for parkas come from the cooperatively owned village store, but if Weir goes off on a long hunting trip, he always wears a caribou parka, pants, and mukluks sewed by Roseanne—they keep him warmer and drier than anything he can buy.

Roseanne prefers to sit on the wooden floor, her back ramrod straight and her legs together in front of her. With a portable sewing machine in her lap, she sews parka covers for herself and her granddaughter and the white cotton snow shirts that Weir puts over his parka to protect the fur and to camouflage him when he goes hunting.

Housebound through most of the long, bitter winter, Roseanne goes out on occasional jaunts with her friends to fish for smelts through tidal cracks in the sea ice. To go jigging, she waits for good weather when no wind blows.

One day in December, I saw her set out into a blue-white world with a vacuum bottle of sweet tea tucked into its own caribou-skin jacket, a jigging stick, a short fishing pole, and an   *Continued on page 145*

140

GUY MARY-ROUSSELIERE, OMI, EDUCATIONAL DEVELOPMENT CENTER

Guns already had begun to replace bows and arrows when the Danish explorer Knud Rasmussen traveled across the ice-gripped wastelands of northern Canada 45 years ago. Today even the long-familiar snow igloos used as dwellings by Canadian Eskimos have disappeared. Cargo planes coming in from the outside world now glide above Rasmussen's dogsled trail, carrying lumber for frame-house settlements and factory-made clothing to stock trading posts. Air travel links the modern world with some 70,000 Eskimos scattered from Siberia's East Cape to Greenland's Scoresby Sund. Writing with the perspective of a dozen years of careful observation among the Eskimos, Dr. Frederick A. Milan, an anthropologist at the University of Wisconsin, records the changing life of the village of Wainwright, Alaska.

Reliving a migration of earlier years, Netsilik Eskimos trek across the bleak tundra toward their autumn fishing camp on Canada's Kellett River. Huskies help transport the group's belongings. The once-nomadic people now lead a settled life.

Netsilik Eskimo woman coaxes flame from the wick of her seal-oil lamp to counter the early morning chill as her husband and son lie naked under caribou-skin blankets. Unmindful of the freezing cold of the igloo, a boy frolics with his grandmother beneath a window of solid ice. Friendly but intent competitors exchange blows to the shoulders in a bout of endurance and pain. In 1965 the Netsiliks of Pelly Bay began to abandon snowhouses for frame dwellings built by the Canadian Government.

GUY MARY-ROUSSELIERE, OMI, EDUCATIONAL DEVELOPMENT CENTER

Exuberant Eskimos in Kotzebue, Alaska, celebrate the Fourth of July: A lively dancer interprets a hunting legend as elders beat a rhythmic accompaniment, tapping sticks against the wooden frames of drums covered with walrus-liver membrane. Catapulted 20 feet into the air from a walrus-hide blanket, a girl (right) deftly maintains her balance, trying to land on her feet. Hunters may have originated the sport by tossing sharp-eyed scouts high overhead to look for game. A teen-age boy (left) slices off a chunk of chewy whale skin and fat in a muktuk-eating contest.

THOMAS J. ABERCROMBIE, NATIONAL GEOGRAPHIC STAFF

ivory fish lure. A mile out on the frozen sea, she joined friends and chiseled through a tidal crack to the water below. Sometimes she used a can-opener key and a piece of red calico for bait. For five hours in −20° F. cold she jigged the stick up and down, chattering and giggling with her companions and filling a skin bag with about 50 of the small, tasty fish.

Men can't always wait for good weather. They must go on with the hunt through the long winter night. The people of Wainwright at 70° N. latitude see the sun disappear about November 21; it will not be seen again for two months. The aurora borealis that often sets the sky aglow with shimmering color gives diffused and unreliable illumination. But the moon, shining half of every month on the snow-white landscape, gives enough light for hunters to search the tundra for caribou or fox, and to cross the turreted sea ice to look for seal sleeping on top of the ice or wheezing through breathing holes.

Each seal swimming below the ice moves among several airholes, for it must get air every 20 minutes. Hunters wait quietly around the holes, a rifle ready in one hand and in the other a harpoon poised to thrust into the wounded seal before it sinks below the ice. A Wainwright Eskimo may sit on a stool for hours waiting for a seal to poke its nose above the ice or to jostle a bobber the hunter has placed in a hole.

Weir supported and cared for two adopted children. Fanny, the older one, had the same Eskimo personal, or soul, name as his wife. Every person in Wainwright has one or two such names in addition to a European-type first and second name in use since the advent of missionaries and census takers three generations ago.

Weir explained the practice to me: "A person has a 'name soul' and a 'breath soul.' When he dies, the breath soul leaves him. His name soul never dies, but stays around until attached to a baby. The virtues of the previous owner of the name then transfer to the baby and protect him throughout his life.

"Around here you will hear an old man say *aapaga,* my father, to a young boy. This means that the little boy has the personal name of the man's father."

At the conclusion of an Eskimo funeral in Greenland some years ago, a villager with a little boy at his side approached the minister. "Don't grieve over our dear friend," the man said, "because he is right here in front of you." The boy had just been given the dead man's name.

Before Christianity, dating from about 1725 in Greenland and 1890 in northern Alaska, each settlement had an *angakok,* a shaman or medicine man, to help the people control the weather and food supply and to protect them from harm or disease. In a trance or ecstasy, induced by fasting or hypnotic drumming, the shaman communicated with the spirits in a frenzy of shrieks, shouts, and whispers.

Eskimos also wore charms and amulets, such as owl claws, caribou ears, and bumblebees, and recited magic formulas and special songs to give them strength and good luck when hunting. Soon after missionaries brought Christianity to the people of Wainwright, Eskimo whalers used pages torn from the Bible for charms. Now they simply say short Christian prayers.

One March morning in Weir's home I watched him prepare to make coffee by melting year-old sea ice, which had lost its salt through natural leaching. Outside, the husky dogs tethered near the storm-porch door yelped sharply, announcing the arrival of a visitor.

These dogs, about six to an Eskimo family, once provided the only means of winter transportation. A dozen dogs can cover 50 to 60 miles in 12 hours, pulling a 300-pound load. Many Eskimos, like Weir, also own motorized toboggans, which have skis on the front and a track under the rear. The vehicles can travel up to 60 miles an hour and can also move over the roughest of surfaces.

The huskies continued yelping as Wesley Ekak crossed the storm porch—a 20-foot-long passageway heavy with the scent of seal oil—that keeps out cold air and serves as a storeroom for hunting gear and frozen meat. Beating the snow off his parka with a mittened hand, Wesley entered the kitchen-living room.

Roseanne greeted Wesley from her seat on the floor and asked, "*Qanoq sila?*"—literally, "How is the universe?"

"Very cold with a strong northeast wind and drifting snow," he replied. Snow had already piled to the eaves.

"I wonder if the mail plane will come today from Barrow," Roseanne said, half to herself.

The nearest settlements to Wainwright lie 100 miles in either direction along the coast, but the airplane links Eskimo villages everywhere to the 20th century.

W ESLEY once told me about seeing Knud Rasmussen, Danish ethnologist and explorer, when he and two Eskimo companions passed near Wainwright in 1924 on their expedition across the North American Arctic by dogsled.

"It was June. Only a little ice was left along the edge of the ocean on the beach. First came Knud's team, and then those of the Eskimo man and woman who traveled with him. Their clothing, their sleds, the way they hitched their dogs were different from anything we had ever seen. They harnessed the dogs on fan-shaped leads. They all sat sideways on the sleds instead of standing on the runners at the back. Knud gave a speech in our language. He told us he had traveled by sled from Greenland and had visited Eskimos all along the way. I remember how happy we were that they had come to visit us."

Knud Rasmussen retraced the route that the Eskimos are believed to have taken about 2,000 years ago in an early migration that distributed them from Alaska across the top of the North American Continent all the way to Greenland.

Wesley could understand Rasmussen because from Greenland to East Cape, Siberia, Eskimos speak variations of the same language. Their dress, eating habits, and houses differ, but racially and culturally, all Eskimos are closely related. Their language contains exact rather than general terms. For example, it has no word for seal but has many specific words for seals of all kinds and ages, and no word for snow but precise words for "snow in the air," "drifting snow," "soft, watery snow," and "snow suitable for building snowhouses."

One winter as I sat with a group of friends in the Wainwright village store, favorite gathering place for the men, I told them how I once had

Greenland Eskimo girls wearing hip-high sealskin boots dance aboard the steamer Roosevelt *during Robert E. Peary's 1908-09 expedition that took him and five companions to the North Pole. Modern versions of Greenlander boots, or* kamik, *dry on a clothesline near the town of Egedesminde.*

ADM. ROBERT E. PEARY COLLECTION (ABOVE) AND VAGN HANSEN NORDISK PRESSPHOTO

Wielding sharp-bladed poles, Eskimo whalers of St. Lawrence Island, 40 miles from the tip of Siberia, flense blubber from a whale as villagers tug lines to steady their craft. Near Point Barrow, Alaska, a whaler (right) fires a miniature bomb at a blowing bowhead. The embedded explosive stuns or kills the mammal. At left, a harpooned whale, with a floating marker attached, dives in an attempt to escape.

STEVE AND DOLORES McCUTCHEON (ABOVE), FROELICH RAINEY (LEFT), AND HARRY GROOM

built a domed snowhouse following the instructions in explorer Vilhjalmur Stefansson's *Arctic Manual.*

I cut wedge-shaped blocks out of firm, but not hard, snow and placed them in a rising spiral on a circular base ten feet in diameter. Each tier leaned inward at what seemed an impossible angle, but the blocks stuck together. After I put the last ceiling block in place, closing myself in, I dug an entrance under the wall. A portable stove raised the inside temperature rapidly. I poked a hole in the roof for the house's "nose." The temperature held at 10° F. near the ground and 45° F. at the ceiling, but it didn't melt because the outside cold, −25° F., penetrated the thin roof and kept it frozen.

"Pretty good house, I suppose," said an old man, "but it must have been a lot of work to make. Why didn't you use a tent with snow blocks piled around it the way we do when we go hunting?"

It amused Weir when I told him that many people think that all Eskimos live in snowhouses. Only Eskimos from northern Canada actually lived in the domed igloos, so often seen in photographs. Eskimos in Greenland made them too, but only as temporary shelters.

THIS RUGGED, SEVERE WORLD imposed its own brutal law on the Eskimo. Living close to death, he measured it by a standard very different from our own. In times of hunger, the Eskimo might abandon aged men and women, or allow them to walk away across the ice; infants might be left outside to die.

All this has changed now with Christian ethics and government welfare payments and old-age pensions. To the people of Wainwright, and to all the other 70,000 Eskimos spread over a million square miles, civilization has brought electricity and rifles, spaghetti and cornflakes, tuberculosis and influenza, radios and schools.

Children in Wainwright go to a school run by the U. S. Bureau of Indian Affairs; there the youngsters learn English, but when they go home they speak Eskimo. Most of the eighth-grade graduates go on to a free public high school near Sitka, on Baranof Island, 1,200 miles to the southeast.

One girl who had just graduated from high school returned to Wainwright while I was there. Dressed in parka, jeans, and mukluks she complained: "There's nothing going on here; there's nothing to do."

Many high-school graduates have no desire to hunt, flesh hides, clean furs, and stitch mukluks. Men seek, but few find, employment at the Distant Early Warning Line installation, at the post office, or in the few local stores.

The Eskimo has come to want and to depend on the white man's goods, but he finds few opportunities in the Arctic to earn a steady income to pay for them. No longer can he make money through whaling, and the fur market fluctuates wildly. Many people leave to seek work in Fairbanks or Anchorage or in other U. S. cities. Those who remain in Wainwright, at the edge of the polar sea, continue to live mostly by hunting and fishing.

But whatever way of life the Eskimo chooses, he will take with him the raw courage, natural genius, and cheerful serenity that have long served him in his battle with nature at its cold, cruel worst.

Straining huskies haul a supply-laden sled over jumbled sea ice near the entrance to Admiralty Inlet in Canada's frozen northlands. Recently, planes and motorized toboggans have begun replacing the dogsleds, spanning the barrier of ice and snow and expanding the world of the once-isolated Eskimos.

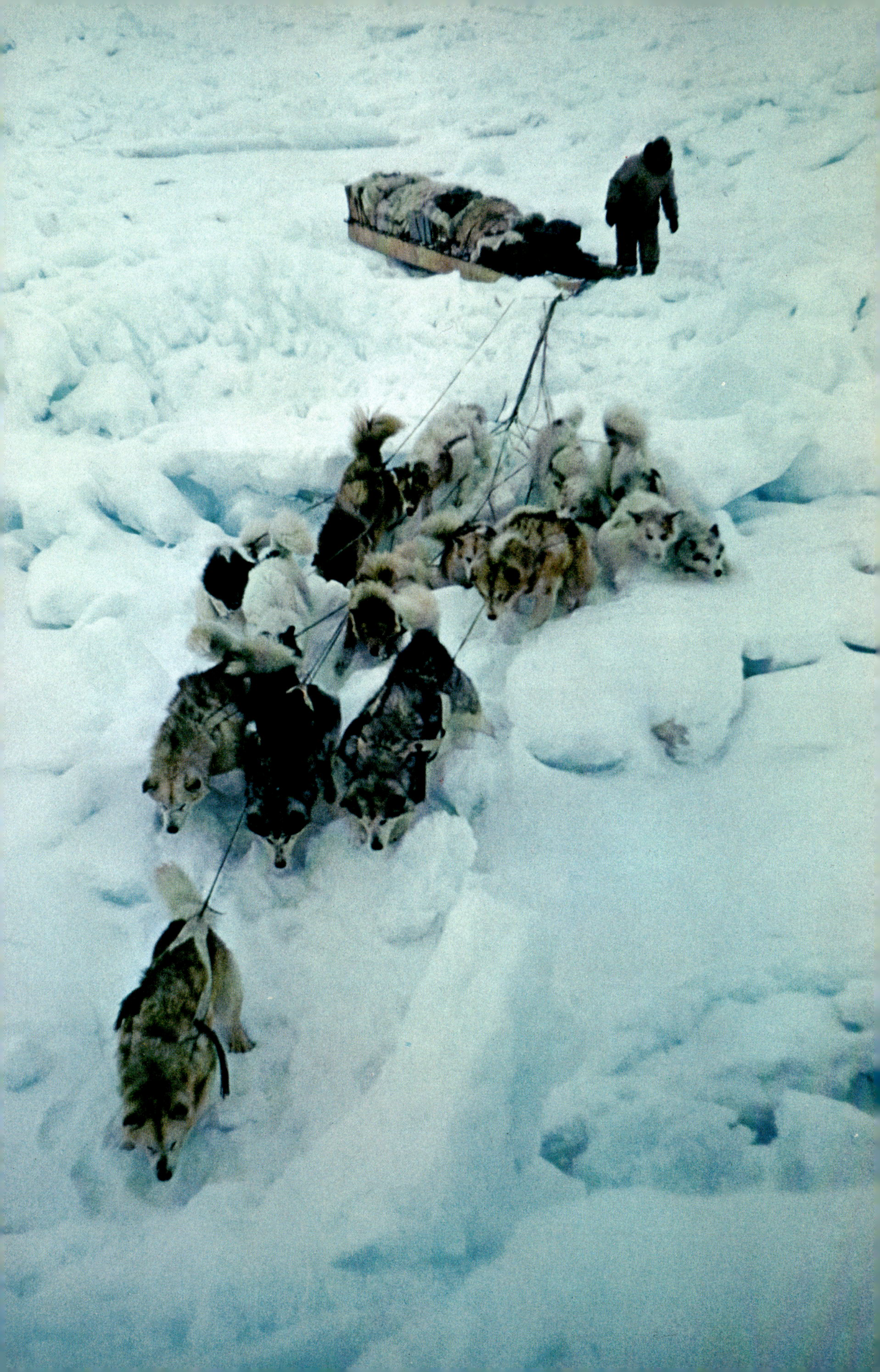

8

Indians of Central Brazil: A Struggle to Survive

By Vilma Chiara Schultz
Illustrations by Harald Schultz

"Where are the xetá indians?" we asked the laborers on the new coffee plantation in central Brazil.

Laughing, one of them answered, "The poor beasts disappeared last month. A tractor toppled a tree on a hut in their settlement, so they moved on."

Over the years the Xetá had emerged, one by one, from the forest to work on farms, where some died of disease and others found a new way of life. However, as a tribal group, they have ceased to exist.

Moved by the tragic disappearance of Indian culture and life, my husband Harald and I studied, documented, and, when possible, gave aid to remote Brazilian tribes for 20 years. The National Geographic Society sponsored many of Harald's expeditions before he died in 1966, and, through the pages of its magazine, reported on his field work with the Kraho, Waurá, Suyá, and others.

In the summer of 1965 Harald and I drove north from Brasília on the dirt highway that stretches 1,370 miles from the ultramodern capital to the seaport city of Belém. Bathed in dust, we bucked along the sun-baked road winding through the lonely savanna, an endless sea of amber grass. Near the Tocantins River, slightly more than 500 miles from Brasília, we turned onto a narrow, rutted lane that led to Itacajá, a small trading center and the nearest town to the Kraho village of Pedra Branca.

Some of the Kraho came to meet us there and helped us carry our supplies as we set out on foot across the sweltering countryside for the village about 15 miles away.

Arriving at the settlement, I saw that since my visit ten years earlier, the garden plots had grown much larger. Agriculture had become a necessity, a villager explained. Manioc, rice, potatoes, and maize, once side dishes for meat, often made the whole meal now, he said. Kraho

Scarlet coiffure of Brazilian tribesman wards off evil spirits. This Waurá decorates himself with red paste made from seeds of the urucú *plant. Lapokitee, friend of the author, proudly wears the regalia for war games — a jaguar-claw necklace and toucan-feather ear pendants.*

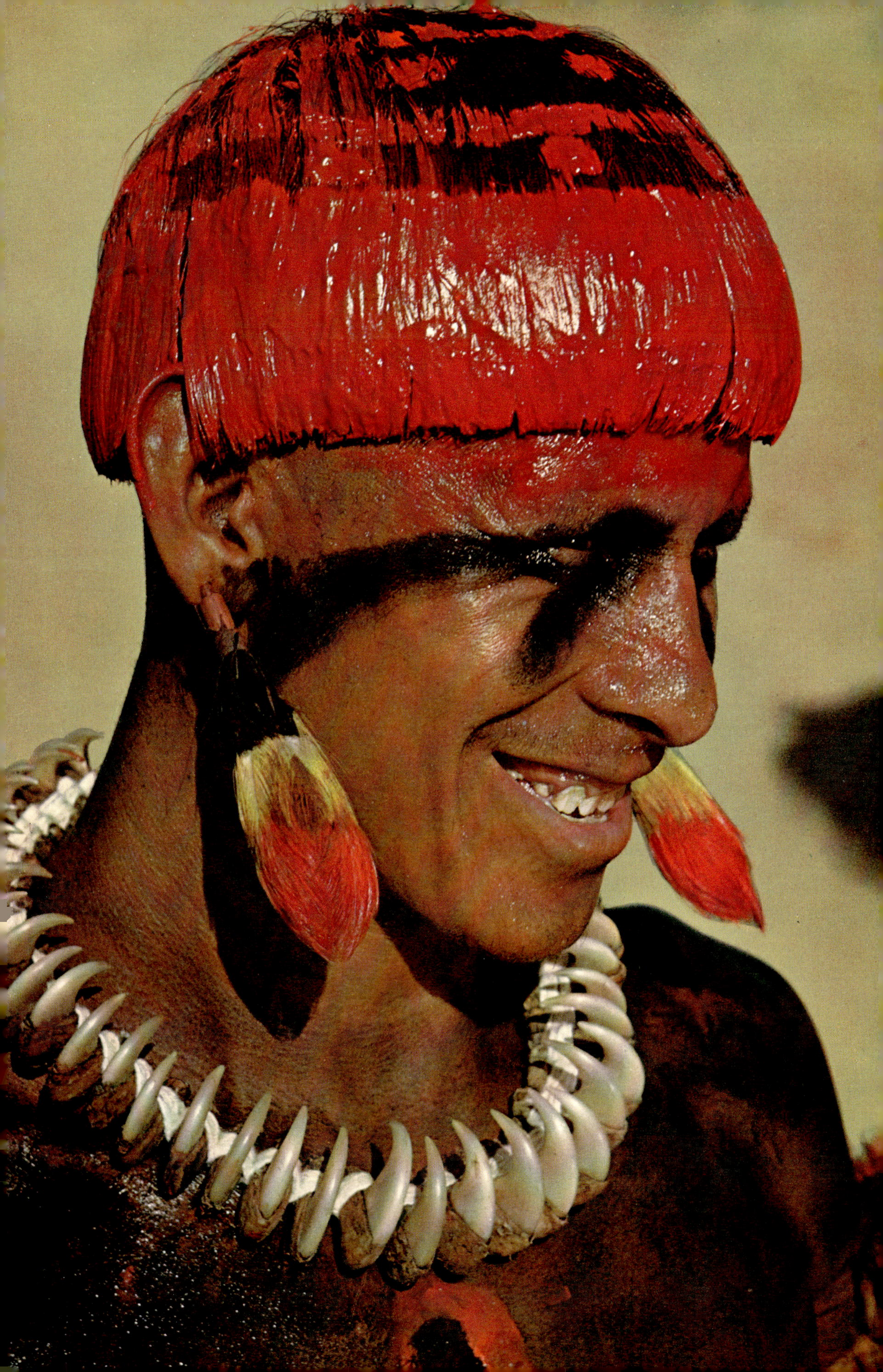

W. JESCO VON PUTTKAMER (ABOVE)

men have always hunted deer, wild pigs, anteaters, and monkeys, but almost all wildlife has disappeared—killed off by white hunters.

The classic circular design of the village had remained beautifully intact. Looking down from a nearby hill, I saw Pedra Branca as a giant wagon wheel in the sand. The rim stood out as a broad, circular boulevard, the outside bordered by huts. Straight paths gave the appearance of spokes, radiating from the center plaza to the houses.

From my vantage point, I also could see another significant change in Kraho culture: cattle-raising. Harald and I were proud to have played a role in getting the project started during our 1958 visit. At that time the tribe wanted herds like the white man's, but the people had problems to solve first.

"We are hungry," one of our Kraho friends had told us. "Our children cry out for meat. We must have cattle to survive. But we don't want to give up our village community and live in scattered families like white people. It is no fun."

The Kraho, committed to a communal life, had to find a way to manage livestock without introducing a system of personal ownership.

154

Young Txukahamei tribesmen shoulder a 300-pound anaconda, food for their village on the Mato Grosso Plateau. Below, a Kraho splashes his coppery skin during a chilly morning bath. Suyá wives (below, left) gather water hyacinths. When burned, the plant yields an ash that the Indians refine and use for salt.

155

They also worried about jeopardizing their complex social structure. Each villager belongs to one of two political groups. One governs during the six summer months, and the other assumes power in winter. Each Kraho is also born into a ceremonial group that divides the settlement into still two more units for feasts and rituals.

Finally, the elders agreed on a plan. They would raise cattle, but in the Kraho way: Everyone would own the herd jointly.

The Kraho had the plan, but no cattle—and little prospect of getting any. When we went home to São Paulo, Harald and I took the Indians' problem to sympathetic friends, who donated 25 animals to give the tribe a start. Now, several years later, I was pleased to see that in spite of their hunger the Indians had resisted slaughtering the small herd.

I went into one of the square, thatched huts to call on Mra-heetee, who had adopted me as her daughter in 1958. She sat on a straw mat

Waurá tribesman (above) practices with his long spear for *javari*, war games between neighboring tribes. In the mock battle, a live opponent becomes the target and tries to dodge the blunted weapon. Left: A Waurá lad plays with wooden airplanes patterned after craft he had seen land in his village.

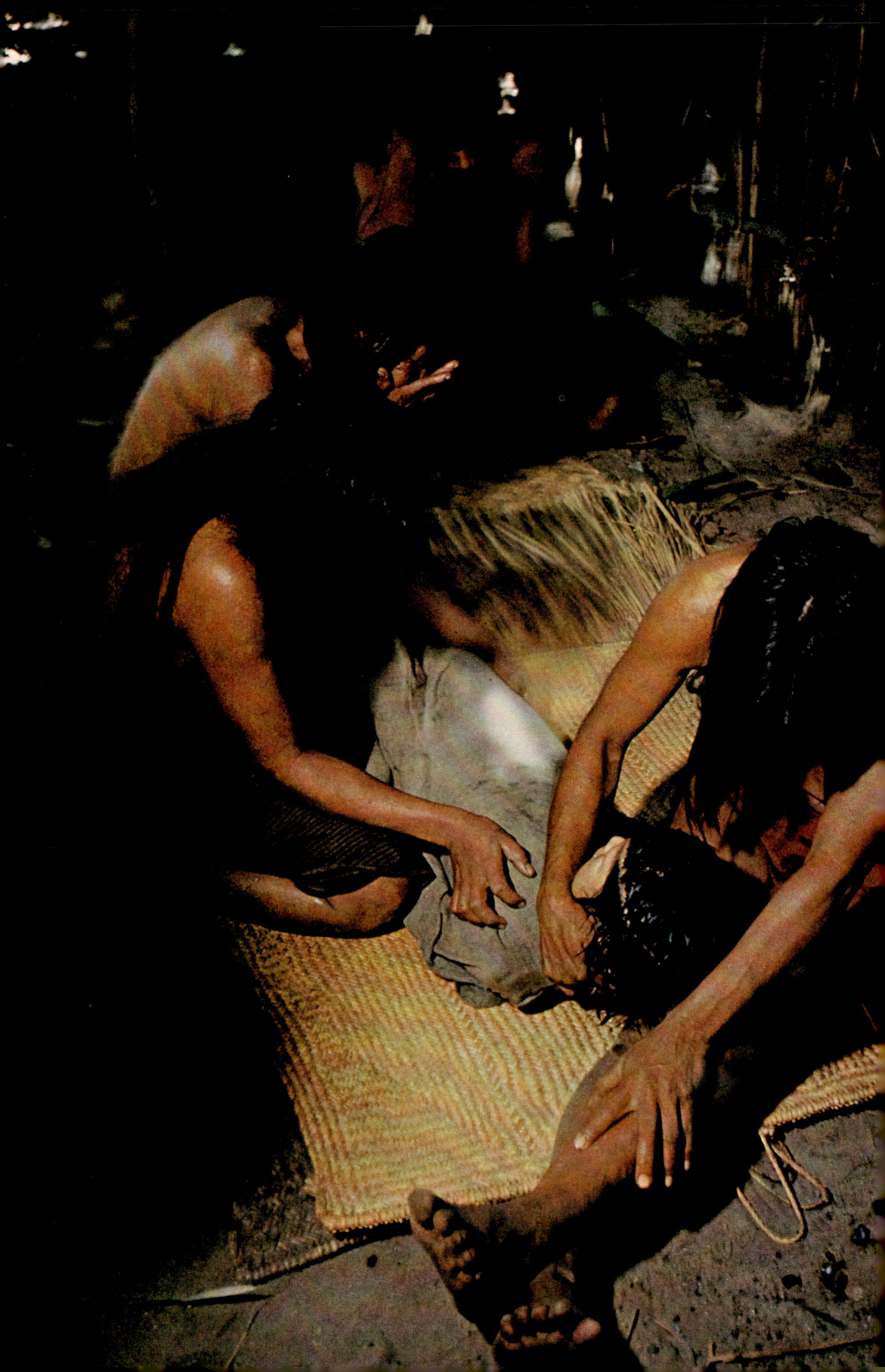

in the middle of the room, and as I greeted her she put her forehead against mine and began to shake and sob. In a singsong lamentation she wailed forth events that had occurred since my last visit. It was the customary Kraho greeting, expressing news, mostly bad, in melody.

"Patricio died ten days ago, Tokôi," Mra-heetee sobbed, calling me by my Kraho name.

I knew what grief this brought the village. Patricio, more than 60 years old, was the tribal counselor, their wisest man. It was he who had instructed the young people in the Kraho ways and customs.

For many days the village mourned. Most activities ceased; nobody adorned himself with paint; nobody sang in the plaza. The silence weighed even heavier since it was summer, the season that usually resounds with song and dance.

Except in time of mourning, Kraho sing at every opportunity. Song begins the day and ends it. When they work in the fields or cross the plain alone or in groups, Kraho serenade the countryside.

It was nearly dawn when I awoke to the sound of a rattle and a soft melodious voice. Standing in the square, Antonio, the religious leader and the best singer, was shaking a gourd filled with small pebbles. An alluring rhythm filled the plaza.

The mourning period had ended. Antonio's song signaled the village to assemble. Then I heard a woman's voice, a deep-throated full contralto, join his.

The predawn duet sounded beautifully strange to my ears. Another woman's voice blended in, followed by still another. Soon all the women and girls of the village had formed a choir. Antonio moved up and down the line of women, who faced east. Swinging, swaying, and stamping his right foot, he coaxed an ever-quickening tempo from them. The choir greeted the rising sun with rapturous song. Then, with the first rays of the sun, the singing ended. The women left in small groups for a nearby creek and the morning bath, as girls began to carry water back to the village. The workday had begun.

That evening Harald and I joined villagers in their nightly songfest. We sat cross-legged on the soft sand of the central plaza. Some of the songs resemble medieval religious music in cadence and melody, some are like love songs, and others have the spirit of a march. Repeating verses countless times, the Kraho sang of nature, of the fruits of the field, and of the animals of the forest and savanna.

As night advanced and the singing waned, families withdrew from the square, one by one. The unmarried young men remained to sleep on the ground in the square near small fires for warmth.

The rains returned in September, and the Indians prepared for the last of a summer-long schedule of ceremonies before returning to work in the fields.

In the heat of one afternoon I heard a flutelike whistle beyond the village. "The first Kraho are coming for *Piegré*," Mra-heetee said. How

Overwhelmed by grief, a Kraho mother cradles the head of her dead son and wails a lament, as relatives arrange a shroud of coarse cotton cloth. Contagious diseases such as tuberculosis, smallpox, and measles have taken a heavy toll of Brazilian Indians, but anemia claimed this child.

Rugged Brazil, sprawling over nearly half of the South American continent, held explorers, adventurers, and settlers from its heart for nearly four centuries after the Portuguese stepped ashore in 1500. Mountain ranges, dense tropical rain forest, vast stretches of savanna, and treacherous rivers barred Europeans from the interior. Then fortune hunters, planters, miners penetrated the wilderness. They drove Indians from their homeland and left behind epidemics that decimated the populations. Historians have recorded the disappearance of about a hundred tribes; no one knows how many more have vanished since the 1500's. Today so few members exist in some tribes that they too face extinction, and it may be only a matter of time before contact with outsiders destroys the structure of their society. Anthropologist Vilma Chiara Schultz, who assisted her husband Harald for more than two decades in his pioneer studies of Brazilian Indians, records here the traditions of the Kraho, Waurá, and Suyá before their way of life passes.

---

fortunate, I thought; it gave me the rare opportunity to witness this cycle of ceremonies, which occurs only about every ten years.

For the next several days numerous whistles pierced the air as families arrived and signaled that friends from neighboring Kraho settlements were entering the village. Each family stopped at a nearby creek to bathe, trim hair, and groom for the occasion.

Dancing and singing filled the festive days. But nothing attracted more attention than the log races, an event that in years past conditioned the Indians for chasing game.

Two teams of men gathered outside the village and cut two buriti palm logs weighing about 40 pounds apiece. A member of each team hoisted a log to his shoulder, and the race began. Running with the ponderous weights toward the village, about a mile away, teammates passed the logs to each other in relay fashion.

Reaching the village, the sweating teams raced counterclockwise around the sandy boulevard. Villagers watched intently and cheered the runner who overtook his opponent. The enthusiasm of the crowd heightened as each racer passed the log to a teammate—the most critical and exciting maneuver in the race. Badly done, it can make a runner break stride and fall behind.

The last event of Piegré began at dawn. I joined the villagers to watch the ritual of the seriema, a relative of the crane. The Kraho built a platform on the boulevard at the edge of the village to represent a seriema nest. Three children, their bodies covered with the down of a parakeet, sat on the structure in the role of young seriemas.

Two groups of men—representing hawks and *iraras*, a weasel-like mammal—enacted a battle that symbolizes the conflict between two opposing forces of nature.

The long ritual ended abruptly, and participants distributed gifts of food to the crowd. This anticlimactic ending left me puzzled; I asked a Kraho friend what it meant.

"We don't know," he shrugged. "We do this because our ancestors have always done it."

Other Kraho ceremonies have failed to survive on the strength of tradition. Once all males between 10 and 14 years of age underwent initiation ceremonies that secluded them for months, transforming the

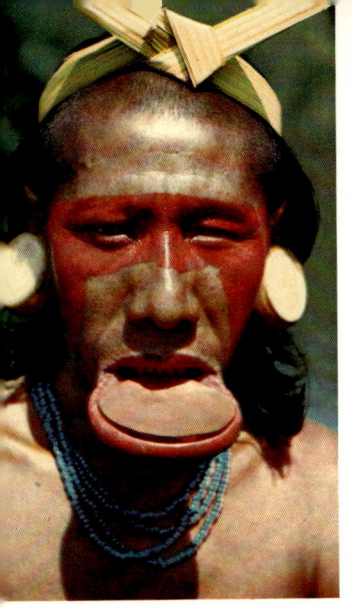

Wooden disks distend the lower lip and earlobes of a painted Suyá—once one of the most feared tribes in Brazil's upper Xingu region.

Young Tchikao carry a prize catch (below). The Indians shoot some fish with bow and arrow, net some, and take others by poisoning the water with timbo vine.
W. JESCO VON PUTTKAMER (BELOW)

boys into adults and warriors. As civilization gradually depopulated surrounding tribes, ending tribal strife, the need for warriors ended. The initiation ritual, its primary purpose gone, gradually became abbreviated. But some tribesmen are working to restore the original rite.

"Our youth are becoming too soft," elders claim.

Many boys resist the return to initiations and also oppose the custom of piercing ears. Traditionally, Kraho males pierce their ears and insert sections of arrow shafts, gradually increasing the size of the openings. Eventually they insert a wooden plug the size of a teacup into the stretched lobes. The men look upon the adornment as giving them romantic appeal—the larger the disk, the greater their success with the girls. Now, some fathers forbid their sons to follow the custom.

"If our children must live and compete in a white man's world, we want them to look as much like the white man as possible," a tribal elder said.

The storm of civilization touches even the remotest tribes of the interior and continues to sweep away traditions that have developed over the centuries. Nearly 500 miles southwest of the Kraho reservation, toward the heart of Brazil, rises the Mato Grosso Plateau. This tabletop region has five major rivers that merge to form the Xingu River, some 1,000 winding miles from its confluence with the Amazon.

In 1965 I journeyed into the little-known world of the Xingu to visit the Waurá—another people struggling desperately to survive. While Harald stayed in Brasília to plan another trip, I flew deep into the immense wilderness in a single-engine plane.

"OVER THERE!" The pilot pointed to the horizon. "See the green beginning? That's the upper Xingu region."

Below, the rolling savanna turned into a mosaic of shining lakes, streams, and towering forests. In 1884, when the German explorer Karl von den Steinen first entered the region, he estimated the Indian population at 3,000; in 1962 the World Health Organization reported a total population of only 500. In an attempt to protect the Xingu tribes from the fatal onrush of disease and greed and to create a sanctuary for the tribes, the Brazilian Government established the 8,500-square-mile Xingu National Park in 1961.

The square white buildings of Pôsto Leonardo Villas Boas stood out prominently as we came in for a landing. The park headquarters bears the name of the late brother of Orlando and Claudio Villas Boas. These men have spent many years befriending, pacifying, and protecting Indians of the Xingu. Orlando and Claudio control entry to the park and enforce rigid admission rules. When I arrived I was asked to show my health records and proof of immunization against smallpox and yellow fever.

We continued our flight along the Tamitatoala River, also known as the Batovi, to the Waurá village. The settlement lies far upstream, but by plane it was only a matter of minutes before I glimpsed a jungle clearing with haystack-shaped huts encircling a wide earth plaza. There live 85 Waurá—the last in the world.

The proud Indians share a culture common to all Xingu tribes. They live in elliptical communal houses. Hammocks are their beds, wooden

161

Wagon-wheel pattern outlines Pedra Branca, one of five remaining Kraho villages in Brazil. Pathways link family houses with the central plaza—tribal assembly ground and political and social center. Every day men gather at points as far away as three miles from the village for a relay race. Carrying logs of buriti palm that may weigh up to 200 pounds each, the racers sprint homeward, passing the logs to teammates as they tire. Arriving at the village, they circle the boulevard counterclockwise twice for the finale (right). Log racing, the Kraho's principal sport, stems from a myth that says the sun and moon began the semireligious event for themselves, then passed it to their descendants the Kraho.

163

benches their chairs, and necklaces of shell and toucan feathers their jewelry. They live mostly on fish and devote much of their leisure time to the sport of wrestling.

In forest clearings they cultivate small plots of land, and in the savanna they collect fruits such as the succulent yellow *piquiá*, and *mangaba*, a delicacy like a small apricot with a taste resembling ripe pear.

Our plane bumped in for a landing on the grassy airstrip, hardly more than a scratch on the plain. As I stepped to the ground, a villager approached.

A 23-year-old Waurá named Lapokitee, who spoke some Portuguese he learned at Pôsto Leonardo, pointed toward a handsome, robust man. "This is our chief." Malakiyauá stepped forward and shook my hand and smiled to put me at ease. His calm presence radiated kindness and nobility, and I knew I was welcome.

"I am Kukoi's wife."

"Ahhhhh." Malakiyauá understood little Portuguese, and I did not speak the Arawakan tongue of the Waurá, but the chief recognized the word "Kukoi," Harald's name among the Waurá. Chief Malakiyauá led me to his village. The center plaza was empty, the village quiet. The morning sun already hung high in the rich blue sky. For hours now, the women had been working in the back of their huts, preparing manioc, staple of the diet for most of the Indians in Brazil.

We went directly to a rectangular building, a departure from the traditional round huts of the Waurá. It was the chief's new house, and he lived in it with his sons and their families. I could see by the way he smiled that he was proud of the home.

Inside, Malakiyauá pointed to two posts in the corner where I could hang my hammock.

"Look, Harald sends presents for you." I opened a bag and produced some fishhooks, a hunting knife, and ammunition for a .44-caliber rifle Harald had given the chief. Malakiyauá smiled with pleasure at the sight of them.

He gestured toward my bag of gifts, curious to see what else I had brought. I opened the bag, and his head nodded in approval as he politely examined glass beads, scissors, and several cartons of ammunition for the .22-caliber rifles used more and more for hunting.

"*Oolookee*," he said. This meant a formal exchange of goods between his tribe and me.

Activities among the Waurá are methodical, carefully planned in advance. Each night the chief and men of the village gather around a small fire in the center of the plaza. Smoking large, strong, homemade cigars, they discuss events of the day and plan the next day's activities. The council would set a date for oolookee.

I hung my hammock and joined the women, who smiled to welcome me. I could not speak their language, but I managed to convey that I wanted to help them prepare manioc. I took a clamshell and began to peel one of the roots.

In the shade of straw festival masks, a Waurá woman strains manioc to separate the pulp from juice containing deadly prussic acid. From the starchy residue, she makes **beiju** *cakes, tribal staff of life.*

165

Almost daily from dawn to dusk during the dry season, Waurá women process the dark brown tubers. One woman peels them while another, seated in front of a large ceramic pot, grates the root on a board set with small, hard teeth made of palmwood. She soaks the shreds in cold water and then squeezes the mixture in a fiber sieve to extract the juice containing poisonous prussic acid and collects the liquid in a pot along with fine particles of starch.

Coarse pulp left on the sieve is rolled into balls, dried in the sun, and used to make *beiju* cakes. Starchy residue left in the pot is dried to make a finer type of cake. The milky liquid, boiled for hours, loses its prussic acid and becomes nutritious soup.

THE HARDWORKING WOMEN sometimes re-enact the myth of the Jamarikumá Amazons—legendary Xingu wives who fled their selfish husbands and led a jungle life without them. Early explorers of the Amazon are said to have named the region for the mythical women after seeing them along the river. In the ceremony I saw, the nearly naked wives, wearing bright paint and yellow feathers, conveyed the story, singing and dancing. Two dancers presented arrows to the village chief to symbolize their gratitude to the old man who helped them gain their freedom in the myth.

The men lead busy lives too, and spend much of their summer fishing for food. Using basketlike traps of plaited vines, they get their biggest catches during the dry season when lakes are low. The Waurá change their technique according to the season: When rivers run full, they shoot the fish with bows and arrows. At other times, they cast fiber nets from dugout canoes received in barter with other tribes.

On the afternoon they set aside to barter with me, the entire village formed a semicircle in front of my bench in the chief's large hut. To begin the oolookee, I took a pair of scissors and laid them beside me. One man stepped forward, placing a bow and arrows beside me. I nodded, and he took the scissors. That made the exchange official.

The Indian would use the scissors to cut cotton for armbands and anklets, or feathers for a headdress, and also to cut his hair. I wondered how the Waurá had cut their hair in ages past. Possibly like other tribes they used sharp piranha teeth, clamshells, bamboo knives, or even hot coals to singe it. Today Waurá men use metal scissors almost exclusively.

The chief decreed that one sack of white glass beads was a fair exchange for one of their small, red ceramic pots decorated with images of Xingu animals.

The Waurá alone supply the other upper Xingu tribes with the giant flat-bottomed pots used to process manioc. The women make the pots by hand and paint red, black, or white geometric designs, representing fishes and snakes, on the large basins.

The enormous size of the manioc vessels has helped preserve pottery making in the Waurá culture. Waurá women prefer the shiny appearance and the durability of aluminum, but fortunately aluminum pots are too small to replace the giant ceramic bowls required for producing manioc flour.

The secret of ceramics brought prestige and wealth to Waurá villages,

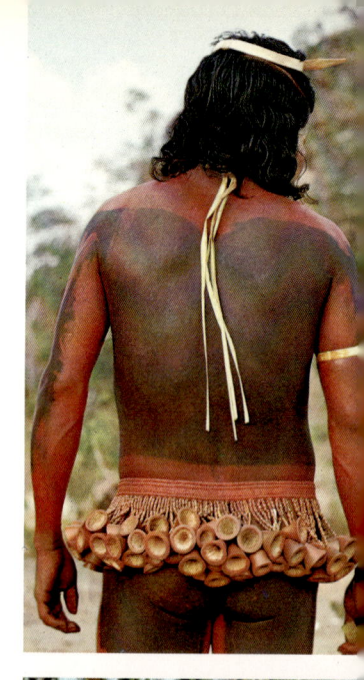

166

Waurá sportsmen sway, dip, and bob in a rousing dance after daily practice for javari, or war games. Geometric designs on their bodies symbolize jungle creatures—hawks, jaguars, armadillos. Left, palm streamers and a belt of bells adorn a Kraho. The wife of a fellow tribesman (right) applies red dye to her husband, indicating he belongs to the ceremonial division of the tribe whose members consider themselves linked to the sun.

but as recently as the 1940's, the Suyá raided their villages for pots and abducted women who knew how to make them.

The Suyá now live in peace in the Xingu National Park. In 1959 the Villas Boas brothers used gifts of tools to persuade the Suyá to move into the park from their village up the Suiá Missu River.

When Harald visited the Suyá in 1962, they were using steel axes, knives, matches, and aluminum pots. They had just moved to a small forest clearing. Huts were not yet built, but hammocks hung between trees with rough thatch over them to shed night moisture. Bows and bundles of arrows—no longer important for battle—lay casually about the camp amid clay pots and wooden mortars and pestles.

"I began to take a census," Harald told me later. "My heart stopped. I counted only 35 individuals, and that would be the very minimum for maintaining Suyá tribal life. With less than that it becomes nearly impossible to carry on the daily chores of food gathering and trading. It also becomes difficult to conduct ceremonies and rituals so vital to social relations between upper Xingu tribes. The Suyá were finished, I thought.

"Some days later, I happily learned that a second party of the village was upstream cutting bamboo for arrow shafts. They numbered 30, bringing the total to 65."

"T HE TRIBE LIVED off the forest temporarily and already had planted new crops," Harald noted in his diary. "Till harvest, the village survived by gathering palm nuts and wild roots. Every day we ate fish, but the Suyá also served me roasted golden hare, water pig, and monkey—meat shunned by other Xingu tribes."

Each adult male wears a large wooden disk that distorts the lower lip. As soon as a man marries, he has his lip pierced and inserts a small disk. Progressively larger ones stretch the hole until he can wear the standard ornament, three inches in diameter. To eat, he must cut or break his food into bits. To drink, he tucks his disk under the rim of a gourd dipper and extends his tongue inside of it as far as possible, coaxing what liquid he can down the throat.

Harald's Suyá friends pointed out several Waurá women to him. Although once seized against their will, they seemed content with Suyá husbands.

Long feared as one of Brazil's fiercest tribes, the Suyá have made peace with civilization. Few in number and lacking the skills to bring to the Xingu marketplace, they may lose the will to live. Dispirited, reduced to a scant 65, the Suyá face the danger of extinction.

The Waurá, on the other hand, enjoy a firm place in Xingu society. Their skill at making the large clay pots gives them a livelihood and a sense of purpose—a reason to endure.

The Kraho too seek economic independence in the struggle to survive. They base their hopes on a small herd of cattle, which represents not only food but also a chance to find a place for themselves in the white man's world.

What is the future for these Brazilian aborigines whose bow-and-arrow customs clash with the Atomic Age? Knowing the plight of others, I try hard not to imagine it.

Bathed in red, the color of life, a Kraho infant wears bracelets and anklets of vine to ward off evil spirits. Both the infant and her young mother face an uncertain future as their tribe seeks to adapt to a new way of life.

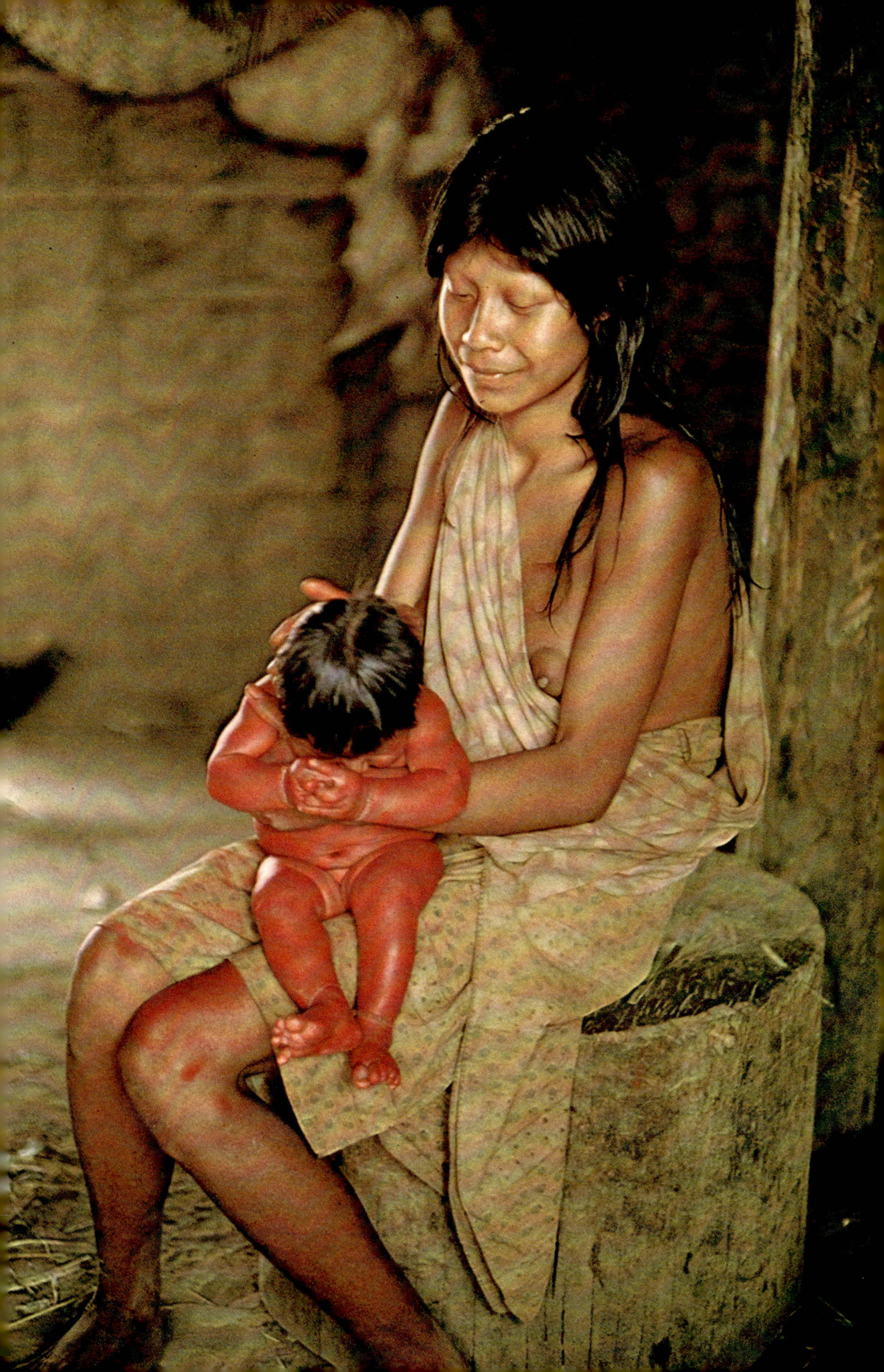

9

Hopis: "The Peaceful Ones" Confront the 20th Century

By Arthur P. Miller, Jr., *National Geographic Staff*

MIDDAY SUN baked the dust of the plaza and the sandstone walls of the one- and two-story homes of Hotevilla. On benches, Hopi matrons quietly waited. To one side, tribal elders sat cross-legged, their graying hair contrasting with red headbands.

Suddenly, a single line of kilted Kachina dancers, marvelously masked and weirdly painted, strode on moccasined feet into the *kisonvi*, the ritual plaza of the Hopi village. Tortoise-shell rattles and sleigh bells dangled from the dancers' legs, and turquoise and silver bracelets encircled their arms. Collars of spruce greens formed the bases for masks with brilliant yellow beaks and crowns of feathers.

With the sound of rattles, the dance began—a living, moving prayer. In perfect rhythm, one behind the other, the men stamped their feet. An Indian prayer song filled the plaza, rising, then falling. In unison the masked figures pivoted, then turned back again.

When the dancers stopped, each of them reached into a box of food and tossed or handed its contents to the villagers. Fresh-baked loaves of bread, ears of corn, oranges, and candy found their way to outstretched hands. So did rolls of *piki*, a paper-thin corn bread used for special occasions and ladled with sweeps of the hand from batter bowl to the hot surface of a flat stone.

I was fortunate to witness this Hopi ceremonial dance with Polingaysi, an indomitable woman whose jet-black hair belied her four-score years. She grew up a Hopi, then left the reservation for many years to teach school. Eventually, she returned to "grow again in native soil" and to help others understand her people.

As the Kachina dancers moved to another side of the plaza to repeat the steps, Polingaysi spoke of Hopi beliefs and folklore.

Kachinas, she explained, are respected supernatural beings—spirits of the dead; spirits of rocks and plants and animals, even of the planets and stars; spirits of all the invisible forces of life. Half of each year the

Seated before a heated cooking stone and following an old tribal recipe, Hopi Indian Vera Pooyama bakes piki, *a crisp, paper-thin corn bread. She demonstrates Hopi cooking skills during a crafts exhibit held annually at the Museum of Northern Arizona in Flagstaff.*

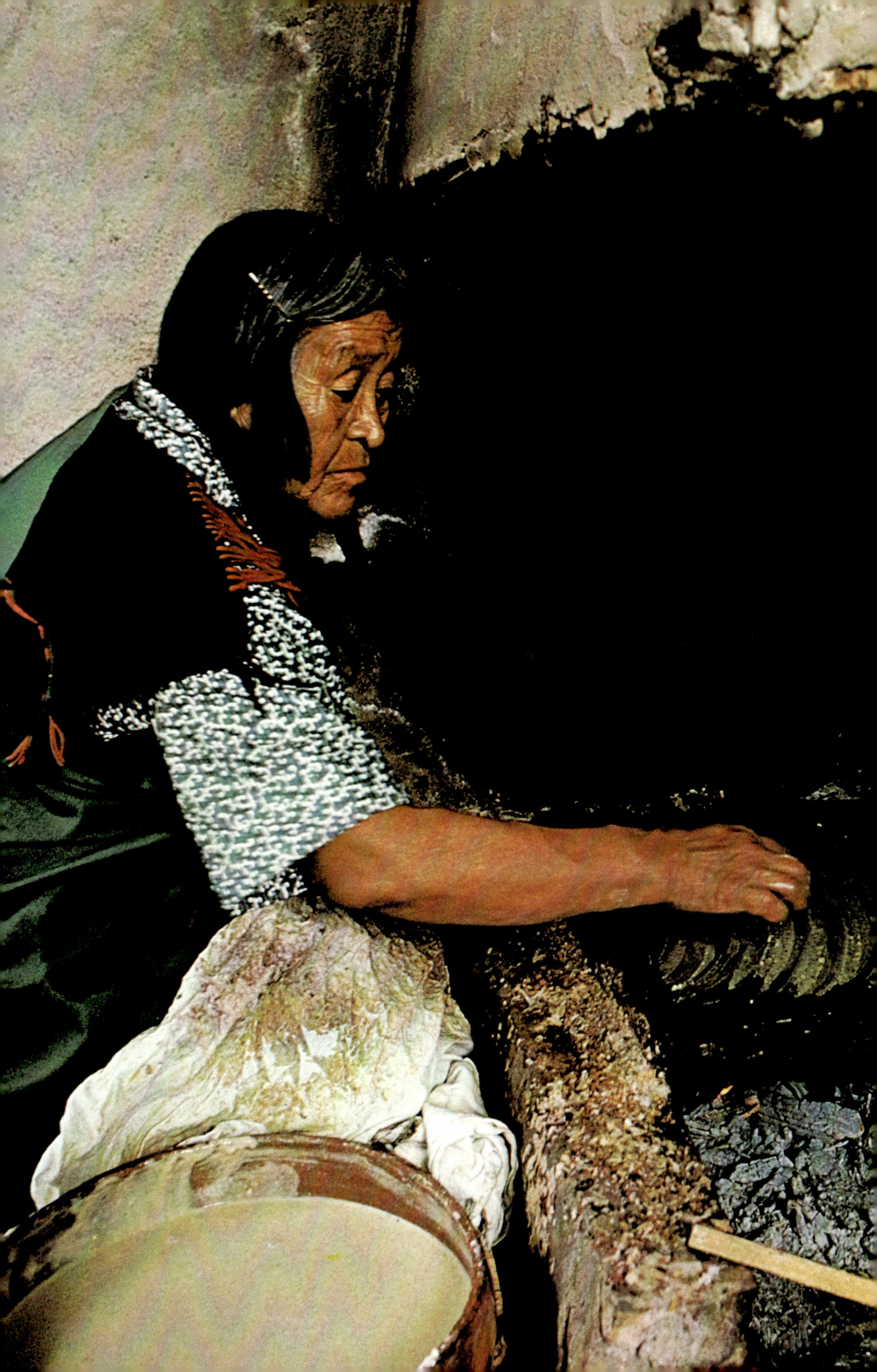

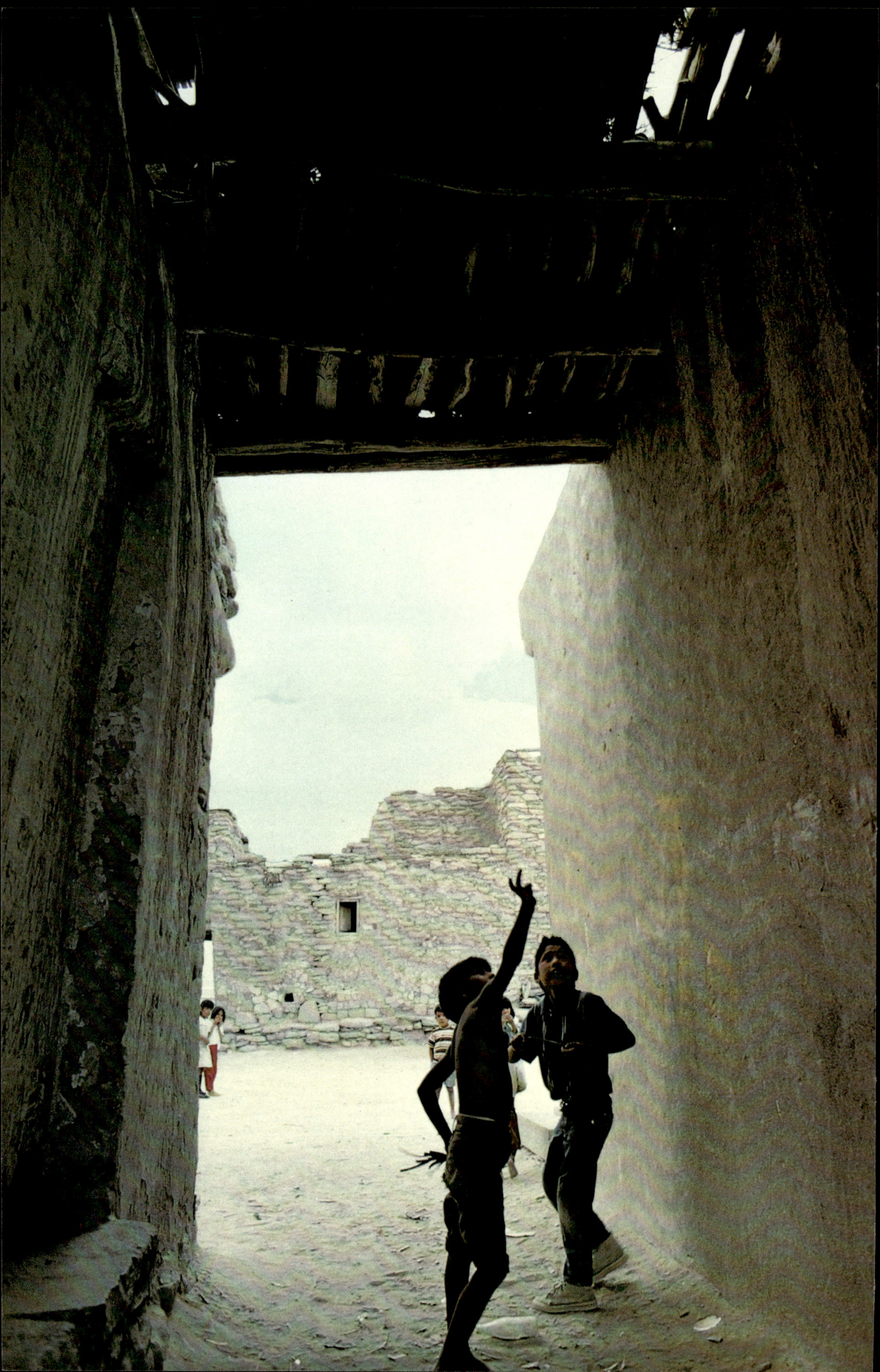

TERRY EILER

Flat-roofed stone houses wall the dusty square in Shongopovi, a village more than 250 years old on the Hopi reservation in northeastern Arizona. In a shadowed corridor boys fire rubber bands at a target in the rafters. Above, youngsters in improvised masks mimic the ceremonial dances of their elders.

Kachinas inhabit the snow-covered San Francisco Peaks near Flagstaff, Arizona. The remainder of the year they visit Hopi villages in the guise of masked dancers to bring happiness, the blessings of rain, and good crops, thus ensuring the harmonious continuation of life.

The Hopis have hundreds of different Kachinas. The dancer believes that when he puts on the Kachina mask he loses his own identity and assumes that of the spirit. He must do each dance to perfection, overlook discomfort, and think pure thoughts as he helps act out the religious myths of his people.

Most dramatic and publicized of Hopi rites is the Snake Dance, a prayer for rain. In 15 days of complex preparation, the celebrants hunt snakes, make feathered prayer sticks called *pâhos*, and conduct religious rites inside kivas, or underground ceremonial chambers. Finally, with writhing serpents—including rattlesnakes—in their mouths, men of the Snake Society begin the dance, circling with jolting steps to the chants of the Antelope Society. When the dance ends, Antelope men place all the snakes in a circle marked with ground corn, sacred to the Hopis; then runners speed into the desert to release the serpents so that they may tell the spirits of the need for rain.

As the Kachina dancers retreated from the plaza at Hotevilla, four clowns appeared. These white-painted comedians kept the crowd

Overleaf: Atop a spur of Arizona's Black Mesa, the tiny fortress villages of Mishongnovi and Shipaulovi blend together, forming a lofty retreat in a stark expanse little altered since Spanish conquistadores saw it in 1540. Late in the 1600's the Hopis moved from the slopes and scrubland below to the mesa top as a defense against the Spanish. Now a road penetrates the old stronghold, and the Hopis' resistance to change has begun to crumble.

NATIONAL GEOGRAPHIC PHOTOGRAPHER WINFIELD PARKS

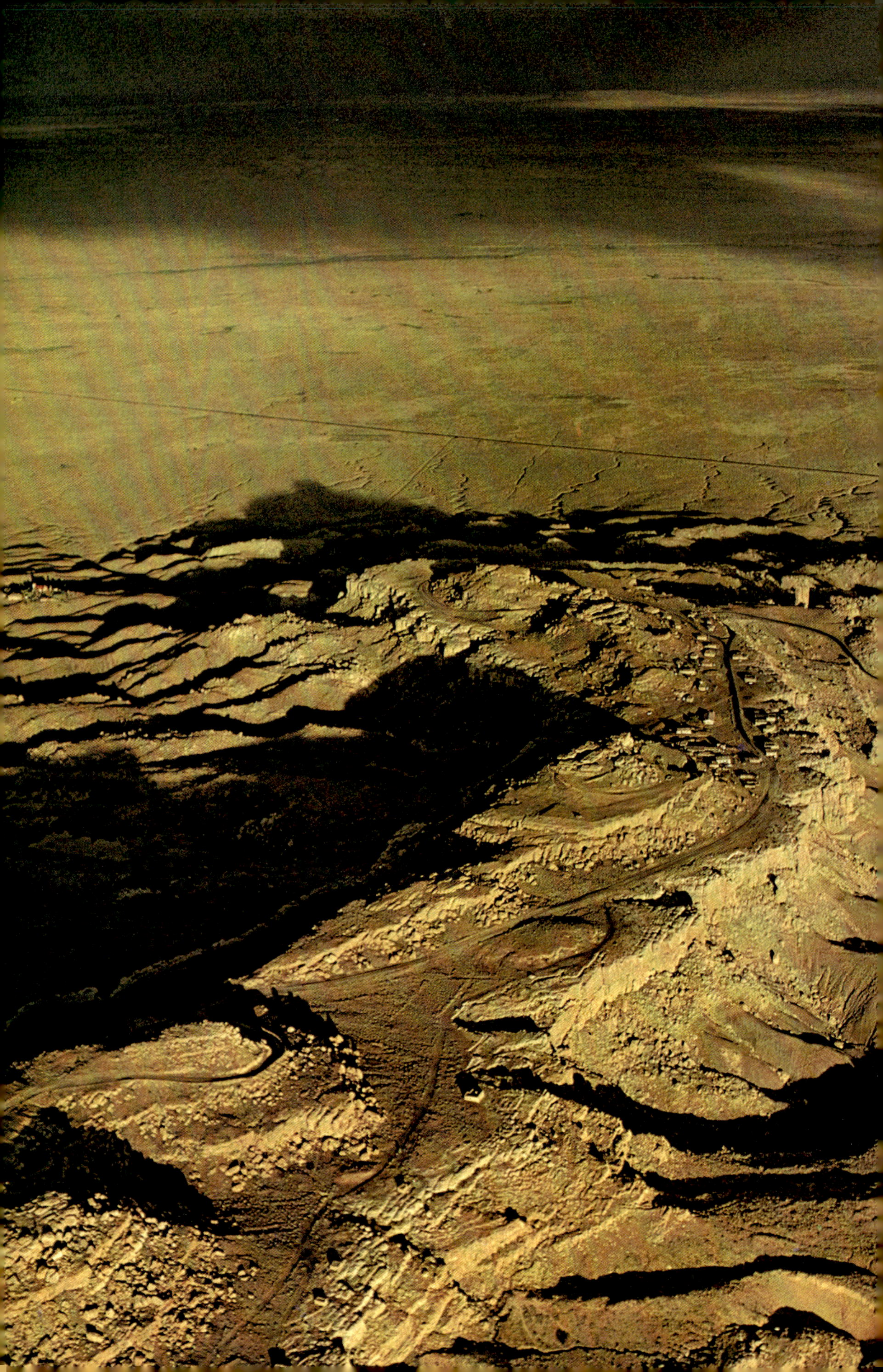

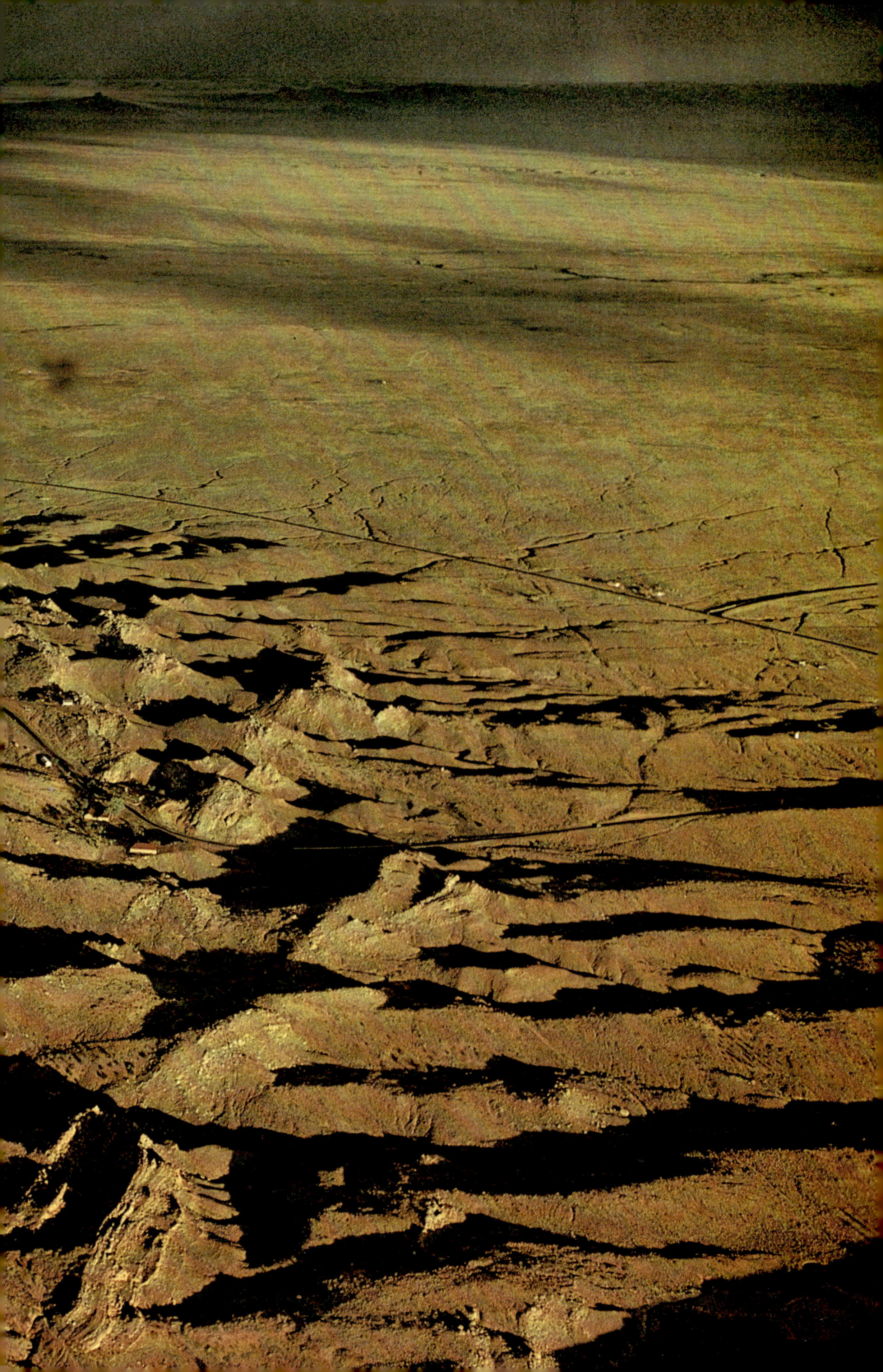

laughing with humorous pantomime and gymnastics, while the dancers rested for their next performance. The clowns have a more serious purpose as well. They mimic bad manners, the use of hair spray, belligerence, and other examples of poor Hopi conduct, such as overindulgence in food and drink.

As I watched the unforgettable Kachinas, I reflected that to visit a Hopi village is to step into history. In 13 villages, 9 of them on three spurs of Black Mesa, live 5,000 Hopi men, women, and children, many of them still clinging to the heritage of their ancestors.

The Hopis have lived in northeastern Arizona for centuries. Archeologists have dated Old Oraibi at about A.D. 1150, making it one of the oldest continuously inhabited places in the United States.

When the Spaniards of Francisco Vásquez de Coronado's expedition discovered the Hopi settlements in 1540, along with those of the Zuni and Acoma, they called them *pueblos,* Spanish for villages. The conquistadores, lured by tales about cities of gold, soon moved on. Beginning in 1629, Spanish priests sought to convert the Hopis, but the Indians rejected the new religion. They did, however, welcome the sheep and cattle brought by the Spanish and have been herding ever since. During the 18th century, the Spanish paid scant attention to the Hopis.

After Mexico declared itself independent of Spain in 1821, the Mexican authorities also left the Hopis to themselves. With the treaty of 1848 ending the Mexican War, most of the Southwest, including the land of the Hopis, became part of the United States. In 1882 President Chester A. Arthur established for the Hopi Indians a 3,863-square-mile reservation centering on the traditional homeland at Black Mesa. The Hopis now have exclusive rights to 1,015 square miles and share the use of the remainder with the Navajos.

As I walked the dusty streets of settlements like Walpi and Shongopovi, I saw Hopis doing their household chores, carrying spring water,

Bleak, inhospitable land of baking sun, infrequent rains, and killing frosts yields an unpredictable harvest to Hopi farmers. At right, 78-year-old Don Talayesva grubs weeds from his bean patch on the edge of a sandy wash that carries runoff from the mesa during rains. Often he begins work before dawn to escape the full heat of the day. With a soft drink (left), he rests in late afternoon at the trading post in the village of New Oraibi. An elaborately masked corn dancer (far left) bears a bountiful harvest of melon and corn.

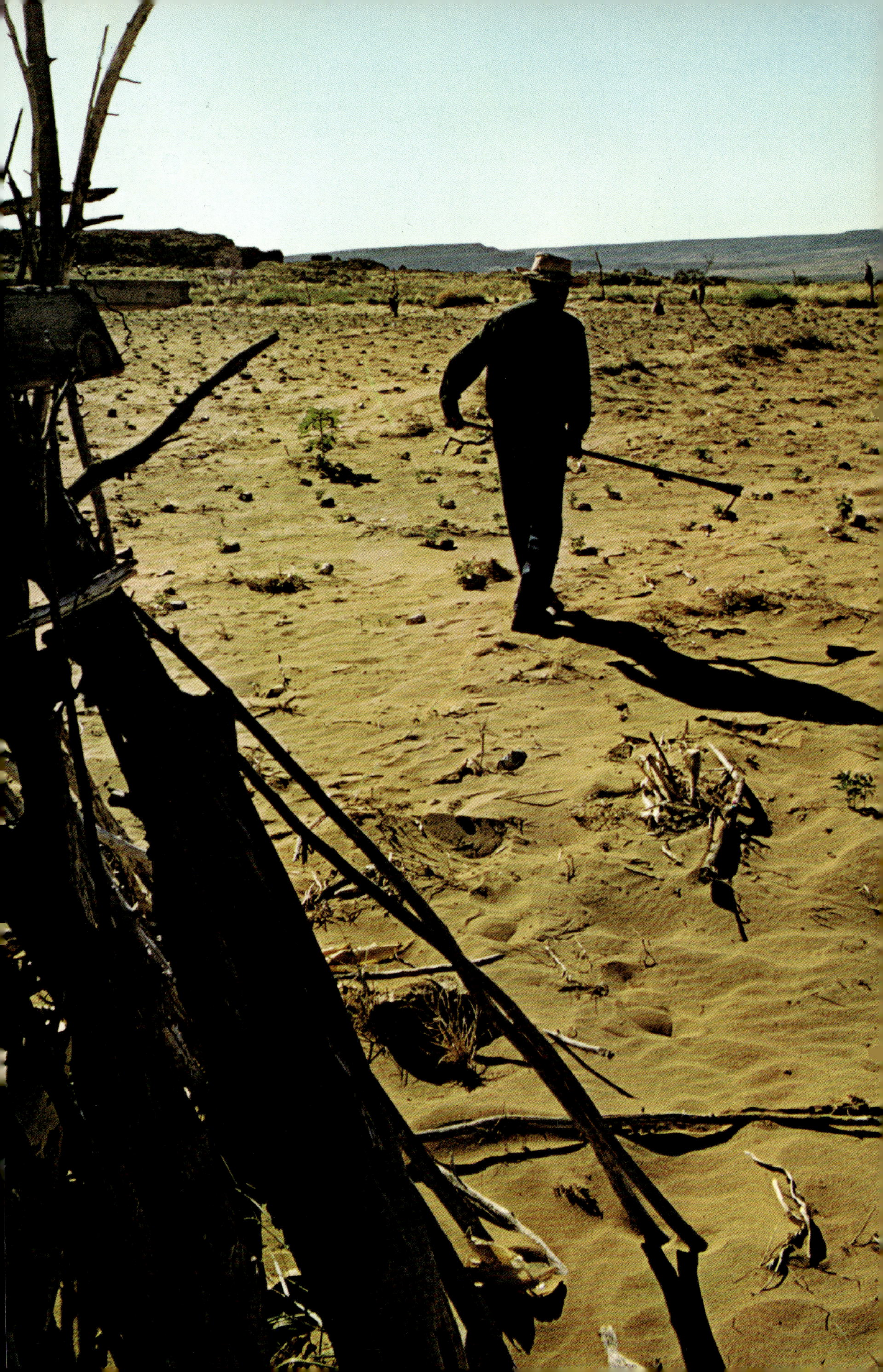

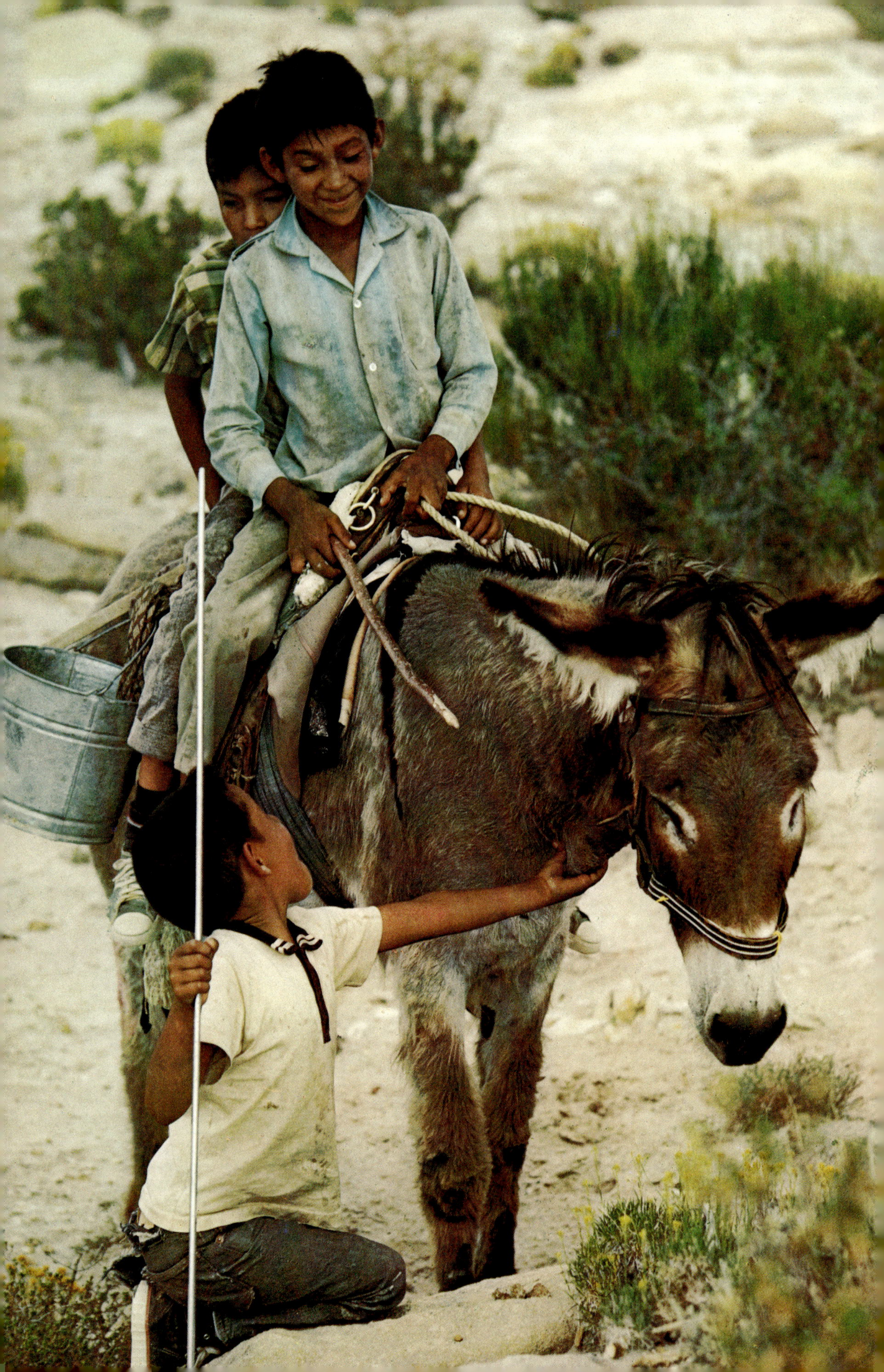

On a sandy, windswept reservation that spreads across 1,015 square miles of semidesert in northeastern Arizona live 5,000 Hopi Indians, many of them holding tenaciously to beliefs and customs followed by their ancestors before the time of Columbus. Once among the most isolated of the North American Indians, the Hopis today confront the complexities of 20th-century life. New wealth from oil leases and mining concessions has led them to embark on a business venture—a clothing plant in nearby Winslow, Arizona. The Tribal Council also plans a combined motel, restaurant, and crafts center on the reservation. Electricity and running water transform some villages, and television antennas have just begun to sprout from rooftops along the mesa. More and more young people seek a place in the modern world, leaving the reservation to complete their education and to find employment. The old religion and the Hopi way exert a deep influence, yet the pull of the future is strong. This timely report by Arthur P. Miller, Jr., of the National Geographic Society's editorial staff, captures a culture in transition as winds of change sweep relentlessly across the high and parched homeland of the Hopis.

and trading gossip—much as Coronado's men must have seen them.

But how long can this way of life persist in a dynamic country of 200 million people? Will traditional Hopi life alter significantly in the years just ahead? I sought answers to questions like these in the weeks I lived among the Hopis.

I found my first clue the day I walked out of Hotevilla to the Kachina dance. On a nearby rooftop flapped a tethered golden eagle, a sacred bird that would be sacrificed the following morning to provide feathers for Kachina masks and pâhos for carrying prayers aloft. In striking contrast, a late-model pickup truck gleamed near a back door. Not far away stood a farm tractor. A boy rode past on his bicycle, snaking between two teen-age girls in cotton print dresses worn stylishly above the knee.

IN SUCH WAYS the 20th century lives side by side with the 17th in Hopi villages, but winds of more drastic change gust across the mesa. Even the Hopi religion, which has stood like a rock through the centuries, is being chipped by changing attitudes. Some Hopis complain that a few ceremonial leaders have deserted their villages for jobs in the cities, leaving their responsibilities in less experienced hands. A number of Kachina dancers practice in town, going to the mesa only for the rituals. The cycle of rituals based on the growing season may begin to lose meaning for a people who no longer depend on agriculture, but have become largely a population of wage earners.

Modern conveniences save backbreaking toil. Eight settlements have accepted electricity and five have access to telephones. Nearly all households have radios, some powered by batteries. Television antennas sprout from a score of homes. The old isolation has begun to fade.

Most Hopis, I found, are in deep doubt about where to draw the line between hallowed teachings and hurrying technology. Different points of view generate dissent within the tribe.

"We must hold fast to our covenant with the Great Spirit and stand guardian over land and life," said a spokesman for one faction on the reservation. "The *bahana*, the white man, invents all kinds of things. If we accept too many, these will bring trouble, maybe destruction."

Setting out to fetch water, Hopi boys urge their burro toward the nearest source, a small spring at the foot of the mesa. Of 13 villages, only 4 have running water. Some Hopis reject this modern convenience, and carry household water, as their ancestors did.

In the half-light of dawn, Myron Polequaptewa drives his sheep through tumbleweed and juniper toward a well two miles from his corral. The 74-year-old Polequaptewa, a leader in Old Oraibi and a shepherd since the age of 12, finds contentment on the reservation, but laments that "our young people are not interested in herding or farming anymore."

NATIONAL GEOGRAPHIC PHOTOGRAPHER WINFIELD PARKS

"We too want to follow the Hopi way," asserted Jean Fredericks, chairman of the Tribal Council which 9 of the 13 villages have joined. "Without our beliefs we would have no identity. But we also feel that each Hopi must find a place for himself in the modern world."

The modern world seemed far away the morning I went with Don Talayesva to his fields. He set to work grubbing weeds that would steal precious moisture from his corn, beans, and watermelons. The sun shone hot on his face, bronzed from more than 50 years of working there in what seems a waterless wasteland.

Hopi farmers choose fields with care. Don's plot nestles on the banks of a wash, or watercourse, formed by the runoff that pours from the mesa during rains. Only by farming such a floodplain, or a field fed by a spring, could Don find moisture enough for his crops in a region with an average precipitation of only 8 to 12 inches a year.

Noting a gap in a row of cornstalks, he beckoned me over. "Want to see how we plant our corn?" I nodded. Dropping to his knees, he gouged a hole in the sandy soil with a metal bar.

"Use a narrow bar so you don't disturb much soil," Don explained. "All right. Dig down six inches, not more, not less. Shallow enough so the seeds sprout. Deep enough so the kangaroo rat doesn't get them." He dropped 12 kernels into the hole, then scooped sand over them.

Next Don placed a crumpled tin can on the windward side of the planting as a windbreak to shield the seedlings when they sprout. During my stay on the reservation, I saw many Hopi fields pockmarked with cans and other debris, unlovely but efficient.

Corn, long the basic Indian crop in the Southwest, remains the staple of Hopi diet. Mutton may join corn on the dinner table; a number of older Hopis still run sheep across the scrubland that stretches from the foot of the mesa. Today, 5,640 sheep and goats share with 3,370 cattle the 624,000 acres of meager pasturelands on the Hopi reservation.

Dawn barely brightened the sky the morning that I helped Myron Polequaptewa untie the gate of his stone corral, allowing 110 sheep to

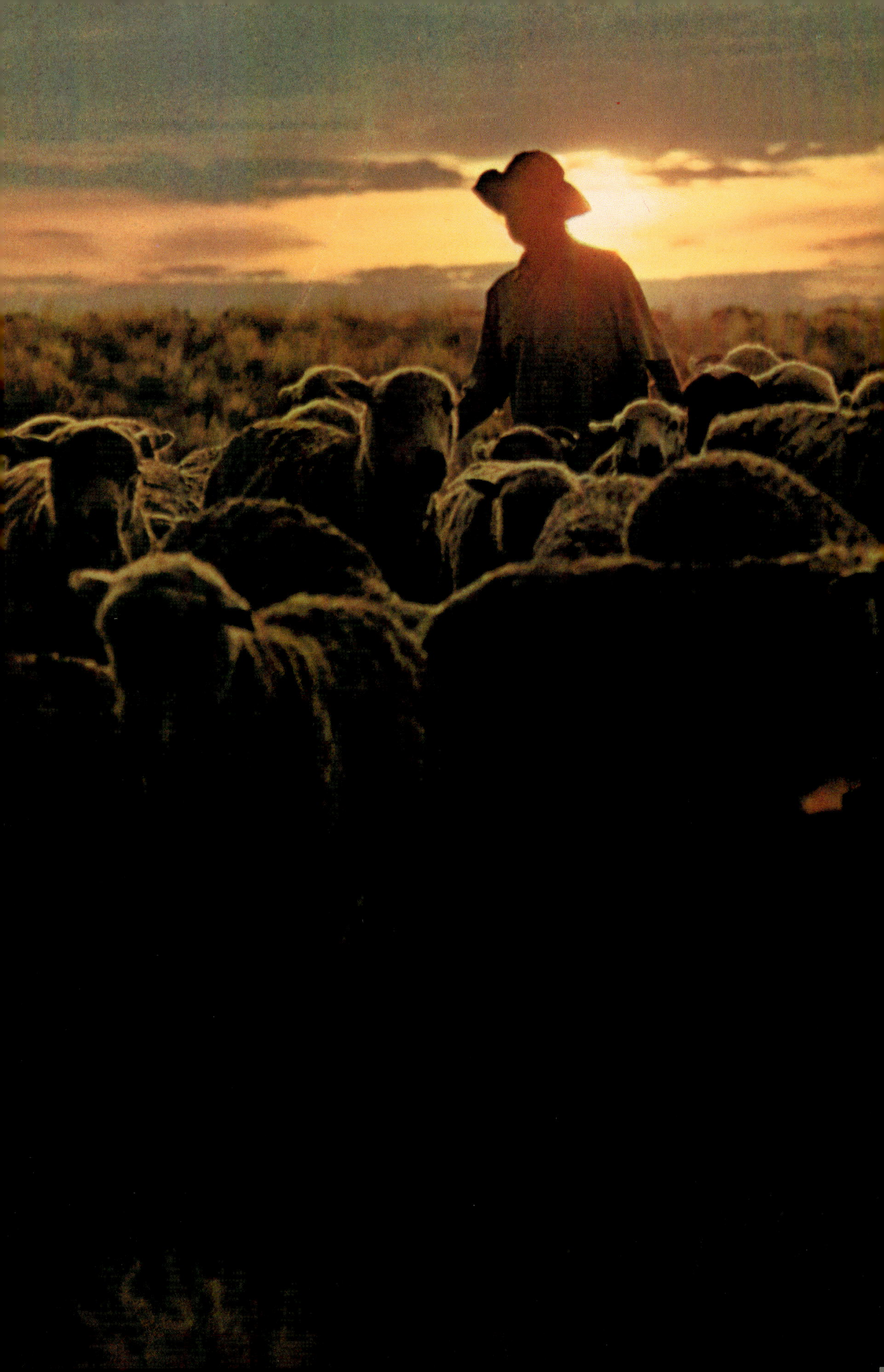

cascade onto the olive-green rangeland. With the practiced skill of a herder more than half a century on the range, Myron trotted from one side of the flock to the other, clapping his hands and hissing to guide his herd two miles to a windmill-fed watering trough.

"The government put in this well for us ten years ago," Myron said. "Before that I had to drive my sheep eight miles to Oraibi Wash to give them a drink—if there was any water.

"Our young people are not interested in herding or farming anymore," Myron said, shaking his head.

The same thought was echoed by Samuel Shing, portly leader from Upper Moenkopi, a Hopi village that lies 21 miles outside the reservation. "When I was a boy, people raised their own food and gave no thought to money. Now they buy groceries at the store. Our children would rather take a job in Tuba City, Winslow, or Flagstaff than farm. Old people die—then nobody works the fields anymore."

But some of the old arts, I found, flourish in spite of the influx of bahana goods. The nimble-fingered women who make Hopi pottery and basketry have bridged the gap from shaping utensils for the family to fashioning articles for trade.

Artisans on the mesa look forward to their crafts exhibit at the Museum of Northern Arizona in Flagstaff on the Fourth of July, when the city holds its All-Indian Pow Wow. During the 1968 exhibit, thousands of visitors crowded onto the museum's sunlit patio, buying all but a few of the hundreds of items created by 250 Hopi artisans. Dr. Harold S. Colton, 87, founder of the museum, recalled that the Hopis had all but stopped making pots and baskets when he and his wife staged their first exhibit in 1930.

"But we did find several Hopi silversmiths imitating Navajo designs. I told them if they would create authentic Hopi designs, the museum would buy all they produced." With the encouragement of Dr. and Mrs. Colton, two Hopi teachers did something about it. Artist Fred Kabotie helped adapt old Hopi designs and silversmith Paul Saufkie helped the young men turn them into jewelry, bringing a resurgence to the art.

Education leads the youth of Black Mesa in new directions. Two generations ago the parents of school-age youngsters were reluctant to allow their children to go to the "white man's school."

Now most of the adults concede that they would be poorly equipped for the modern world if they spoke no English and knew no arithmetic. Consequently, they permit their sons and daughters to go to school and learn a trade. In 1967, more than 870 children trooped off each morning to the five reservation elementary schools, and some 550 of their older brothers and sisters left the reservation to study. Aided by grants and scholarships, 102 Hopis also attended college last year.

Some parents have mixed feelings as their offspring leave the reservation for school. They wonder: Will the youth ever be content to return?

The reservation offers few jobs. But the pull of the homeland and the old religion remains strong, and the young men usually take the jobs that keep them closest to the reservation so that they may return to visit their families and take part in the ceremonies.

Twenty-five years ago, Helen and Loki Tewa moved to Flagstaff, but

TERRY EILER

Kachina figures symbolize the spirits of the dead, and all the invisible forces of life that stand at the heart of Hopi beliefs. The Kachinas, Hopis say, visit the pueblos in the guise of masked dancers, bringing rain and abundant crops and carry messages and prayers to the gods. Below stand Kachina dolls, foot-tall wood carvings meant not for play but to familiarize children with the appearance of the spirits. At left, a clay wind chime and the design on a plaque of coiled yucca fibers represent mudheads—witty Kachinas who bestow the blessing of laughter.

183

they have kept their family home on the reservation. There they returned for the ceremonial naming of their daughter's new baby. I was invited to witness the event.

The plaza lay dim in the dawn as an elderly aunt, accompanied by the mother, Lorrinda Kay, carried the infant from the house. Slowly, reverently, the aunt raised the infant toward the east, presenting her for the first time to the life-giving sun. She said a prayer, asking the Sun God to set this child on the Hopi road of life.

Like all Hopis, the baby was born into one of more than 30 tribal clans. Dozens of relatives and fellow members of her Eagle clan envelop her with warmth and love. And they will educate her in the Hopi way. To be *kahopi* (un-Hopi) is the worst of conditions. The Hopi seeks happiness and security within clan and tribe.

SOME PEOPLE MIGHT CALL Hopi child-rearing permissive. Young children play with almost no supervision. They are not even required to come home for meals, although they usually do. But by the age of six or seven a boy is helping his father work in the field and fetching wood for the ovens, and a girl is tending her younger brothers and sisters and learning to cook.

Once, all the children could be disciplined by the So'yoko Kachina and a band of masked ogres, who went from house to house, ferreting out wayward children and reciting details of each misdemeanor: stealing fruit from a tree, failing to do a household chore. For such sins, the ogres threatened to carry the child away and eat him.

When the youngster appeared penitent, his parents would try to ransom him by offering the Kachinas food. The ogres would stand unmoved, and the child might offer a small gift to please them. Finally, the mother would offer up a sweet cake, piki, or a basket of cornmeal. Then the Kachinas would agree to leave—after the child had promised never to misbehave again. Today, So'yoko and the disciplinarians visit most of the villages.

Economic as well as social change marches across Black Mesa. In 1964 the tribe's leaders allowed oil companies to explore their land. No oil has gushed as yet, but $3,247,790 paid for the leases has poured into the Hopi treasury. The tribe also receives royalties from a strip coal mine on the reservation and plans to develop a crafts center combined with a restaurant and a motel.

Inexorably, the world crowds in on Hopi villages. The unhurried tempo of the ageless Kachina dance gives way to the urgent throb of modern life.

"No one can control the passage of time," Emory Sekaquaptewa said. A college graduate, he is executive director of the Tribal Council. "Hopi prophecy, you know, tells us that one day we will wake up in the morning and find ourselves in the midst of the white man."

Aura of timelessness and serenity pervades the village of Walpi, moved to the mesa top at the end of the 17th century. Isolated on their arid land, the Hopis remained remarkably unchanged as a developing country passed them by. Today, Walpi stands as a living relic, where some 100 Indians hold on to the traditions and values of the past.

NATIONAL GEOGRAPHIC PHOTOGRAPHER WINFIELD PARKS

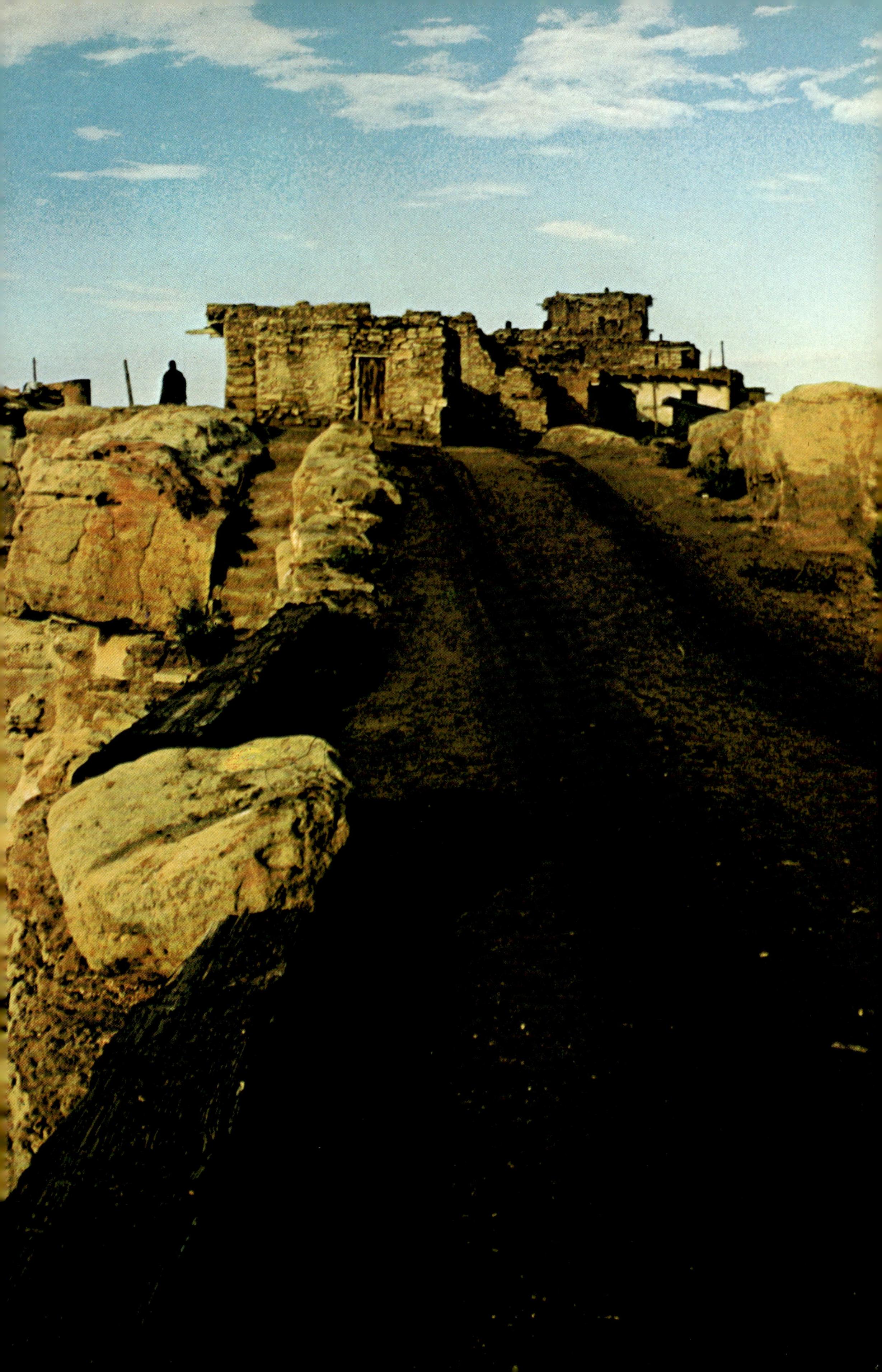

10

New Guinea's Fierce Asmat: A Heritage of Headhunting

By FATHER ALPHONSE SOWADA, O.S.C.

SWAMPS! Jungles! Mud! Headhunters! With a feeling of apprehension, I stood on the deck of the small Dutch cargo vessel *Letong*, bobbing dangerously on its way across the treacherous Arafura Sea along the southwest shore of New Guinea. As the ship approached Flamingo Bay, the wind tossed patches of foam over the mahogany water. Through a blanket of hot, dank air, I could see the Asmat coast, a vast mud plain with jungle growth of huge trees imprisoned in the tangle of vines.

Inland, not far beyond those trees, I knew men lived who had taken the heads of their enemies in battle or in ambush, eaten their flesh, and then used their skulls as pillows. These same people had a deep and obsessive fear of their ancestors' spirits and wore some part of a forebear's skeleton to ward off his ghost—a skull as a huge pendant, a vertebra on a necklace, or some other bone as a nose ornament.

For centuries these Asmat cannibals, Papuans whose forefathers migrated from Southeast Asia, had linked their pride, manhood, art, and religious rites to headhunting. How much, I wondered, had the coming of outsiders changed all that?

Suddenly an opening broke the monotony of the jungle wall, and I caught my first glimpse of the little town of Agats, its buildings set on poles and roofed with corrugated metal. On their stilt legs, with doorways and windows gaping seaward, the houses looked like mammoth spiders patiently awaiting their prey.

Not long after the *Letong* anchored at Agats, headquarters for the Roman Catholic mission, I set out on a 50-mile journey with Father Frank Pitka up the Northwest River for the twin villages of Saowa and Erma. Although no outsider before me had ever settled permanently in either village, members of my order, the Crosier Fathers, had made trips there and had told the people of my coming. Crocodiles slid off the riverbank as our boat passed by. The "chug chug" of the motor startled

Paddling their dugout toward a favorite fishing area, Asmat men and their wives glide down the Ewta River, near New Guinea's southwest coast. The women will drag woven-bark nets for catfish and share the catch with relatives, among them warriors who have taken human heads and eaten the flesh of victims in religious rituals.

JOHN SCOFIELD, NATIONAL GEOGRAPHIC STAFF

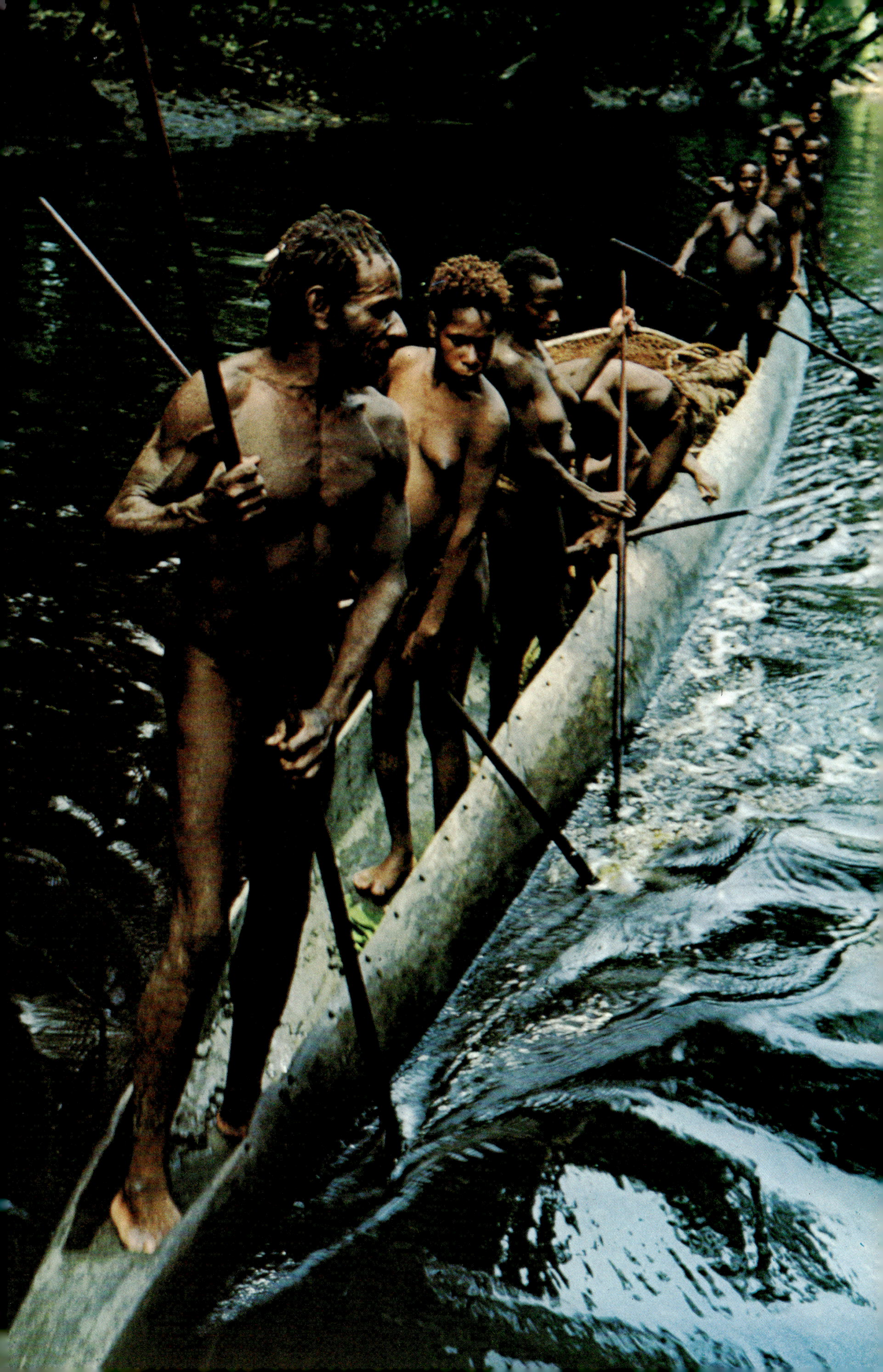

flamingos searching for crayfish and lizards on the mud flats. Occasionally, a cockatoo flew off, screeching at the sight of our craft.

As we neared the villages, I saw dugouts filled with firewood, coconuts, bananas, and fish. A family—husband, wife or wives, and children—rode in each dugout. Naked except for woven armbands that held bone daggers, the men stood at the prows of the boats and paddled. The women, wearing aprons of grass drawn between their legs and tied to plaited belts, rowed in unison with their husbands.

I soon saw a row of houses along each bank of the river; we had arrived at Saowa and Erma. The thatched huts, resting on thin poles, stood more than four feet off the ground.

After bidding Father Pitka farewell, I went to the hut of Saati, eldest of the elders, and a man who had gained great prestige from his success as a headhunter during his younger days. I climbed a notched log, the

Mock battle to honor visitors rages between spear-wielding warriors. In a continuous cycle of warfare and revenge, men once preyed on villages or attacked from ambush in head-hunting raids. The Asmat referred to the flesh of victims as maneowé—"our food." At right, a father carries a bag of woven grass to hold tobacco, fishhooks, and matches; if worn on his chest during important ceremonies, it would identify him as a great headhunter.

JOHN SCOFIELD, N.G.S. STAFF (ABOVE) AND MICHAEL
ROCKEFELLER, COURTESY MUSEUM OF PRIMITIVE ART

stairway to the floor of the hut, knocked, and identified myself in the Keendok dialect of the Asmat language I had learned after I arrived in Agats. From inside, a deep voice told me to enter. Saati, sitting naked and cross-legged in the center of the hut, immediately arose and commanded me to sit on his mat as he began to don a well-worn pair of short trousers. He sat down facing me and recrossed his legs. Without saying a word, he rummaged through a bag of woven grass hanging by a strap from his neck and removed a hollowed-out pig bone about an inch in diameter and finely engraved with an intricate design.

Saati moistened his forefinger with spittle, then moved the finger to and fro through a hole in the septum of his nose, and, with a sigh of satisfaction, placed the pig bone in the hole. Thereupon he solemnly appraised me and announced, "Pastor, I welcome you to remain with us. The people wish you to stay. Our village is good. We possess abundant sago palms, fish, wild boar, cassowary birds, rats, sago grubs, snakes, and much jungle fruit. These we will give you, but also we would like to share what you have, especially tobacco."

I THANKED HIM profusely, and handed him a piece of tobacco. As he slowly rolled it into a nipa-palm leaf, I looked about his home. Three women, Saati's wives, sat nearby, each tending a fire. Close to the main wife's fireplace hung Saati's hourglass-shaped drum. Its head of lizard skin had been glued with a mixture of lime and human blood. On the rafters I saw Saati's bow and arrows. His spears and two shields looked as if they had been long in disuse. Elsewhere lay fishing nets and traps, two stone axes and a metal one, paddles, carrying bags, bamboo water containers, and huge chunks of sago, a starchy food staple made of pulp taken from the heart of sago palm. I turned to Saati and started to praise the craftsmanship of his arrows and drum.

"Woman, fire!" he shouted abruptly. Quickly his second wife brought a burning piece of wood, and Saati ignited his tobacco. "Woman, prepare sago and other things."

Later I realized why Saati had interrupted me. To praise an Asmat's property equals requesting it. The owner must give it away to avoid the stigma of a stingy man.

The principal wife removed a huge hunk of pasty white sago from the loft. She broke off two pieces, poured a little water over them, and gently rolled them on her thigh. After she had formed two almost perfect spheres, she placed them on the hot coals of her fireplace. When the sago turned a brownish black, she offered the first portion to Saati, and the other to me. As we ate, Saati's wife took a number of lively sago grubs from a leaf container, placed them on spits, roasted them, and served them to us.

The Asmat share what they have with a visitor. They consider it an insult to send a person away empty-handed. Fellow villagers would call such a selfish person *mban doso ipir,* a man with a putrid hand. How rude we westerners must have seemed to the Asmat when we arrived with all sorts of goods yet did not divide them among the people. A man, if he possesses, shares; but he also realizes that at sometime or other he will receive something in return.

After we ate, Saati invited me to see his longhouse, one of the 11

Grisly relics shield an Asmat from ancestral spirits—still an obsessive fear among some of his people. His mother's skull protects him from her ghost; her vertebra forms part of a necklace. He carries a dagger of human bone in his woven armband and wears two pig-tusk armlets, one for each human head he has taken.

JOHN SCOFIELD, NATIONAL GEOGRAPHIC STAFF

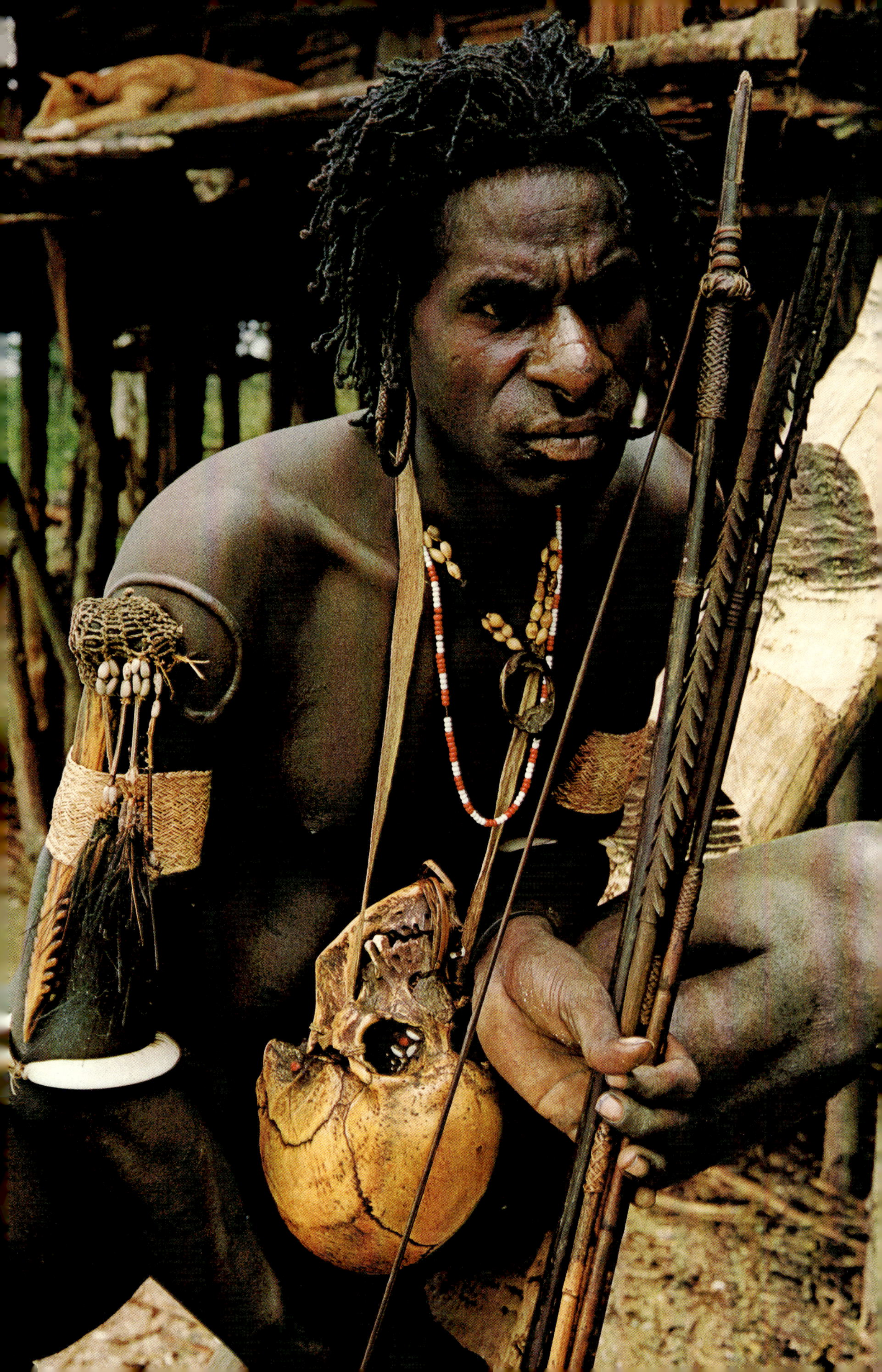

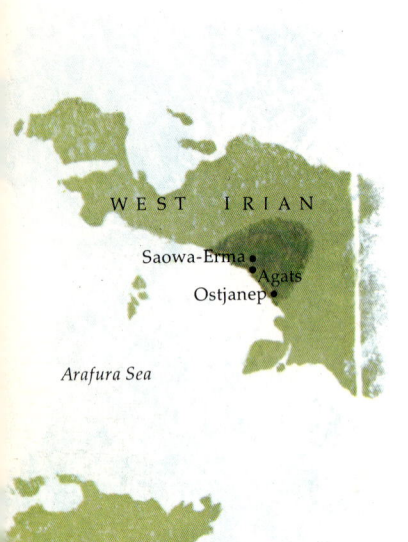

A wilderness of mud, mangrove swamps, gloomy rain forests, and crocodile-infested rivers locked the Asmat in a nightmare of headhunting, black magic, and fear. Until November 1954, when the Dutch administration established a permanent post at the village of Agats, in southwestern New Guinea, the Asmat dedicated themselves to a cult that appeased the spirits of the dead and demanded rites of revenge. Headhunting served their religion, governed their lives, and inspired extraordinary art. Administrative control, first by the Dutch and then by the Indonesians, effectively curbed the fierce raids and grisly practices. As these threads in Asmat religion were severed, the whole fabric of the traditional life of the people began to disintegrate, and today the old culture has virtually disappeared, preserved only in memories. Father Alphonse Sowada, a trained anthropologist who has lived among the Asmat since 1961, writes their story with sympathy and understanding as they make a desperate effort to catch up with the 20th century.

---

ceremonial centers for some 800 people of Erma. Saati's thatched longhouse, some 50 feet in length, contained nine fireplaces, each with one of its corner poles exquisitely carved with stylized ancestral figures. The fireplace at either end of the longhouse belonged to the oldest husbands and wives of the clan, who guarded and instructed the young married couples and children at the remaining fireplaces.

In the longhouse, children learned how to drum, dance, and sing, and heard the myths and stories of their people. It was the place where the Asmat wished to die, and where man was created. In the creation legend of the Saowa-Erma people, a mythological hero decided to populate the Asmat area. He went from river to river building longhouses and placing carved wooden figures, both male and female, inside. Then he beat upon his ceremonial drum, and brought them to life.

The Asmat believed that every longhouse on earth had an associated longhouse on the "other side," the spirit world where the ancestors live. Man, by continuously exchanging locations, kept membership relatively equal. If a longhouse on earth became overpopulated, some members would die. If the clan on the other side became too large, some would seek out clan women on earth to be reborn.

I soon familiarized myself with the daily routine of the Asmat. They arose before sunrise. Those out of food left the village with their children for the sago grounds, or went fishing. Normally, the men sat in groups, talking or fashioning hunting implements, and the women wove fishing nets, made sleeping mats, or cared for the small children. The young girls remained with the women to learn their skills, or to care for younger sisters and brothers. The boys formed into respective age groups from 6 to 16, to play or to hunt. But about noon, when the heat and humidity reached a peak, the village became quiet.

The people roused again about four in the afternoon and resumed their work or play until dark. Some men gathered again to continue their discussions; others played with small sons or daughters. Festivals, however, often broke the daily routine, and some ceremonies and feasts lasted for as long as three months.

Almost every major festival or religious ceremony once required the taking of a head. But the life of the Asmat started to change in 1955, when the Dutch began to suppress headhunting in a few villages. The

Still-wild Asmat wears a bone nose ornament, feathers, and face paint to frighten his enemies and give himself inner strength and courage. Warsékomen (lower), an Asmat elder, took at least nine heads before he abandoned his ceremonial life.

TONY SAULNIER AND
FATHER DAVID GALLUS, O.S.C. (LOWER)

Indonesians assumed control of the government in 1963 and continued to outlaw headhunting. They also prohibited feasts and the construction of longhouses.

The introduction of schools, alien values, and work programs upset the old order in which headhunting permeated all life and society. The Asmat believed that headhunting, and the cannibal feasts associated with it, appeased ancestral spirits and assured continued good health and fertility. It inspired elaborate wood carvings and became the fountainhead of prestige and authority.

No Asmat boy could cross the threshold into manhood without a complex initiation rite that lasted many days. The sacred ritual first demanded the taking of a head by his relatives, who often ambushed their victim. They decapitated him, skinned his head, and painted the skull with ash, ocher, and chalk. Then the boy sat with the skull between his legs to absorb the strength and courage of the dead man.

Afterward, the boy journeyed downriver in a dugout on a symbolic voyage to the "other side" with his father, uncles, and older brothers. On the trip, in a pantomime of death, the boy grew weaker and weaker; finally he lay motionless. To bring him back to life in a ritual rebirth, the men immersed the boy several times in water. Slowly he responded, and on the homeward trip he acted like a child, pretending to learn again the simple things his parents had taught him years before: how to stand and paddle a canoe, and the names of rivers, plants, and familiar landmarks.

Through the initiation ceremony the boy assumed all the powers of the dead person. In a sense he became the dead man, and even took his name. If he later traveled to the village of his namesake, the relatives of the victim addressed him as their father, brother, or uncle and treated him as if he actually were their departed kinsman. The Asmat learned the names of their intended victims through trickery or by earlier contact with people of other villages.

Ancestral spirits, especially the decapitated, demanded revenge. To remind themselves of their obligation, the Asmat carved figures of their ancestors on longhouse fireplace columns, prows of dugouts, memorial poles, and shields.

An Asmat gained prestige and authority through his achievements in war. No individual could wield any influence unless he had taken a few heads, and a truly accomplished headhunter enjoyed many privileges. A man could avoid heavy tasks through success in headhunting. He also won the admiration of women and assured his status on the "other side." A man could marry even though he had not obtained a head, but his wife would ridicule him as a *ndese nimfi,* a worthless hunk of flesh. Understandably, the man either separated from her or, in a fit of frenzy, found a victim.

Today the majority of the Asmat seem ashamed when questioned about past headhunting exploits. Many times I urged Saati to tell me how many heads he had collected, and he always replied, "I have never killed a man." I knew this had to be false because of the high

Overleaf: Children splash near dugouts—the Asmat's only means of transportation—hollowed by craftsmen with fire and stone axes.

TONY SAULNIER

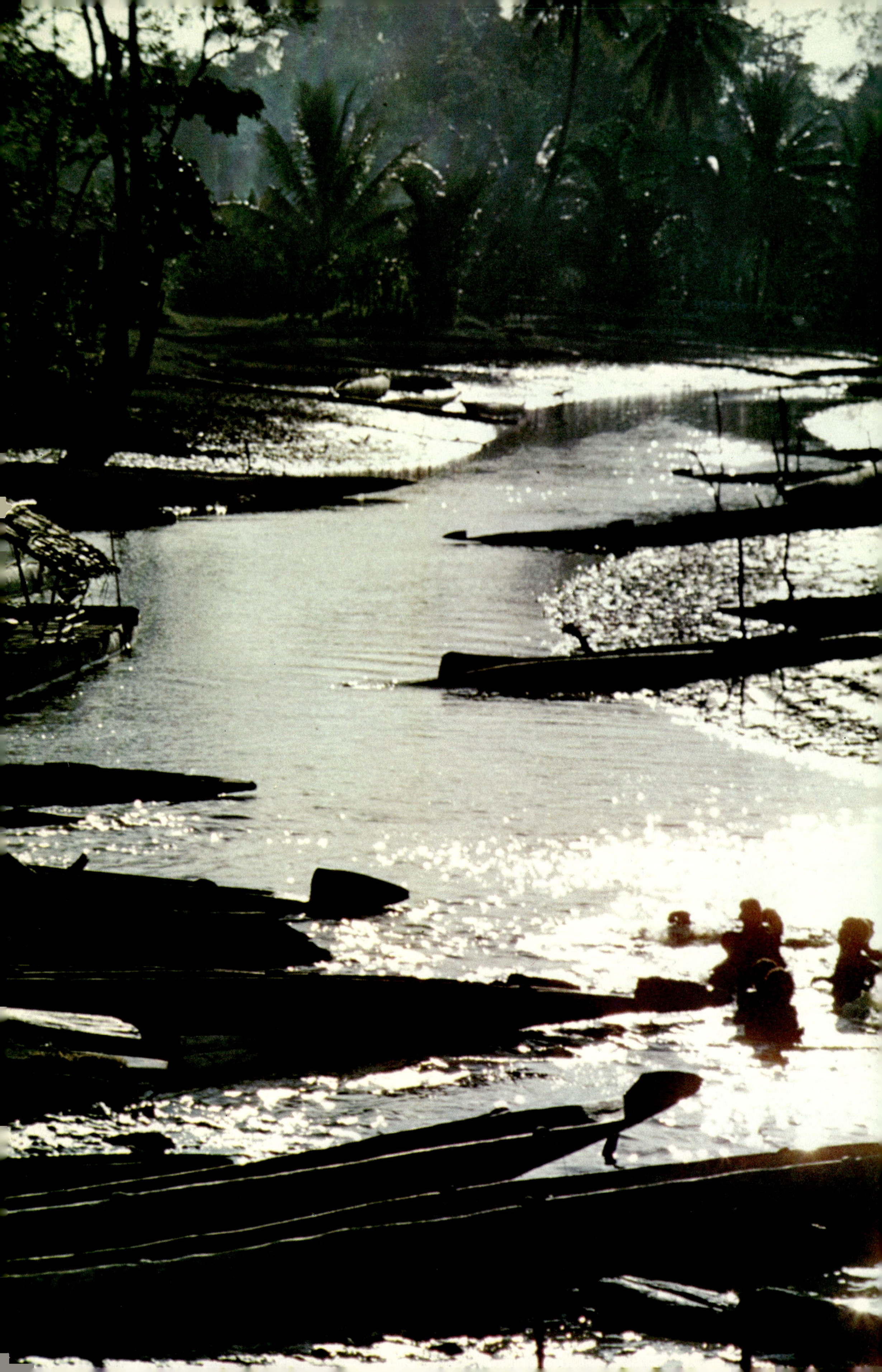

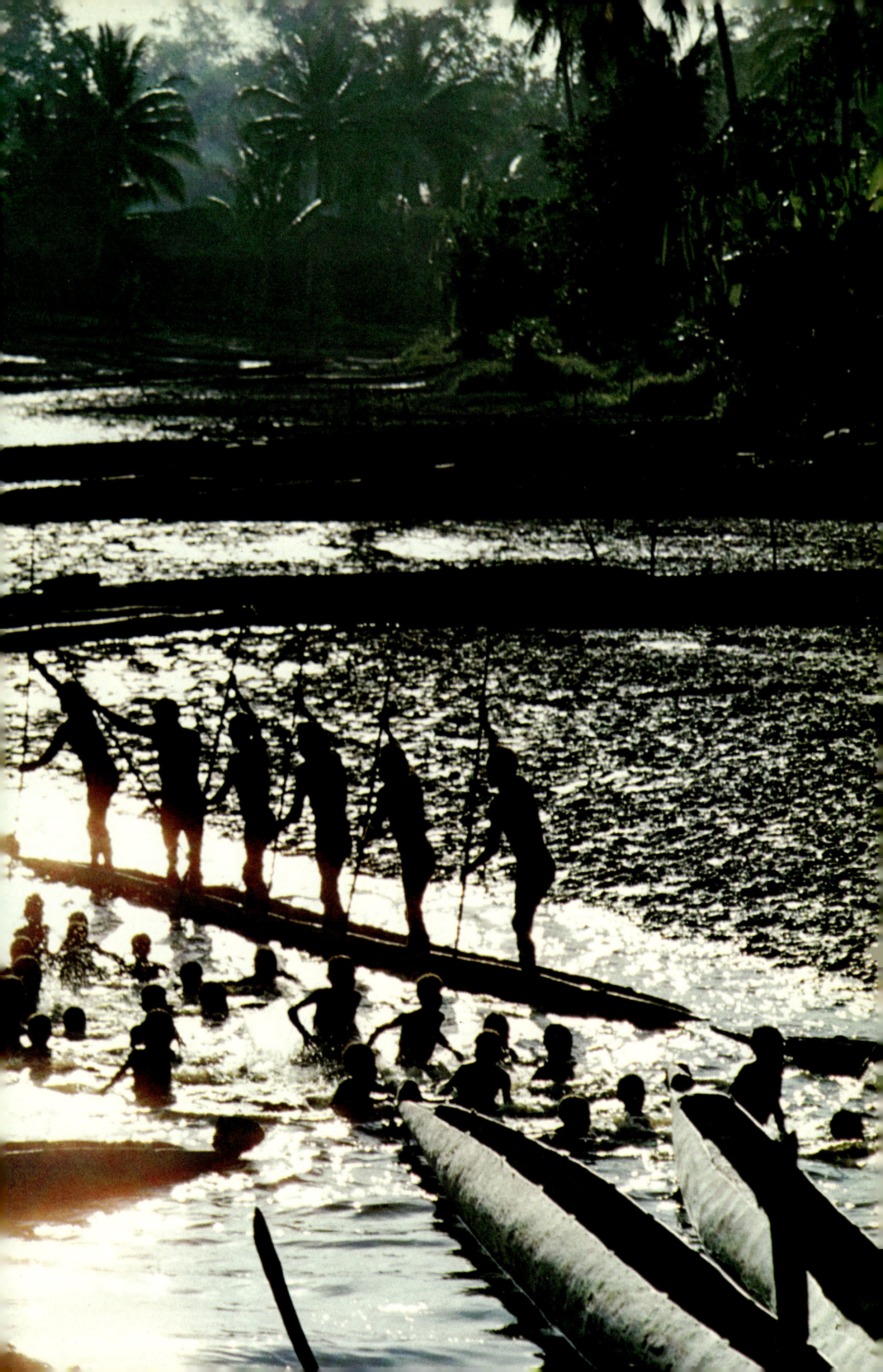

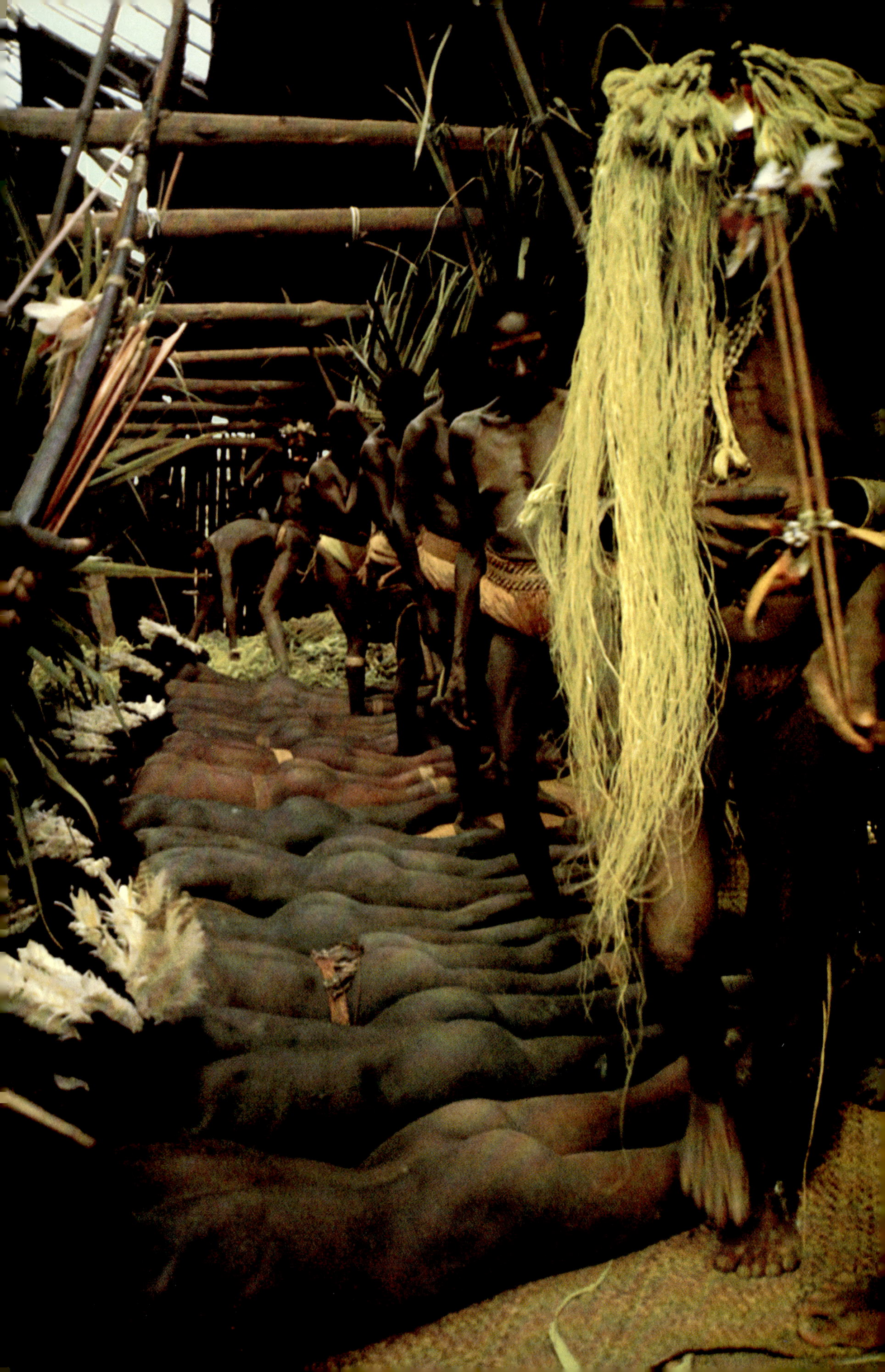

prestige Saati enjoyed. One day I called him over and confidently said, "Now I know how many heads you have taken in your expeditions—35!" I indicated the amount by showing my fingers and toes for the number 20, then his fingers and toes to make the number 35. Saati reacted abruptly. "No, not that many," he shouted, "only this many!" The fingers and toes totaled 17.

IN THE MISSION SCHOOL at Erma, we have taught the children of Saati's village to count in a different fashion from their elders. The youngsters readily accepted school, where teachers emphasized basic skills and gardening in the hope that the Asmat would begin to grow their own food instead of gathering it in the forests.

Girls attended class beyond the age at which marriages had been arranged by their parents in the past. After leaving school, some strongly opposed the preplanned marriages, completely baffling their elders. One indignant father complained, "The girls are stubborn, hardheaded, and disobedient! In the old days a woman knew her place. Now they are shameless. Before, a woman walked down the village path with her head bowed. Today, these females cast their eyes all over the place, at this man, at that one, at all of them! Unprincipled, shameless things!"

"Since the females have changed so, perhaps you might let them marry the boys they like," I cautiously suggested to one of the men.

"Impossible!" he responded. "Why? Deipir, my son, many years ago married the daughter of Tokonomok. Now Tokonomok's son needs a wife. If my daughter does not consent to remain with Tokonomok's boy, Deipir's wife will become angry, also her family, and she may leave my son." Later, the daughter reluctantly agreed to the marriage.

Many girls endured parental criticism—some for more than two years—before gaining their own way or finally succumbing to adult and social pressure. If a girl married as she wished, her kin had to patch up severed ties, either by searching for another bride for the insulted boy or by paying out a considerable amount in reparations to dampen the anger of the boy's family.

TONY SAULNIER

Trailing streamers of coconut fiber, a woman rises in a ritual of rebirth, a ceremony that will seal a peace pact between two hostile villages. Each warring Asmat clan adopted a man and woman from the other as a gesture of goodwill. In a symbolic re-enactment of their birth, among members of both villages, the two couples crawled over the backs of men and through the legs of women. A reborn man at right mimics the sleep of infancy.

Elaborately carved ancestor poles lie in the village of Ostjanep. Made from fully grown mangrove trees, each represents a pledge of revenge for a dead kinsman killed by enemies or evil spirits. Some craftsmen add tiny dugouts near the feet of the figures, symbolizing soul ships that carry a spirit to the afterlife across the sea. At right, wood carvers decorate battle shields with stylized figures of the cannibalistic praying mantis, an important religious motif that occurs often in Asmat art. Government authorities outlawed wood carving because of its close association with headhunting. Michael Rockefeller, collecting works for New York's Museum of Primitive Art, photographed the large wooden head (opposite) in a small village not far from the area where he disappeared in 1962. Search parties found no trace of the young anthropologist.

TONY SAULNIER (BELOW), ADRIAN GERBRANDS (LEFT), AND MICHAEL ROCKEFELLER

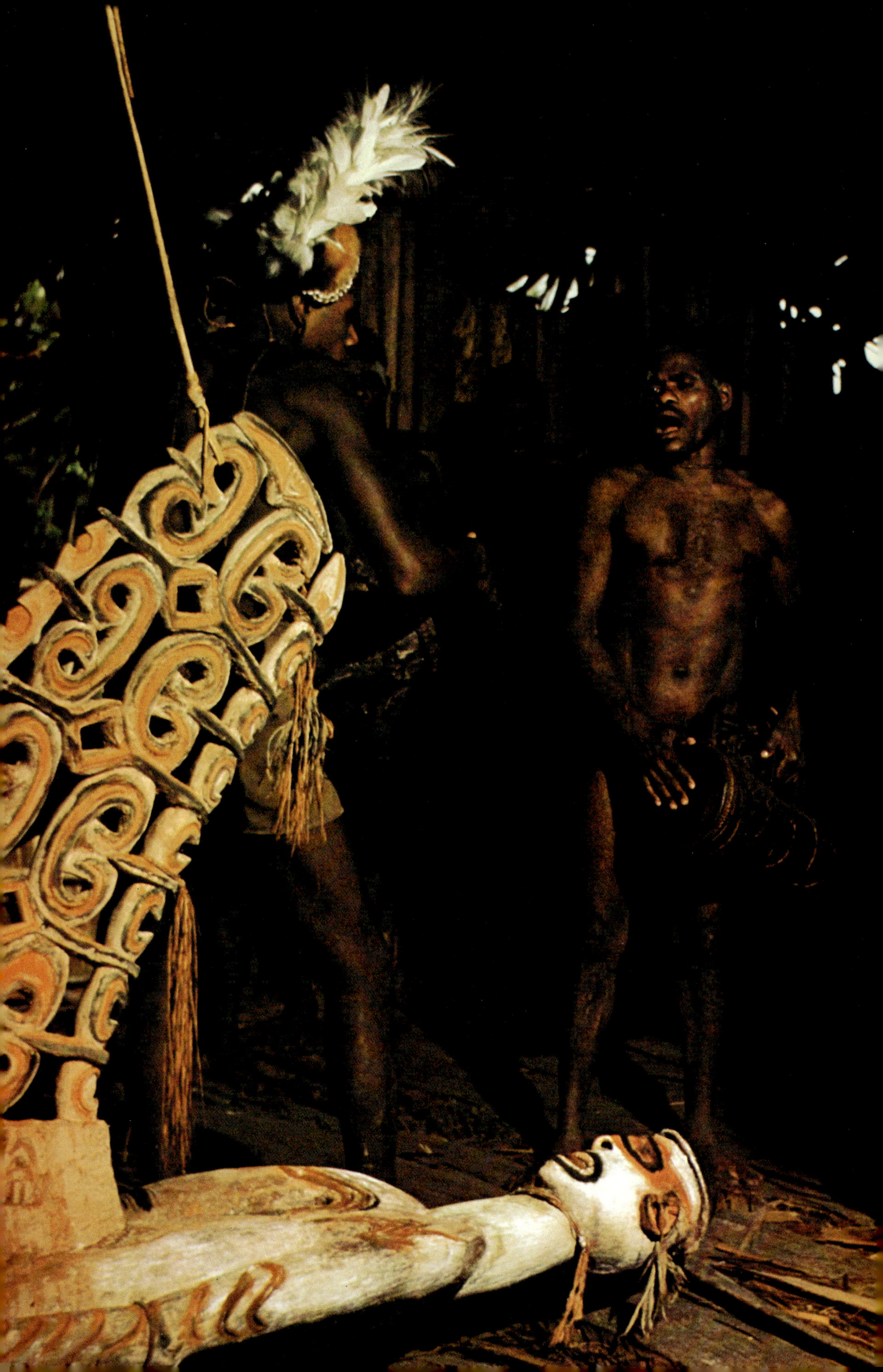

Fear of ancestral spirits and malevolent magic have terrified the Asmat. A man did not die of a disease—he died because he ignored the ghosts of forebears, or he fell victim to sorcery. A person struck by pneumonia or amoebic dysentery seldom recovered; the Asmat saw him as someone doomed to pass away. But with the advent of modern medicine, most of the afflicted lived on. This created the villagers' first doubts about magic, and a guarded respect for medicine.

*I*N MY EARLY DAYS at Erma, Saati and others had told me that drugs— even the most powerful—could not counteract malevolent magic. Once under the spell, the victim "carried it around" until it produced death. No one could name a person who had survived its ravages.

Normally the older Asmat women possess the power of creating black magic. A woman sits quietly and meditates in an area behind her home, and at some point she may determine that she needs the aid of a companion. Men explained to me that the efforts of two or even three women together are better than those of one. The men had not learned all the ingredients for the potent mixture, but they knew some: dog's tooth and liver, snake's tooth and head, pig's hoof, bird's beak, frog's eye, man's hair and nail parings. In proper sequence, the sorceress combines all or a selection of these in a small grass bag that she hides in the thatch of her house to "ripen." Meanwhile, the malevolent power seeps into an imaginary arrow also in the bag. The female avenger patiently awaits the proper moment to inflict the magic on the victim, for sooner or later he must pass her home, and when he does, she shoots him with the invisible arrow. The news soon spreads, and the victim, hypnotized by fear, dies within a day, a week, or a month.

Dekes, a healthy man of about 25, had worked every day sawing lumber at a project started by the mission for the Asmat. One morning when he failed to report, I asked his whereabouts.

"He is sick," one of the men told me. "Very likely he will not be coming to work again."

"Why? What ails him?" I inquired.

"Dekes was inflicted with *aro pok* [black magic] yesterday afternoon," he replied as he turned away.

I immediately walked toward Dekes's hut; as I neared it, I heard his female relatives wailing the death chant. When I climbed into the house, I found Dekes lying on a mat, immobile, and deaf to my shouts. I began to slap his face, and soon his eyes fluttered open. I sat him up, rolled him some tobacco, and ordered him to smoke it. Then I told him to follow me. I pointed to the lumberyard and commanded, "Now work; your sickness is gone." Dekes complied without any ill effects, much to the surprise, I'm sure, of some of his fellow villagers.

On another occasion I asked Paulus Pamup whether he still believed in magic.

"No, I am already Christian," he explained.

"Pamup," I said, "What are your notions on baptism? What do other people think of it?"

Pamup thought for a few moments. Then he said, "Pastor, we all want baptism. It gives us great strength; it protects us. Before, we received a head name which made us strong, but now we get baptism."

Near a freshly carved ancestor pole inside a ceremonial longhouse, two Asmat warriors pound hourglass-shaped drums, their heads of lizard skin glued on with human blood and lime. Longhouses once served as social and religious centers. There children learned to drum, sing, and dance, and heard legends of their people.

MICHAEL ROCKEFELLER, COURTESY MUSEUM OF PRIMITIVE ART

Many of the Asmat today find themselves in a dilemma. They seriously doubt the old, but do not quite believe or trust the new. This creates a painful vacuum for them.

Once the people learned that they must work to get goods from the outside, most of them eagerly sought jobs. Initially, an Asmat would work a few days, receive his pay, and leave his job feeling completely satisfied. Whether one man worked six days, and another but a few hours, each man thought payment should be equal. "We both worked, didn't we?"

The Asmat believed strongly in equality. When we taught the schoolchildren to play soccer, the game invariably ended in a tie. Only after much prompting did the children learn to play to win the game. The spirit of competition soon began to infringe upon other aspects of Asmat culture. Every year the men of Erma built new dugouts, and each clan entered one of its canoes in a race. With gusto the expert rowers paddled their dugouts across the river, but they reached the opposite bank almost at the same instant. During one annual race, however, a dugout arrived two lengths ahead of the others. Such great consternation resulted among the people that they did not hold the event again.

WHEN I first introduced the project of hand-sawing ironwood logs into lumber, I made up crews of sawyers, adz men, and hand-planers. I even attempted to coax some of the prestigious men to join, but silence greeted me every time. Finally, one Asmat said, "I am an organizer. Others are free to work."

Once the project began, however, almost every male in the village gathered around, including the organizers. Work progressed at an extremely leisurely pace, but crews increased fourfold. On the third day, everyone demanded payment. I carefully pointed out that only those whose names I had previously inscribed in my book would receive pay after three weeks of work. When payday arrived, everyone demanded payment. Finally, after I went through hours of patient explanation, the original crews could work in peace. Soon other difficulties arose. After getting their pay—tobacco, a steel axhead, razor blades, nylon fishing line, a pair of shorts—the men felt obligated to divide their hard-earned items among relatives. "They ask. I am ashamed not to give," the workers told me. But as time went on, the men requested boxes with locks so that "others will not steal or admire the goods."

Prestige in the villages now goes to the responsible workers. They dress well, they possess the desirable skills, and the women admire them. Only this year, a man of Atsj, who not long ago had proudly hung skull trophies from the rafters of his house, explained to me, "When we headhunted we were in constant fear. We did not know when our wives and children would be killed. Then, the government and missionaries arrived in our land to stop that. Peace was much better. Still we felt empty. There was nothing to do. Now we produce wood, which makes us happy again."

It is a pleasure to see the Asmat with carpenter tools in his hand finding satisfaction and a new purpose in life. However, the valiant headhunter, a man like Saati, gripping his bow and arrows, totally bewildered, presents a picture that elicits the profoundest sympathy.

Somber and forlorn, an Asmat evokes the dilemma of his people: With their centuries-old headhunting culture denounced as wrong and evil, they face an age with no place for plumes and war paint, symbols of a way of life that newcomers to the Asmat jungle home have abolished.

TONY SAULNIER

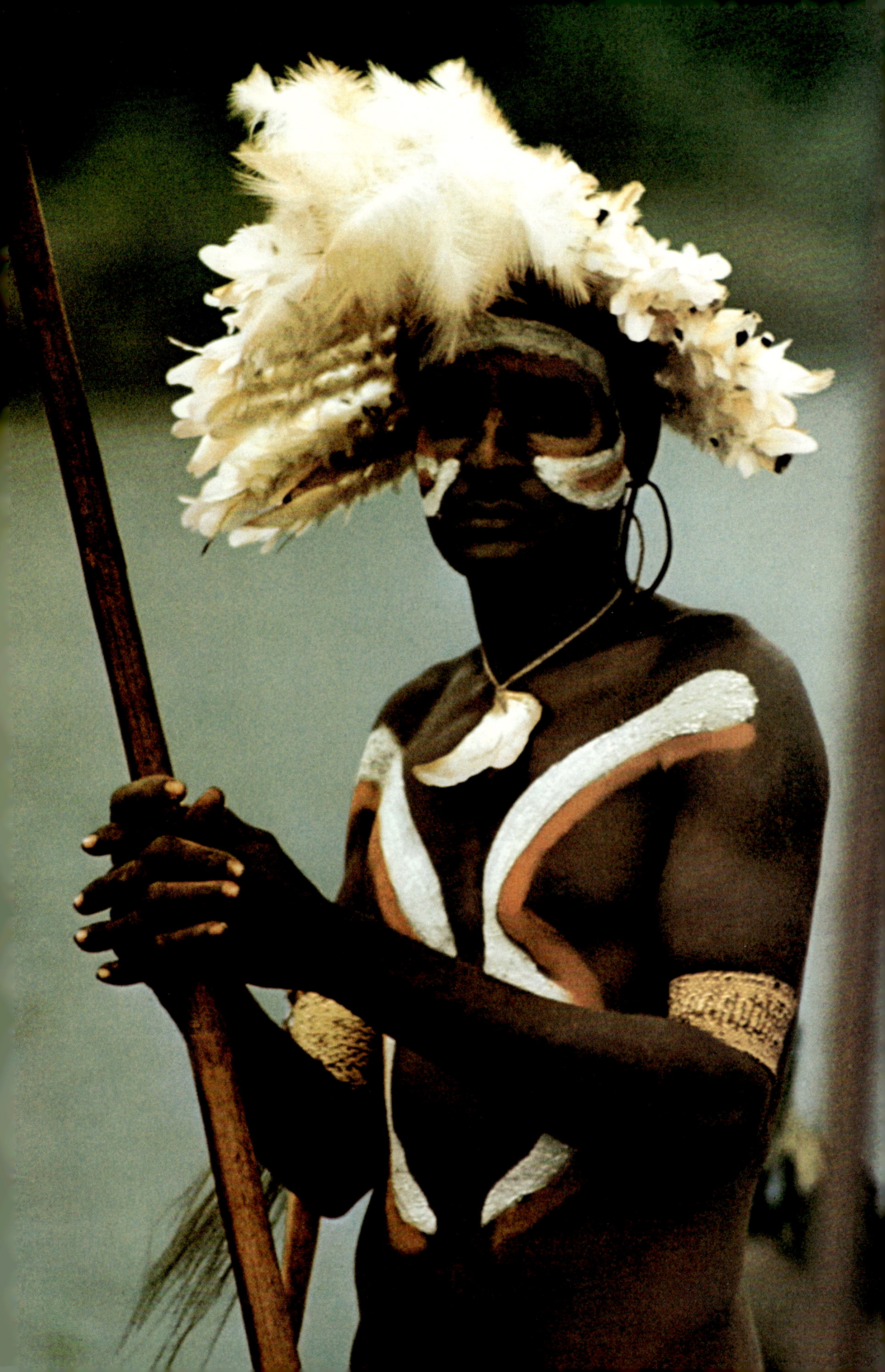

Index

Illustrations references appear in *italics*.

Afghanistan 23
Africa, peoples of: Biras *12*; Bushmen 58-75; Danakils *10-11*; Elmolos *12, 13*; Hadzas 29, 32
Agats, West Irian, New Guinea 186, *192*; map *192*
Agriculture: Ainu 95, *106-107, 108*,112; Asmat 197; Badaga *78-79*, 80; Danakil *11*; Hadza 32; Hopi *176, 177*, 180, 182; Kota 88; Kraho 152; Lua *30-31*; Naga 32; Suyá *168*; Waurá *164*
Ainu 92-112; agriculture 95, *106-107, 108*, 112; clothing *92-93*, 97, *98-99*, 103, 108, *108-109*; dancing *94*, 97, *98-99*; elders 92, *94*, 96, *102-103*, 103, 110-111; fishing 112; food 97, *100*; houses 92, *100-101*, 103; Japanese influence 104, 108, 112, *112*; language 104; legends 95, *96-97, 99, 104-108*; marriage customs 103; medicine 103-104, *111*; number of 92, 95, 97; origin 95, 97, 99; physical characteristics 92, 95, 97, 99; rituals 92, *94*, 95, 96, 97, *102-103*, 103-104, *110-111*; tattooing 96, 103, *113*; trade 108, *109*
Airplane, impact of 26, 29, *34, 141, 146, 150*, 161, 164
Akan, lake, Hokkaido *110-111*; map *97*
Akan National Park, Hokkaido *99*
All-Indian Pow Wow, Flagstaff, Arizona 182
Altar, bear-skull *95*,97, 103
Amazon, river, South America 161; map *160*
Amazons, Jamarikumá, myth of the 166
Amnodr, Toda afterworld *84*
Amulets: Ainu 97; Eskimo 145
Anaconda, snake *154-155*
Ancestor poles 193, *198-200*
Ancestral spirits 25, 186, *190*, 192, 193, 201
Angakok, shaman 145
Animal spirits 96, 97, 103, *111, 134*, 138
Apaches 32, 34
Arafura Sea 114, 186; map *192*
Arawak language 164
Armbands, hide *59*; pig-tusk *191*; woven 188, *191*
Arnhem Land, Australia 114, *119*, 121, 122, 124, *126, 127, 129*; map *119*
Arnøy, island, Norway 40, *46*, 55, *55*; map *43*
Art, examples of: Asmat *192, 198-199, 200*; Australian Aborigines *117, 126-127, 128-129*; Cheyenne *16*; Japanese *93, 102-103, 108-109*; Kafir *15*; Tibetan *33*
Asmat 186-203; art 192, *192, 198-199, 200*; black magic *192*, 201; cannibalism 186, 193; Christianity 201; clans 192, *197*; clothing 188, 190; daily routine 192; equality *202*; food *186*, 188, 190, 192, 197; generosity of 190, 202; headhunting 186, *189, 192*, 192-193, 197, *198*, 202; houses 188, 190; land of 186, map of West Irian *192*; language 190; longhouses 190-192, 193, *201*; marriage customs 193, 197; myths 192, *201*; religion 186, *186, 192, 192*, 193, *198, 201*; rituals 186,

193, *196, 197*; suppression of headhunting *192*, 192, 193, *198, 202*, 202; tools 190, *193, 202*; weapons *188-189*, 190, *191*, 199
Australia 11; map *119*
Australian Aborigines 114-131; art *117*, 121, 122, 124, *126-127, 128-129*, 130; circumcision ceremony 122; civilization, effect of *119*, 124, 127, 130; dances and songs 114, *116-117*, 119, 121, *126*, 127, 128; education 124, 127, 130; family bands *120*, 122, *123*, 127; fishing 122, 124, *124*; food 114, *119*, 122, *123*, 128; food gathering 122, 127-128; funeral customs *126-127*; history *119*, 122; hunting *119, 120*, 122, *123*, 127, 128; land of 114, *119, 120*, 121, 122, 127, 128; marriage customs 119, 124, 128; migration *119*; myths 114, *117, 119*, 119-121, *126, 128, 129*, 130; population *119, 130*; sacred boards 114, 121; sacred rituals 114, *117*, 119, 121, 122, *126, 127*, 130; shelters 124, 128; tools *119, 120-121, 127*; village councils 124

Badagas *76, 78*, 80, *83*, 90; agriculture *78-79*, 80; funeral customs 80; population 80
Bag, woven grass, neckpiece *189*, 190
Bamboo milk container *86*
Bantu people 58, *64*, 65, 74
Bark painting 124, *129*
Basket dance *126*
Basketry: Australian Aborigines 122, 124; Hopi 182; Kadazan *28*
Beads *26*;ostrich-eggshell *59*, 66
Bear Festival 97, *102-103*
Bears, skulls *95*, 97, 103
Beiju, cakes *165*, 166
Bells, belt of *166*
Berbers 23
Berndt, Catherine H. and Ronald M. 114, *119*
Bhutanese *35*
Bira woman *12*
Birth: ritual of rebirth 192, 193, *196, 197*
Black Mesa, Arizona *174-175*, 176, 182, 184
Black Wars (1804-1830) 12, 23
Blanket toss 138, *145*
Boards, sacred 114, 121
Bondo woman: Orissa, India *6*
Boomerangs *116, 119, 127*, 128
Boots: Eskimo 138, *146-147*; Lapp *42*, 43
Bow and arrows 12, 58, *60*, 64-65, *93, 94, 161, 166*, 168, *190, 191*; ceremonial 97; symbolic use 84, *89*
Bowl, lacquered 92, *102, 103*, 104
Brazil: Indians 152-169; map *160*
Buffalo, sacred 76, *78*, 81, *86*, 88, *90*; sacrifice of *84-85*
Bunun tribe, Taiwan 26
Bushmen 58-75; child rearing 67, 70; clothing 64, 65, 67, *75*; family bands *62-63*, 68, *72-73*; food *60-61*, 67, *72-73*; food gathering 58, *72*, *75*; headmen 70; history 58, *64*; hunting 58, *60-61*, 64-65, *72*; land of, *see* Kalahari;

language groups 65, 67; manhood, initiation into 70; marriage customs 67, 70; medicine 70, 74; migration *62-63*, 64; music and dance *59*, *70-71, 72*, 74; name giving 70; number of *64*; "ownership" *63*, 67, 70; origin 65; physical characteristics 64, 65, *65*, *70-71*; sharing *61*, 67; shelters 65, 70; social characteristics 67; taboos 58, 65; territorial rights 68, 70; trade 67; water sources 65, 67, *68-69*, 72, 73

California 12, *17*
Cannibalism 11, 23, 186, 193
Canoes 8, 23, 34; *see also* Dugouts
Cargo cults 26-29
Caribals, family settlements 25
Caribou-skin clothing *133*, 138
Cattle raising 34, 154, 156, 168, 180
Cemetery: Eskimo *134*; Kafir *15*
Ceylon 25
Chamula Indians *20-21*, 25
Cheyenne Indians *17*; book *16*
Chiapas, state, Mexico 25
Child rearing: Ainu 108; Australian Aborigines 128; Bushman *66*, 70; Hopi 184
Chiricahua Apaches 32, 34
Christianity 25, 132, 145, 201
Chukchi Sea, Alaska-U.S.S.R. *135*
Circumcision ceremony 122
Clowns, Hopi 173, 176
Clubs: punishment *96*; war 23
Colton, Harold S. and Mrs. 182
Conquistadores 173, 176
Cook, Capt. James 11
Cooking methods: Asmat 190; Australian Aborigines *128*; Bushman 72; Hopi *171*; Lapp 40, *49*
Copts 23
Corn 173, *176*, 180
Corn bread, *piki* 170, *171*, 184
Corn dancer *176*
Coronado, Francisco Vásquez de 176
Corroborees *116-117*, 127
Courtship, Lapp 40
Cradles: Ainu *100*, 108; Lapp *44*
Creation myths: Ainu 97, 99; Asmat 192; Australian Aborigines (Dreamtime) 114, 119, 121, *129*
Cremation 80, 88

Dairy products *76*, 81, *86*
Danakils *10*, 11
Dances: Ainu *94*, 97, *98-99*; Australian Aborigines 114, *116-117*, 121, *126*; Bushman *71*, 72, 74; cargo cult 26; Eskimo 139, *144, 146-147*; Hopi 170, 173, *176*, 179, *182-183*, 184; Kafir 23; Kota 82-83; Kraho *160*; Marquesan 24; Toda 83, *87*; Waurá 166, *166-167*
Darwin, Charles 11
Dead, spirits of the 25, 74, 104, 186, *190*, 192, 193, 201
Didgeridoo, musical instrument 122
Digging sticks 72, 127
Disease 11, 12, *17*, 24, 25, 32, *32*, 34, 84, 90, *159, 160*, 161
Djanggau Sisters 119, *129*
Dogs *46-47*, 51, 55, *140-141, 146, 151*
Dolls, Kachina *183*
Drums: Asmat 190, *200*; Australian Aborigines *126*; Eskimo *134*, 139, *144*; Hopi *173*; Kota 82, *83*
Dugouts: Ainu *110-111*, 112; Asmat *187*, 188, 193, *194-195*, 202, "soul ships" *198*; Australian Aborigines *125*, toy *124*; Seminole Indian *34*

204

Dusun *see* Kadazans

Ear pendants 153, 161, *161*
Ekak, Wesley 132, 139, 146
Eland dance 71
Elcho Island, Australia 114, 121-122, 124, 127; map *119*
Elmolos *12*, 13
Embroidery: Ainu 108; Toda 81, *81*
Emu *119*, 123
Erma, West Irian 186, 188, 192, 197, 201, 202; map *192*
Eskimos 132-150; Alaskan Eskimos 132, 134, *136-137*, 138, 139, *139*, *144-145*, 145, 146, *148-149*, *150*; Canadian Eskimos 133, *138*, *139*, *140-141*, *142-143*, *151*; Greenland Eskimos 145, *146-147*, 150; Christianity 132, *134*, 145; civilization, effect of 139, *141*, 150, *150*; clothing *133*, 138, *138*, 139, *139*, *141*; dances 139, *144*, *146-147*; education 150; elderly, treatment of 150; folklore 134, *144*; food 132, 134, *136*, 138, *144*; history *134*; houses 133, 139, *141*, *143*, 150; hunting and fishing 132, 133, 134, *136-137*, 139, 145, *148-149*, 150; language 146, 150; name giving 145; physical characteristics *138*, *139*; population *138*, 141, 150; range of 134, *141*, 150, map *140*; sharing 138-139; tools and implements 134, *136*, 138, 139; word, Eskimo, meaning of 138
Ethiopia 10, *11*
Ewta River, West Irian *187*
Eye fold, Mongolian 64, *65*

Face paint 153, *154-155*, 161, *193*, *203*
Feasts: Ainu 97; Asmat 193; Chamula 25; Kafir 23; Lapp 39, 40
Feathers, worn by: Asmat *193*, *203*; Maya 25; Waurá *153*, 164, 166
Fertility rites 119, 193
Festivals: Ainu *110-111*; Chamula 21, 25; Eskimo 138-139, *144-145*; Hopi 182; Kraho 159-160
Finland: Lapland 36, *39*, *40-41*, 43, 51, map *43*
Finnmark, Norway 36, 40, 44
Finnmarks Vidda, Norway 36, 42, 44, 56
Fire, spirit of 92, 96, *111*
Fire making 12, 65
Fishing: bow and arrow 161, 166; jigging stick 139, 145; nets 27, 112, 161, 166, 187, 190, 192; poison 161; spears 112, 122, *125*; traps 166, 190
Flagstaff, Arizona *170*, 182
Food *see* Agriculture, Fishing, Food gathering, Hunting, *and* names of peoples and tribes
Food gathering: Australian Aborigines 122, 127-128; Bushman 58, 72, *75*; Eskimo 138; Hadza 29, 32; Suyá *154-155*, 168; Waurá 164; Yahi 17
Funeral customs: Australian Aborigines *126-127*; Badaga 80; Kafir 15, 23; Kota 88, 90; Toda *84-85*
Furlong, Col. Charles W. 8

Gaup, Isak and Karen Anna 37, 38, 40, 42, 43, 44, *46-47*, 48, *50*, 51, 54, 55, 56, *57*
Gautscha Pan 70, 74; map *64*
Geronimo, Apache chief 34
Ghee 76, 80, 81, *86*

Gibson Desert, Australia *120-121*; map *119*
Gifts: exchange of 67, 164; to spirits 97; to the dead *126-127*
Goats 18, 180
Grass: spinifex 128; tundra 138
Grave markers: Australian Aborigines *126-127*; Eskimo *134*; Kafir *15*
Green Corn Dance 34
Greenland Eskimos 134, 141, 145, 146, *146-147*, 150
Greeting, Toda *81*, 83
Groote Eylandt, Australia *124*
Gwikwe, Bushmen 65, 67, 68, 70, 72, 74

Hadza, Tanzania 29, 32
Hair styles: Bushman *66-67*; Danakil *11*; Kota 90; Tasmanian *12*; Toda 77, 81; Waurá *153*, 166; Yahi *12*
Harpooning 134, 145, *148*
Harpoons 134, *139*, 145
Harps, wooden *20-21*
Headdress: Ainu 92, 103; Bunun *26*; Kafir *15*; Lapp *43*; Maya 25
Headhunting *8*, 29, 32, 186, *189*, *192*, *192-193*, *197*, *198*, 202
Hidatsa tribe 32
Hilger, Sister Mary Inez 92, *97*
Hindu Kush, mountains, Asia 15, 23
Hokkaido, island, Japan 92-112; map *97*
Hopis 170-184; clans 184; crafts 182, *182-183*, 184; dances, ceremonial 170, 173, 179; education 179, 182; farming 177, 180, *180-181*, 182; food 170, *171*, 180, 182; history 176; livestock 176, 180, *180-181*, 182; modernization 179, *179*, 180, 182, 184; number of 176, *179*; religion 170, 173, 176, 179, 182, *183*, 184; reservation 176, *179*, 180, map *179*; Tribal Council *179*, 180, 184; water supply 176, *178*, *179*, 180, 182
Horse, effect on Plains Indians 32
Hotevilla, Arizona 170, 173, 179
Houses: bamboo and thatch *30-31*; log *41*; reed *2-3*; round 161; snow *133*, *141-143*, 150; sod 139; stone *172*, *185*; thatched 34, *100*, 156, *162-163*, 188; windbreaks *12*, 29, 65, 124; wood and thatch 77, *100-101*, 103
Hunting: Ainu *93*; Australian Aborigines 119, *120*, 127, 128; Bushmen 58, *60-61*, 64-65; Eskimos 132, 134; *136-137*, *139*, 145, *148-149*, 150; Krahos 154; Tasmanians *12*; Txukahamei *154-155*; Waurá 164; Yahis 17
Huskies *140-141*, 146, *151*

Ibans: island of Borneo *9*
Igloos *see* Snowhouses
Inau, prayer sticks 96, *97*, *100*, *102*, 103
Incense burning 25, 26
India 7, 32, 76, *76*, 80, 81, 84; map *83*
Indians: North America 12, *16-21*, 21, 25-26, 32, 34, 170-184; South America *1*, *8*, *11*, *32*, 152-168
Infant: bathed in red *169*; ceremonial naming 184; head shaven 66; introduction ritual 76, 79
Initiation rites 12, 70, 122, *126*, 160-161, 193; women *12*
Iomande, ritual 97, *102-103*
Ishi 12, *17*, 21

Islam 15, 23

Javari, mock combat 152, *156*, *157*, *167*
Jewelry: Bunun *26*, Bushman 59, 66; Elmolo 13; Hopi 170, 182; Lapp *45*
Josdalen, valley, Norway *52-53*
Juoigos, folk songs 44

Kachinas 170, 173, 176, *176*, 179, *182-183*, 184; So'yoko 184; mudheads *182-183*
Kadazans: Sabah, island of Borneo, 28
Kafirs *14-15*, 23; funeral customs 23; religious beliefs 23
Kalahari region, Africa 58-74; area 58; map *64*; rainfall 58, 68, *68*; temperatures 65, 68
Kamui, spirits 92, 95, 96, 111
Kangaroo *23*, *119*, 122, 128
Karens 31
Kautokeino, Norway 36, 38, *38-39*, 42, *46-47*; church *45*, *46*; map *43*
Kautokeino River, Norway: reindeer races 38, *38-39*
Keendok Asmat, dialect 190
Kinabalu, peak, Sabah, island of Borneo 29
Kitti, Jouni *43*, 51
Kivas, ceremonial chambers 173
Kotagiri, India 90
Kotas 76, 80, *83*; crops 88; dancing *82*; dress *82*, 90; education 90; ceremonies: funeral 88, 90, salt-giving 90; music 80, *82*, 88; number of 90; occupations 80, 88, 90
Kotzebue, Alaska 144
Kraho Indians 152-161, *155*, *158-159*, 160, *162-163*, 166, *167*, *169*; cattle raising 154, 156, 168; communal life 154, 156; diseases *158-159*, 160; festival (*Piegré*) 159-160; food 152; map *160*; mourning *158-159*, *159*; myths *162*; races, log 160, *162-163*; rituals 160-161; social structure 156; songs *159*, 160; tribal counselor *159*; village 152, 154, *162-163*
Krichauff Range, Australia *118-119*
Kroeber, Alfred 12
Kung Bushmen *62-63*, 65, 66, 67, 69, 70, 71, *72*, 73, 74
Kurumbas, Nilgiri people 76, 80, *83*

Lacandon Indians 25-26
Lamps 76, *138*, *142*; clamshell 103
Lapland 36; map *43*
Lapokitee *153*, 164
Lapps 36-56; clothing 38, *40*, *42*, *43*, *43*, *45*, *54*; courtship and marriage 39, 40, *45*; dwellings 36, *41*, 42, 44, 48, *49*; food 40, *40*, *41*, 43; map *43*; migration, reason for 40, 42, 46; number of 36, *42*; origin 42, 56; reindeer 36, 38, *38-39*, 40, 42-44, *46-48*, *50-54*, 55-56, *56*; songs 44; superstitions 44, 48, 51; transportation 36, *39*, 40, 48, *55*; types: coastal *42*; forest *42*; mountain *42*, *43*; village dwellers *40-41*, 51
Lardil tribesmen *116-117*
Leahy, Daniel 24
Legends *see* Myths
Lévi-Strauss, Claude 34
Libation wand 92, *102*, 103, 104
Lip disks *12*, 161, 168
Lip tattoos 96, 103, *106*, 113
Lisma, Finland *40-41*, 51; map *43*

205

Additional References

For additional reading, you may wish to refer to the following NATIONAL GEOGRAPHIC articles and to check the Cumulative Index for related material:

"Saving Brazil's Stone Age Tribes From Extinction," by Orlando and Claudio Villas Boas, Sept. 1968. "Vanished Mystery Men of Hudson Bay," by Henry B. Collins, Nov. 1956. "Kachinas: Masked Dancers of the Southwest," by Paul Coze, Aug. 1957. "Banks Island: Eskimo Life on the Polar Sea," by William O. Douglas, May 1964. "Africa's Bushman Art Treasures," by Alfred Friendly, June 1963. "Finland: Plucky Neighbor of Soviet Russia," by William Graves, May 1968. "Alaska Proudly Joins the Union," July 1959, and "Lonely Wonders of Katmai," June 1963, both by Ernest Gruening. "Japan's 'Sky People,' the Vanishing Ainu," by Sister Mary Inez Hilger, Feb. 1967. "Milestones in My Arctic Journeys," by Willie Knutsen, Oct. 1949.

"Queensland: Young Titan of Australia's Tropic North," by Kenneth MacLeish, Nov. 1968. "Canada's Caribou Eskimos," by Donald B. Marsh, Jan. 1947. "Alaska's Russian Frontier: Little Diomede," by Audrey and Frank Morgan, Apr. 1951. "Earth's Most Primitive People: A Journey with the Aborigines of Central Australia," by Charles P. Mountford, Jan. 1946. "Cliff Dwellers of the Bering Sea," by Juan Muñoz, Jan. 1954. "The Snake Dance," by Marion L. Oliver, Feb. 1911. "Discovering Alaska's Oldest Arctic Town," by Froelich G. Rainey, Sept. 1942.

"Blue-eyed Indian," July 1961; "Brazil's Big-lipped Indians" (Suyá), Jan. 1962; "Children of the Sun and Moon" (Kraho), Mar. 1959; "Indians of the Amazon Darkness" (Erigbaagtsa), May 1964; "The Waurá: Brazilian Indians of the Hidden Xingu," Jan. 1966; "Tukuna Maidens Come of Age," Nov. 1959, all by Harald Schultz.

"Netherlands New Guinea," by John Scofield, May 1962. "North With Finland's Lapps," by Jean and Franc Shor, Aug. 1954. "Nomads of the Far North," by Matthew W. Stirling, Oct. 1949. "Bushmen of the Kalahari," by Elizabeth Marshall Thomas, June 1963. "'The Alice' in Australia's Wonderland," by Alan Villiers, Feb. 1966.

Logje, Aslak 42, 44, 48, 55, 56, *56-57*
Logje, Johan 42, 48, 55
Logje, Marit 42, 44, *49*, 55
Longhouses 190, 192, *193, 200*
Lua people: Thailand *30-31*
Lumber projects 201, 202

Macpherson, Lt. Evans 80
Magic: black *192*, 201; protective 51, 80, *83*, 145
Mandan Indians 32
Mandelbaum, David G. 76, *83*
Manhood initiation rites: Asmat *193*; Australian Aborigines 119, 122; Bushman 70; Kraho 160-161
Manioc 152, 164, *165*, 166
Maneowé *189*
Maps: Arctic (Western Hemisphere) *140*; Australia *119*; Brazil *160*; Hokkaido, island, Japan *97*; Hopi reservation, Arizona *179*; Kalahari region, Africa *64*; Lapland *43*; Nilgiri Hills, India *83*; West Irian, Indonesia *192*; World *endsheets*
Marquesans 23-24
Marriage customs: Ainu *103*; Asmat *193*, 197; Australian Aborigines 119, 124, 128; Bushman 67, 70; Suyá *168*; Toda 83, 85
Marsh Arabs: Iraq *2-3*
Masks: Kachina 170, 173, *176, 179, 183*;

Waurá *164-165*
Mato Grosso Plateau, Brazil *155*, 161
Maursund, channel, Norway 55, 56, *56-57*
Mawulan 122, *129*
Maya Indians *20-21*, 25-26; sculpture of *21*
Medicine: Ainu 97, 104, *111*; modern: Asmat 201; Bushman 70, 74; Lacandon 26; Nilgiri *80*, 84, 85, 88, 90
Medicine man: Bushman 74; Eskimo 146; Yahgan 8
Melons 65, 72, 73, *176*, 180
Melville Island, Australia *125, 129*
Mexican War 176
Mexico *20-21*, 25, 176
Middle East 23
Migration see Nomads
Milan, Frederick A. 132, *141*
Miller, Arthur P., Jr. 170, *179*
Mishongnovi, Arizona *174-175*
Missions: Australia 114, 120, 122, 124, 125, 127, 130; New Guinea 186, 187, 201; Tierra del Fuego 11
Miyazawa, Eiji 92
Mobley, George F. 36, *42*
Mohawks 18
Moldvay, Albert 76
Monument Valley, Arizona *18-19*
Mukluks 138
Muktuk 138, 139, *144*

Museum of Anthropology, San Francisco 12, *17*
Museum of Northern Arizona, crafts exhibit *170, 182*
Musical instruments: Ainu *98*; Asmat *190, 200*; Australian Aborigines *116, 122, 126*; Bushman *59*, 74; Chamula *20-21*; Eskimo 134, 139, *144*; Hopi *170*; Kota *82-83*
Myths: Ainu 95, 96-97, *99*, 104, 108; Asmat *192, 201*; Australian Aborigines 114, *117*, 119, 121, *126*, 127, *128*, 130; Hopi *173*; Kraho *162*; Waurá *166*

Naga tribes: India 32
Naluqataq see Spring Whale Festival
National Geographic Society: grants 92, 152
Navajos *18-19*, 176
Necklaces: bead *26, 59, 66*; human vertebra *186, 191*; jaguar-claw *153*; shell and toucan feathers *164*
Negovanna, Weir 138, 139, 145; and Roseanne 139, 145
Nehru, Jawaharlal, Prime Minister 84-85
Netsilik Eskimos *133, 138, 140-143*, 151
New Guinea Highlanders *24-25*, 26, 29; cargo cult 26, 29
New Oraibi, Arizona *176*
Nilgiri Hills, India 76, 79-80; map *83*
Nilgiri peoples 76-90; interdependence 76, *78, 80, 83*, 88
Nomads: Australian Aborigines 114-131; Bushmen 58-74; Danakils *10, 11*; Hadzas 29, 32; Lapps 36-56; Tasmanians 11-12, *22*; Veddas 25; Yahgans 8, 11
Northern Territory, Australia 114, *117*, 130
Northwest River, West Irian 186
Norway: Lapland 36-40, *42*, 42-56; map *43*
Nose ornaments *186, 190, 193*
Nuristanis 23
Nyae Nyae region, Kalahari 65, 68

Oil leases: Hopi reservation *179*, 184
Old Oraibi, Arizona 176, *180*
Oolдea, Australia 127, 128, 130; map *119*
Ootacamund, Nilgiri Hills 79, 80, 84; map *83*
Ostjanep, West Irian *198-199*; map *192*
Ostrich eggshells *59, 66-67*, 73

Painting, body 11, 114, *116-117*, 121, *129, 166, 166-167, 169*, 170, *203*
Paintings 8, 22, *102-103*; bark *129*; rock *117*; silk scroll *93*
Pakistan 15, 23
Parkas *138*, 138, 139, *139*, 150
Paternity ceremony, Toda 83, 84, *89*
Peary, Robert E. *146-147*
Pedra Branca, Brazil 152, 154, *162-163*
Pelly Bay, Canada *132, 139, 142-143*; map *140*
Peter, Prince, of Greece and Denmark 84
Petroglyphs *56, 70*
Piegré, festival 159-160
Piljain, Evam *80*, 84-85, 88
Pitka, Father Frank 186, *188*
Plaque, yucca fiber, Hopi *182*
Plains Indians 32
Poems: Ainu 104, 108, 112; Toda 83
Point Hope, Alaska *134, 135*; map *140*

Poisons *60-61*, 65, 67, *161*; prussic acid *164*, 166
Polequaptewa, Myron 180, *180, 181*, 182
Polyandry 83, 84-85
Polynesian civilization 23
Pooyama, Vera 171
Pôsto Leonardo Villas Boas, Brazil 161
Pottery: Hopi 182; Lacandon 25; Waurá *165*, 166, 168
Prayer sticks: Ainu 96, 97, *100, 102, 103*; Hopi 173, 179
Praying mantis, motif *199*
Priests: Kota 88; Toda 76, 81, *86*
Pueblos 32, *172, 174-175*, 176, *185*

Q uechua woman *1*

R aces: dugout 202; log 160, *162-163*; reindeer 38, *38-39*
Rafts, bamboo 27
Rasmussen, Knud *141*, 146
Rebirth, ritual of 192, 193, *196, 197*
Reindeer *42*, 56, 139; calves *54*, 55, 56; food 40, 42, 43, *49*; identification notches 51; migration 36, *36*, 38, 40, 42-44, *46-48, 50-53*, 55-56; milking 43; races 38, *38-39*; summer pasture 40, *46*, 55; swimming 55, 56; winter pasture 42, *46-47*
Reisa River and Valley, Norway 48, 51, 55
Rice 30, *106-107*
Roads, impact of 25, 34, *34*, 36, 48, 74, *174-175*
Robertson, Sir George 23
Rockefeller, Michael *198*

S acrifices: animal 51, *84*, 90, 97, *102-103*; bird 179; human 23
Sago 190, 192
Saki, rice wine 92, 96, *102*, 104
Salt *10, 155*; salt-giving ceremony 90
Sano, Chiye 92
Saowa and Erma, villages, West Irian 186, 188, 192, 197, 201, 202; map *192*
Sarawak, Malaysia *8*
Schools: Ainu 108, *112*; Asmat 193, 197; Australian Aborigines 124; Bhutanese *35*; Eskimos 150; Hopi attendance 182; Naga tribes 32; New Guinea Highlanders 26
Schultz, Harald 152, 154, 159, *160*, 161, 164, 168
Schultz, Vilma Chiara 152, *160*
Seal hunting 132, *132*, *139*, 145
Seminole Indians 34
Sevettijärvi, Finland: herder *39*
Shaman 145
Sheep raising *18-19*, 180, *180-181*, 182
Sherpas: Nepal *4-5*
Shields 190, *199*
Shipaulovi, Arizona *174-175*
Shongopovi, Arizona *172*, 176
Sieide, holy place, Lapp 51
Silverwork, Hopi 182
Skulls: bear, altars *95*, 97, 103; human, pendants 186, *191*
"Sky People" *see* Ainu
Sleds: dog 138, 146, *151*; reindeer-drawn 36, *39*, 40, 42, *46-47, 51*, 55
Snake Dance 173
Snow scooters *39*, 40, 55
Snowhouses *133, 141, 142-143*, 150
Songs: Ainu 108; Australian Aborigines 114, *117, 127*, 128; Bushman 74; Eskimo 139, 145; Kraho 159, *160*; Lapp 44

Sorcery: Asmat 192, 201; Kurumba 80, *83*
South America 8, 11, *32*, 152-168
Sowada, Father Alphonse 186, *192*
Spears: Asmat *188-189*, 190; Australian Aborigines *121*, 122, toy *122*; Waurá *156-157*
Spirits: ancestral 25, 104, 186, *190, 192*, 193, 201; animal 96, 97, 103, *111*, 134, 138; evil *95*, 96, 103, 104, *111, 152, 168*; fire 92, 96, *111*; good 96, *111*; of the dead 74, 104, *192*
Spring Whale Festival 138-139
Steatopygia 71
Steinen, Karl von den 161
Stirling, Matthew W. 8
Suiá Missu River, Brazil 168
Suyá Indians 152, *155, 160, 161*, 168; food gathering *154-155*, 168; map *160*; number of 168; raids by 168
Sweden: Lapland 36, *42*; map *43*

T aboos 12, *17*, 25, 58, 65, 76, 96, 114, 122
Taiwan aborigines *26, 27*
Talayesva, Don C. *176, 177*, 180
Tanzania 29
Tasmanian aborigines 11-12, *22-23*; decline of population 11, 12, *23*
Tattoos: Ainu 95, 96, 103, *106, 113*; Eskimo 139; Lua *30*; Marquesan 23; Toda 77, 81
Tchikao Indians 161
Temple-dairies, Toda 76, 81, 83, *86, 87*
Tents: Eskimo 150; Lapp *36*, 42, 44, *48, 49*
Terrace farming 31, *32, 78-79*
Thailand *30-31*
Thomas, Elizabeth Marshall 58, *64*
Tibetans 33
Tierra del Fuego, Argentina and Chile 8, *32*
Tiwis *125, 126*
Tobacco, use of 25, 26, 32, 108, 112, 164, *189*, 190, 202
Tocantins River, Brazil 152, map *160*
Todas 77, 80, *83*, 90, *91*; buffalo *78-79*; clan system 79, 83, *87*; clothing 76, 77, 81, *81*; concept of beauty 81; council of elders 84, 88; dairy products 76, 81, *86*; dances 83, *87*; economy *78*, 81; food 81; funeral ceremony 83, *84-85*; greeting *81, 83*; houses 77; land of 76, 79-80; marriage customs 83, 85; medicine 88; modern 80, *84*, 85, 88, 90; paternity ceremony 83, 84, *89*; physical description 80-81; population 84; priests 76, 81, *86*; religion 76, 81, 86; sacred buffalo 76, 81, *86*, 88, *90*, sacrifice of *84-85*; temples 76, 81, 83, *86, 87*; thatching ceremony 83, *87*
Tools: Asmat 190, *193*, 202; Australian Aborigines 119, *121, 127*; Eskimo 134, *136*, 138, 139; Kota 80, 88; Suyá 168; Toda 81, 86; Waurá 164, 166
Tundra, plant life 40, 42, *48*, 138, *140-141*
Tuneri, India *78-79*
Turtle Man, mythological figure *128*

Txukahamei Indians *154-155*

U mbrella, split bamboo *30*
Umiak, boat 132, 139

V eddas: Ceylon 25
Villas Boas, Orlando and Claudio 161, 168

W addy, stick 12
Wainwright, Alaska 132, *138-139, 141*, 145, 146; map *140*
Walbiri tribesman *131*
Walpi, Arizona 176, *184-185*
Walrus 132, 134, *136-137*
War games 152, *156-157, 167*
Warburton Mission, Australia 120
Water hyacinths *154-155*
Watson, James B. 26
Waurá Indians 152, *160*, 161-168; adornment *153*, 164, *166-167*; chief 164, 166; food 164, *165*, 166; houses 161; language 164; myths 166; number of 161; pottery 166, 168; song and dance 166, *166-167*; trade (*oolookee*) 164, 166; village 161; war games (*javari*) 152, *156-157, 167*; women abducted 168
Wedding customs: Bushman 70; Lapp *39*, 40, *45*
Whale festival 138-139
Whaling 138, *148-149*
Wildebeest *60-61*
Wind chime, clay *183*
Winnowing *123*, 128
Women: abduction of 12, 168; role of: Ainu 96, 103, 108; Asmat *187*, 188, 192, *196*, 197, 201; Australian Aborigines 122, 124, 128; Bushman 58, *72, 74*; Eskimo 139, 150; Lapp 42, 43, 44, 48, *49, 54*, 55, 56; Kafir *15*; Navajo *18*; Toda 81, *81*, 83; Yahgan 8; status of: Asmat 190, 197; Bushmen 58, 65; Lacandon 25; Toda 76, 88; *and* taboos 25, 58, 65, 76, 96, 114, 122
Wood carvings: Asmat 192, 193, *198-200*; Australian Aborigines *126-127, 128, 129*; Hopi *183*; Kafir *15*
World Health Organization 161

X etá Indians 152
Xingu Indians 161, *161*, 164, *165*, 166, *166-167*, 168; fishing methods 161, 166; food 164, 166; houses, communal 161; mythical Amazons 166; population 161
Xingu National Park, Brazil 161, 168
Xingu region, Brazil 161, *161*
Xingu River, Brazil *160*, 161

Y ahgan Indians 8, 11, *32*
Yahi Indians 12, *17*, 21
Yamaha, Midori 92
Yana Indians 12
Yirkalla, Australia 114, *117*, 121, 122, 124, 127, 130; bark painting *129*
Yucca fiber plaque *182*
Yukar, Ainu epic 104, 108

Z oroastrians 23

Composition for *Vanishing Peoples of the Earth* by National Geographic's Photo-typographic Division, Herman J.A.C. Arens, Director; John E. McConnell, Manager. Printed and bound by Fawcett-Haynes Printing Corp., Rockville, Md. Lithographic color separations by Beck Engraving Co., Philadelphia, Pa.; R. R. Donnelley & Sons, Inc., Chicago, Ill.; Graphic Color Plate, Inc., Stamford, Conn.; The Lanman Co., Alexandria, Va.; and Progressive Color Corp., Rockville, Md.

NATIONAL GEOGRAPHIC SOCIETY
WASHINGTON, D. C.

Organized "for the increase and diffusion of geographic knowledge"

GILBERT HOVEY GROSVENOR
Editor, 1899-1954; President, 1920-1954
Chairman of the Board, 1954-1966

THE NATIONAL GEOGRAPHIC SOCIETY is chartered in Washington, D. C., in accordance with the laws of the United States, as a nonprofit scientific and educational organization for increasing and diffusing geographic knowledge and promoting research and exploration. Since 1890 the Society has supported 455 explorations and research projects, adding immeasurably to man's knowledge of earth, sea, and sky. It diffuses this knowledge through its monthly journal, NATIONAL GEOGRAPHIC; more than 24 million maps distributed each year; its books, globes, atlases, and filmstrips; 30 School Bulletins a year in color; information services to press, radio, and television; technical reports; exhibits from around the world in Explorers Hall; and a nationwide series of programs on television.

Articles and photographs of travel, natural history, and expeditions to far places are desired. For material used, generous remuneration is made.

MELVIN M. PAYNE, President
FREDERICK G. VOSBURGH, Vice President and Editor
LEONARD CARMICHAEL, Vice President for Research and Exploration
ROBERT E. DOYLE, Vice President and Secretary
THOMAS M. BEERS, Vice President and Associate Secretary
GILBERT M. GROSVENOR, Vice President and Associate Editor
HILLEARY F. HOSKINSON, Treasurer
OWEN R. ANDERSON, HERMAN J. A. C. ARENS, WILLIAM T. BELL,
HERBERT T. HENDERSON, W. EDWARD ROSCHER,
C. VERNON SANDERS, Associate Secretaries

BOARD OF TRUSTEES

MELVILLE BELL GROSVENOR
Chairman of the Board and Editor-in-Chief
THOMAS W. McKNEW, Advisory Chairman of the Board

LEONARD CARMICHAEL, Former Secretary, Smithsonian Institution

LEO OTIS COLBERT, Rear Admiral, U. S. Coast and Geodetic Survey (Ret.)

LLOYD H. ELLIOTT, President, George Washington University

CRAWFORD H. GREENEWALT Chairman, Finance Committee, E. I. du Pont de Nemours & Company

GILBERT M. GROSVENOR Associate Editor, National Geographic

ARTHUR B. HANSON, General Counsel, National Geographic Society

CARYL P. HASKINS, President, Carnegie Institution of Washington

EMORY S. LAND, Vice Admiral, U. S. Navy (Ret.), Former President, Air Transport Association

CURTIS E. LeMAY, Former Chief of Staff, U. S. Air Force

H. RANDOLPH MADDOX Vice President, American Telephone & Telegraph Company (Ret.)

WM. McCHESNEY MARTIN, JR. Chairman, Board of Governors, Federal Reserve System

BENJAMIN M. McKELWAY Editorial Chairman, Washington *Star*

MELVIN M. PAYNE, President, National Geographic Society

LAURANCE S. ROCKEFELLER President, Rockefeller Brothers Fund

JUAN T. TRIPPE, Honorary Chairman of the Board, Pan American World Airways

FREDERICK G. VOSBURGH Editor, National Geographic

JAMES H. WAKELIN, JR., Former Assistant Secretary of the Navy

EARL WARREN Chief Justice of the United States

JAMES E. WEBB, Former Administrator, National Aeronautics and Space Administration

ALEXANDER WETMORE Research Associate, Smithsonian Institution

LLOYD B. WILSON (Emeritus) Honorary Board Chairman, Chesapeake & Potomac Telephone Company

CONRAD L. WIRTH, Former Director, National Park Service

LOUIS B. WRIGHT, Former Director, Folger Shakespeare Library

COMMITTEE FOR RESEARCH AND EXPLORATION

LEONARD CARMICHAEL, Chairman
ALEXANDER WETMORE and MELVIN M. PAYNE, Vice Chairmen
LEO OTIS COLBERT, CARYL P. HASKINS, A. REMINGTON KELLOGG, Research Associate, Smithsonian Institution, EMORY S. LAND, T. DALE STEWART, Senior Scientist, Office of Anthropology, Smithsonian Institution, MATTHEW W. STIRLING, Research Associate, Smithsonian Institution, JAMES H. WAKELIN, JR., CONRAD L. WIRTH, PAUL A. ZAHL, and the senior officers of the Society; BARRY C. BISHOP, Secretary on leave; EDWIN W. SNIDER, Secretary

Assistant Secretaries of the Society: CHARLES P. BIXEL, FRANK S. DELK, JOSEPH B. HOGAN, RAYMOND T. McELLIGOTT, JR.
Assistant Treasurer: WILLIAM H. McCAULEY

Leonard J. Grant, Editorial Assistant to the President; Edwin W. Snider, Richard E. Pearson, Administrative Assistants to the President; Judith N. Dixon, Administrative Assistant to the Chairman and Editor-in-Chief; Lenore W. Kessler, Administrative Assistant to the Advisory Chairman of the Board

SECRETARY'S STAFF: *Administrative:* Earl Corliss, Jr., Ward S. Phelps. *Accounting:* Jay H. Givans, George F. Fogle, Alfred J. Hayre, William G. McGhee, Martha Allen Baggett. *Statistics:* Everett C. Brown, Thomas M. Kent. *Retirement:* Mary L. Whitmore (Assistant Supervisor). *Payroll:* Dorothy L. Dameron (Assistant Supervisor). *Procurement:* J. P. M. Johnston, Robert G. Corey, Robert C. Ellis, Jr., Sheila H. Immel, Margaret A. Shearer. *Membership Research:* Charles T. Kneeland. *Membership Fulfillment:* Roy J. Klockenbrink. *Member Relations:* Paul F. Moize. *Computer Center:* John Goedel. *Secretary's Files:* Mozelle L. Downs. *Promotion:* Stan Jennings, E. M. Pusey, Jr., Robert J. Warfel. *Printing:* Joe M. Barlett, Frank S. Oliverio. *Production Control:* James P. Kelly. *Personnel:* James B. Mahon, Adrian L. Loftin, Jr., Glenn G. Pepperman, Nellie E. Sinclair. *Medical:* Thomas L. Hartman, M. D. *Translation:* Zbigniew Jan Lutyk

NATIONAL GEOGRAPHIC MAGAZINE

MELVILLE BELL GROSVENOR
Editor-in-Chief and Board Chairman
MELVIN M. PAYNE
President of the Society

FREDERICK G. VOSBURGH, Editor
GILBERT M. GROSVENOR, FRANC SHOR, Associate Editors

Senior Assistant Editors
Allan C. Fisher, Jr., Kenneth MacLeish, John Scofield

Assistant Editors: Andrew H. Brown, James Cerruti, Robert L. Conly, W. E. Garrett, Edward J. Linehan, Carolyn Bennett Patterson, Howell Walker, Kenneth F. Weaver

Senior Editorial Staff: Lonnelle Aikman, Jules B. Billard, Rowe Findley, William Graves, Stuart E. Jones, Robert P. Jordan, Joseph Judge, Nathaniel T. Kenney, Samuel W. Matthews, Bart McDowell; Senior Natural Scientist Paul A. Zahl

Foreign Editorial Staff: Luis Marden (Chief); Thomas J. Abercrombie, Howard La Fay, Helen and Frank Schreider, Volkmar Wentzel, Peter T. White

Editorial Staff: Thomas Y. Canby, Louis de la Haba, Alice J. Hall, Werner Janney, Jay Johnston, Elizabeth A. Moize, Ethel A. Starbird, Gordon Young

Editorial Layout: Howard E. Paine (Chief); Charles C. Uhl, John M. Lavery

Geographic Art: William N. Palmstrom (Chief). *Artists:* Lisa Biganzoli, William H. Bond, John W. Lothers, Robert C. Magis, Robert W. Nicholson, Ned M. Seidler. *Cartographic Artists:* Victor J. Kelley, Snejinka Stefanoff. *Research:* Walter Q. Crowe (Supervisor), George W. Beatty, John D. Garst, Jean B. McConville, Dorothy A. Nicholson, Eugene M. Scheel, Isaac Ortiz (Production). Marie L. Barnes (Administrative Assistant)

Editorial Research: Margaret G. Bledsoe (Chief); Ann K. Wendt (Associate Chief), Elisabeth J. Chappell, Ledlie L. Dinsmore, Margery G. Dunn, Jan Holderness, Levenia Loder, Frances H. Parker, Patricia Rosenborg, Elizabeth C. Wagner

Geographic Research: George Crossette (Chief); Newton V. Blakeslee (Assistant Chief), Virginia L. Baza, Leon J. Canova, John A. Weeks

Phototypography: John McConnell (Chief)

Library: Virginia Carter Hills (Librarian); Margery K. Barkdull (Assistant Librarian), Melba Barnes, Vera Cassilly, Louise A. Robinson, Esther Ann Manion (Librarian Emeritus)

Administration: Betty T. Sanborne, Administrative Assistant to the Editor; Harriet Carey, Virginia H. Finnegan, Joyce W. McKean, Winifred M. Myers, Shirley Neff (Editorial Assistants); Dorothy M. Corson (Indexes); Rosalie F. Millerd, Jeanne S. Duiker (Files); Evelyn Fox (Transportation)

ILLUSTRATIONS STAFF: *Illustrations Editor:* Herbert S. Wilburn, Jr. *Associate Illustrations Editor:* Thomas R. Smith. *Art Editor:* Andrew Poggenpohl. *Assistant Illustrations Editors:* Mary S. Griswold, O. Louis Mazzatenta, Charles Allmon (Incoming Photographs). *Senior Picture Editors:* Charlene Murphy, Robert S. Patton. *Picture Editors:* Manuel L. Lopez, Jon Schneeberger. *Research:* Paula C. Simmons, Barbara A. Shattuck (Assistant)

Artists: Walter A. Weber (Naturalist), Peter V. Bianchi

Engraving and Printing: Dee J. Andella (Chief); William W. Smith, James R. Whitney

PHOTOGRAPHIC STAFF: *Director of Photography:* Robert E. Gilka. *Assistant Directors:* B. Anthony Stewart, Dean Conger. *Film Review:* Albert Moldvay (Chief); Guy W. Starling (Assistant Chief). *Pictorial Research:* Walter Meayers Edwards (Chief). *Photographers:* James P. Blair, Bruce Dale, John E. Fletcher, Otis Imboden, Emory Kristof, Bates Littlehales, George F. Mobley, Robert S. Oakes, Winfield Parks, Joseph J. Scherschel, Robert F. Sisson, James L. Stanfield

Photographic Laboratory: Edwin L. Wisherd (Chief); Milton A. Ford, Donald McBain, Claude E. Petrone, Carl M. Shrader

RELATED EDUCATIONAL SERVICES OF THE SOCIETY

Cartography—Maps, atlases, and globes: *Chief Cartographer:* Wellman Chamberlin. *Associate Chief Cartographer:* Athos D. Grazzini. *Assistant Chief:* William T. Peele. *Base Compilation:* Charles L. Stern (Supervisor), James W. Killion. *Name Compilation:* Donald A. Jaeger (Supervisor), Manuela C. Kogutowicz, George E. Stuart. *Map Drawings:* Douglas A. Strobel (Supervisor), Robert W. Northrop, Thomas A. Wall. *Map Editing:* Ted Dachtera (Supervisor), Russel G. Fritz, Richard K. Rogers, Thomas A. Walsh. *Projections:* David W. Cook. *Layout and Design:* John F. Dorr, Harry C. Siddeley. *Revisions:* Richard J. Darley. *Administrative Assistant:* Catherine M. Hart

Books: Merle Severy (Chief); Edwards Park (Associate Chief); Seymour L. Fishbein (Assistant Chief), Thomas B. Allen, Ross Bennett, Charles O. Hyman, Anne Dirkes Kobor, John J. Putman, Berry L. Reece, Jr., David F. Robinson, Werner L. Weber

Special Publications: Robert L. Breeden (Chief); Donald J. Crump (Assistant Chief), Josephine B. Bolt, David R. Bridge, Johanna G. Farren, Ronald M. Fisher, Mary Ann Harrell, Bryan Hodgson, Geraldine Linder, Michael J. Long, Philip B. Silcott, Joseph A. Taney

School Service: Ralph Gray (Chief, and Editor of National Geographic School Bulletin); Arthur P. Miller, Jr. (Assistant Chief, and Associate Editor School Bulletin), Richard M. Crum, Jeanne A. Davis, Joseph B. Goodwin, Phyllis Greene, Charles H. Sloan, Janis Knudsen Wheat. *Educational Filmstrips:* David S. Boyer (Chief)

News Service: Windsor P. Booth (Chief); Paul Sampson (Assistant Chief), Edward Cornish, Donald J. Frederick, Sabin Robbins; Isabel Clarke (Assistant)

Television: Robert C. Doyle (Chief); Dennis B. Kane (Assistant Chief), David Cooper; Patricia F. Northrop (Administrative Assistant)

Lectures: Joanne M. Hess (Chief); Robert G. Fleegal, Mary W. McKinney, Gerald L. Wiley

Explorers Hall: T. Keilor Bentley (Curator-Director)

EUROPEAN OFFICES: W. Edward Roscher (Associate Secretary and Director), 11 Stanhope Gate, Mayfair, London, W. 1, England; Jacques Ostier, 6 rue des Petits-Pères, 75-Paris 2e, France

ADVERTISING: *Director:* Harley L. McDevitt; *Manager:* William A. Boeger, Jr., 630 Fifth Ave., New York, N.Y. 10020. *Regional managers—Eastern:* Joseph T. Feeney, New York. *Midwestern:* William Turgeon, Chicago. *Los Angeles:* Jack V. Sheehan. *San Francisco:* Thomas Martz. *Automotive:* John F. Grant, New York. *Travel:* Gerald A. Van Splinter, New York. *International:* James L. Till, New York

1. Eskimos—Siberia to Greenland
2. Mohawks—Northeastern North America
3. Florida Seminoles
4. Hopis—Arizona
5. Navajos—Arizona, New Mexico, Utah
6. Apaches—Arizona, New Mexico, Oklahoma
7. Marquesans—South Pacific
8. Lacandons—Mexico and Guatemala
9. Quechuas—Peru, Bolivia
10. Brazilian Indians
11. Lapps—Norway, Sweden, Finland, Russia
12. Danakils—Ethiopia, French Somaliland
13. Elmolos—Kenya
14. Biras—Democratic Republic of the Congo